THAILAND'S
BOOM AND BU

PASUK PHONGPAICHIT
CHRIS BAKER

SILKWORM BOOKS

ISBN 974-7100-57-6

First published in April 1998, reprinted (twice) in 1998, 1999 and 2001 by
Silkworm Books
104/5 Chiang Mai–Hot Road, Suthep, Chiang Mai 50200, Thailand
E-mail: silkworm@pobox.com

Set in Palatino 10.5 pt. by Silk Type

Printed in Thailand by O.S. Printing House, Bangkok

CONTENTS

1 A DIFFERENT COUNTRY

This book is about the transformation of a country over one roller-coaster decade. It is about the economics of boom and bust, but also about the politics, the social changes, and the popular culture.

Thailand today is a very different country from Thailand a decade ago. The economic boom that began after 1985 changed so much. Understanding Thailand today means understanding the boom – where it came from, what it did, why it ended, and what may follow.

For a decade, Thailand was the world's fastest-growing economy.[1] At the start of the decade, almost no-one predicted this. Very, very few had Thailand marked down as Asia's next economic success story. Outside the country, few were really aware of it. Inside, many were scarcely aware how quickly and how much the country was changing before their eyes.

From the 1960s, the Asian economies had divided into two camps. The Four Tigers of Korea, Taiwan, Hong Kong, and Singapore plunged into export industrialization and flooded the world with cheap clothes, shoes, and electronics. The other countries moved at a more sedate pace. Even among the others, Thailand seemed less promising. The Philippines had its US links. Malaysia had its old colonial industries. Indonesia had lots of oil.

Thailand seemed less modern, less likely to leap ahead. Its politics were an old-fashioned mix of kings, coups, and generals. Its economy was a classic third-world blend of agriculture and tourism. It had grown quite strongly in the 1960s and 1970s but many believed it had been pumped up by

US aid during the Vietnam war. After the Americans left, they expected the balloon to deflate.

In the early 1980s, these expectations appeared correct. The Thai economy slowed down and grew less stable. The second oil price hike swelled the foreign debt and triggered inflation. In 1984-5, the country slipped towards a crisis of recession and political disorder.

One bank went under. Three others teetered. In two others the top executive fled. In another, the chief executive was jailed for handing out large sums to tide his cronies over the business crisis. A housewife started a pyramid loan scheme which grew so large it threatened to destabilize the whole economy. The military chief tried to reverse a currency devaluation by threatening a coup on prime-time TV. Two foreign newsmen were killed in a street skirmish during a later coup attempt.

Against this backdrop, predictions about the future of the Thai economy were filled with gloom. The World Bank advised the economy would need major surgery to regain its health. Government suspected its target of 5 percent annual growth for the period 1987-92 was hopelessly ambitious. A conference of academics, technocrats, and businessmen concluded: "Thailand's future does not look rosy with the economy in the worst shape it has ever been in."[2] Within eighteen months, the economy was racing along at double-digit pace. In seven years, it doubled in size.

Thailand's boom came as a surprise. But Thailand was not the only Asian economy which spurted ahead in the late 1980s. Malaysia and Indonesia were on the upswing. Vietnam began to move. The Philippines picked up. Even Myanmar stirred.

The common reason lay in Japan. To overcome the second oil crisis, Japan held down its exchange rate and exported its way out of trouble. In so doing, Japan built up huge trade surpluses with its trading partners, especially the US. The partners then ganged up to force Japan to revalue the yen. In four years after the Plaza Accords of October 1985, the yen rose 89 percent against the dollar.

In 1985, the slogan for Japanese firms was "Escape the value of the yen!" Many firms moved manufacturing directly to the US and European markets where they sold their products. Others looked around for low-cost sites in Asia. After the first oil crisis, many had moved into the four Tiger economies. But now the Tigers were facing rising currencies and rising costs just like Japan. Firms from Japan and the Tigers looked to Malaysia, Indonesia, and Thailand.

Between 1986 and 1993, Japanese firms invested US$47 billion in Asia, mainly to manufacture goods for export. To stay competitive, many firms from the Tigers were forced to follow suit. These investment flows spread export-oriented growth into other countries of the region.

For many years, Japanese economists had predicted that the Japanese economic miracle would radiate across Asia in this way, rather like England's industrial revolution had radiated out through neighbouring Europe.

These economists described the process with an image of flying geese.[3] Japan headed the echelon. From the 1960s, the Tigers started flying in Japan's wake. They copied some of Japan's strategies and they benefited from some Japanese investment. Now in the 1980s another set of countries was being tacked onto the back of the flight.

So far, so neat and simple. It would be easy just to attribute Thailand's boom to the migration of Japanese manufacturing. But some tricky questions remain.

First of all, *why this goose?* How come such a large portion of this migrant capital settled in Thailand? Between 1985 and 1990, the flow of foreign investment into Thailand multiplied ten times. *The total inflow of the last three years of the decade was greater than the total foreign investment in Thailand over the past thirty.*

Next, *how come this goose took off so fast?* While the increase in foreign investment was impressive, the upsurge in local investment was larger. Foreign investment accounted for only one-eighth of the increase in investment between 1985 and

1990. Thousands of local firms joined in the surge of export-oriented manufacture. The products were not limited to the textiles and electronics which were the principal migrants. The export boom spread to jewellery, leather goods, wood products, processed foods, computer components, auto parts, and a whole host of items. *In ten years, manufactured exports multiplied twelve times* and drove up total exports seven times.

	1985	1996	% annual growth
Population (million)	52	60	1.3
GDP (billion baht at 1988 prices)	1,191	3,117	9.1
GNP per head (baht at 1988 prices)	22,731	50,565	7.5
Manufacturing percent of GDP	22	33	
Exports (billion baht at current prices)	193	1,412	19.8
Manufactured exports	96	1,151	25.3
as percent of total	49	82	
Manufacturing employment (million)	2.0	4.5	7.7
as percent of total	8.2	13.8	

In a very short period the whole shape of the Thai economy altered. In 1980, three-fifths of exports originated from agriculture. By 1995, over four-fifths came from manufacturing. Over a decade the urban population doubled and the average per capita income doubled. The changes were much more dramatic than the foreign investment flows alone warranted, much more startling than in other countries of the region.

Finally, *how come this goose flew so well?* Through four years of double-digit growth (1987-90), inflation averaged 4 percent. With a quadrupling of foreign trade, the balance of payments stayed under control. Despite a sharp rise in the demand for urban labour and new skills, the boom was not seriously disrupted by labour shortages or labour agitation. For ten speeding years, the economy stayed on a relatively even keel.

In 1993, the World Bank highlighted Thailand as a case which "shows how openness towards foreign investment, combined with export orientation, can contribute to a dynamic export-push strategy."[4] In early 1995, *The Economist* projected Thailand as the world's eighth largest economy in 2020. In 1996, Thailand's planners wrote 8 percent growth into the next five-year plan.

Then it all fell apart, even more suddenly than it began.

In 1996, export growth slumped from over 20 percent to zero. The stock market lost two-thirds of its value. In 1997, the currency was battered by speculators into a sharp depreciation. The biggest finance company collapsed. Two-thirds of all finance firms were suspended. The IMF was called in to arrange its second-largest-ever bailout.

The crash sent shock-waves through Asia. Journalists spun images of sick geese, trembling tigers, and exhausted dragons. *The Economist* and many others now asked if this crisis signalled the end of the Asian miracle.

Like the upswing, the downturn had an international explanation. The Japanese economy had been struggling with recession for seven years. This too had radiated across Asia, pulling investment and exports gradually down. The strength of the European and, especially, the US economies was drawing investment funds back to the profit opportunities at home base. The strengthening of the EU and NAFTA trade blocs was closing off export opportunities. A new bunch of geese had hitched onto the rear of the flight. China, India, Indochina offered even cheaper export platforms.

But these conditions were the same for other Southeast Asian countries. They too suffered but not as badly as Thailand. For many both inside and outside the country, the vicious downturn of 1997 pointed to failures in the bureaucracy and politics. The Bank of Thailand, which had long been seen as the bedrock of Thailand's economic stability, came in for sharp criticism. The politicians fell to blaming one another. Many urban people pinned their hope on a new constitution which promised to overhaul the way the country was run.

The boom ended. But it had changed Thailand forever.

The single outstanding theme of social change in the boom decade was the rise of the city. Even in the early 1980s, despite the size and importance of Bangkok, Thailand liked to think of itself as a rural nation at heart. But as the millennium approaches, the city is rampant.

And within the city, business is clearly the dynamic force. Until quite recently, Bangkok felt more like a political capital than a commercial metropolis. Palaces, temples, and government offices overshadowed the commercial shophouses. But now glittering towers of commerce dominate the skyline. The ethos of the civil servant has been overwhelmed by the spirit of the marketplace. The bureaucracy's grip over government is challenged by a parliament stacked with businessmen.

In Japan and the Tigers, governments dragged businessmen into export-led industrialization by pushing and pulling, bullying and bribing. In Thailand, by contrast, the businessmen have made most of the running. The government's role was to provide support and not to offer many restrictions. Business revelled in the atmosphere of free-for-all, and this revelling contributed to the speed and strength of the boom.

But free-for-all is not the same as good-for-all. Indeed, *free-for-all tends to mean good-for-some*. In simple income terms, the boom converted Thailand into one of the developing world's most unequal societies. This fact is still something of a secret. To many it would be quite a shock. Thailand has long prided itself on being a relatively fair society. "Thailand," the King once said, "was built on compassion."

The problem of inequity goes beyond this income skew in two major ways.

First, the rapid dash to industrialization has had a devastating impact on the environment. The social impact of this devastation is very unequal. Urban pollution weighs heaviest on those who cannot defend themselves. The destruction of forests is most critical for those who rely on the forest for a major part of their livelihood.

Second, Thailand was scarcely prepared for the rush to industrialization. It has few of the social controls which an industrializing society needs. The framework of law, police, and justice belongs to a bygone age. It provides the individual with little defence against state, employer, rich neighbour, gangster. It offers society little help in controlling business's carelessness about the environment, or politicians' schemes to loot the public purse.

The boom made business a dominant social force. But what sort of society would it build? The end of the boom prompted rethinking about Thailand's political structure, development strategies, social values, and cultural core.

The Pattaya road, 1985-97

In 1985, the highway from Bangkok to the resort of Pattaya was two-lanes wide most of the way. From Bangkok to Chonburi it was flanked by paddy fields and swamp, and beyond Chonburi by dry scrub and cassava. In the light traffic of local delivery trucks and tourist minivans, the 140 kilometres usually took only 1:30 hours. Only the two traffic lights in the bustling town of Chonburi could sometimes cause delay.

Pattaya was built on sun, sea, and sex – sold first to the USA's Vietnam troops on R&R, then to the package tours of Europe, and then to the oil-rich Arabs of the Gulf. The resort was a monument to the forces of the Cold-War period: Asian underdevelopment, US military power, post-war Europe's mass prosperity, and Arab oil wealth. The resort itself had a tacky, makeshift air – like a temporary exhibition hall or a refugee camp.

By 1997, the highway is four, six, eight and ten-lanes wide. Six more lanes are being built over-head. And another six on a parallel toll-road. The journey takes two hours at least (often much more), through a stream of construction lorries, pick-up trucks, air-conditioned buses, container transporters, and Mercedes Benz. The road evades Chonburi's growing traffic jams on a new ring road complete with soaring interchanges. A

---

new spur leads off south from Pattaya to a shiny new refinery and petrochemical complex in Rayong.

The paddy fields have almost completely disappeared behind housing projects, advertising billboards, shophouses, and factories. Especially factories: Nissan, Mitsubishi, Sharp, National Panasonic, Volvo, Master Toy, Michelin, Itokin, Maisto, Tabuchi, Koyo, Hitachi, On Star, Yokorei, Venus, Sohbi Kohgei. A new town is emerging at Bang Pakong, sparked by industrial estates, and now spreading into retail complexes, housing projects, and 30-storey condominiums springing abruptly up from the flat delta landscape.

Along the road you now pass thirty golf courses (only two there in 1985), three universities (none in 1985), ten hospitals, a boat marina, a power station. At points which had recently seemed quite remote now stand Mercedes Benz showrooms, gleaming temples to wealth and power.

Beyond Laem Chabang, an expanse of some four hundred hectare has been bulldozed flat, planted with factories, and bounded by a container port and a refinery complex. The rapid development of this Eastern Seaboard industrial zone prompted one Pattaya hotelier to complain that industrialization was ruining Thailand's tourist industry. Her guests did not want to drive to their holiday destination through a landscape of the late twentieth century's satanic mills.

With the energetic promotion of tourism ("Visit Thailand Year", "The Most Exotic Destination in Asia", "Amazing Thailand"), Pattaya itself has become bigger and more solid. The coastline is studded with high-rise hotels. The resort offers any amusement imaginable — go-kart tracks, rifle-shooting ranges, crocodile farms, paintball war-games, transvestite shows, discos, elephant rides, bunjee jumps, jet-ski ponds, skating rinks, archery schools, and every size, shape, and subcategory of bar and brothel.

But Pattaya has also begun to change. Its tourist lure has been terminally damaged by sewage, concrete, and greed. More and more, it is developing into a residential suburb of the industrial city spreading down the coast from Bangkok. The hotels and entertainment places are being overwhelmed by residential condominiums, housing estates, supermarkets, department stores, international schools, sports clubs, and all the ornaments of the global city.

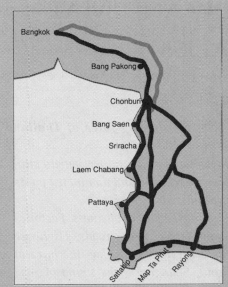

Over the 1985-95 decade, the population of the Bangkok area ballooned to nine million. More dramatically, the city is rapidly spreading along the Pattaya road, linking Bangkok, Bang Pakong, Chonburi, the Eastern Seaboard, Pattaya, and Rayong into one ribbon conurbation. By the early twenty-first century, this mega-city will probably house over twenty million people.

Watching Thailand in the boom decade was like seeing history condensed for a TV documentary. The Pattaya road has changed from a rural seaside route into the artery of an emerging industrial megalopolis. Scenes along the road give glimpses into the human dimension of the boom.

In the evening, workers emerge from the roadside factory. All are dressed in a jacket overall of the same pastel colour. The informal sector is there to meet them. Along the path stretching away from the factory gate, they pass through rows of stalls selling T-shirts, shampoo, instant noodles, comic books, make-up – the toys and trinkets of the new consumerism.

The path ends at a klong, one of the canals built to expand the rice economy a century ago. From the path they step into a long-tailed boat and are whisked back to their village. The pastel overall gradually disappears among the natural colours of the landscape.

2 "Pillow and Mat" Capitalism

Private enterprise has been the driving force of Thailand's boom.

Not so long ago, Bangkok was still a rather courtly city, famed for its palaces, temples, canals, and dominated by its population of government officials.

Today Bangkok is very much a city of business. Factories ring the outskirts. Commuters clog the roads. High-rise office towers crown the centre. The city has the buzz of Hong Kong, Taipei, Seoul, Shanghai – the sound of Asia making money.

The rise of Bangkok business over the past generation is the central story of the boom. The story has three main themes. First, the business community is totally dominated by the immigrant Chinese. In Bangkok they have become more secure and more expansive than elsewhere in Southeast Asia.

Second, this community rose through the classic techniques of such migrant businessmen. They stuck together, saved hard, and suborned the rulers.

Third, they prospered by linking up with powerful forces in the global economy – with the USA's military-economic expansion, with Japan's economic miracle, with the globalizing forces of the 1980s and 1990s. This combination of a secure base and far-flung connections was at the core of the boom.

In 1940, three brothers were running a seed shop in Bangkok's Chinatown. They had been born in China and had immigrated with their father in the 1920s. They grew up speaking Thai and attending Thai schools. During the 1940s, they began to import animal feed and fertilizer. In 1954, they launched a feedmill business.[1]

By the 1970s, their Charoen Pokphand (CP) company had a virtual monopoly on the supply of chickens and eggs. By the 1980s, they had over sixty companies in Thailand spread across poultry, pig-raising, feedmills, and related agribusinesses. They had started similar ventures in Hong Kong, Indonesia, Malaysia, Taiwan, Singapore.

By the 1990s, CP had diversified much more widely. It had become the key player in the booming telecommunications industry in Thailand and had ambitions to spread into neighbouring countries of the region. It had launched into retailing through joint ventures with Japanese Sunny, Dutch Makro, and American 7-Eleven, KFC, and Wal-Mart.

More remarkably, CP had become one of the largest foreign investors in mainland China. The China ventures included their heartland of agribusiness but extended into making motorcycles, distributing petroleum, brewing beer, developing industrial estates, running hypermarkets, and building petrochemical complexes.

By 1995 the CP group claimed to employ over eighty thousand people in over three hundred companies across twenty countries.[2] During their 75-year round trip out from China and back again, the Chiaravanont family had been transformed from poor migrants into a major corporate player in Asia.

The CP story captures the main themes of Thailand's urban growth. The dynamism came from the ambitions of the migrant Chinese. The first take-off point came in the 1940s. For the successful firms and families, the growth from then on was spectacular. For many, success in Thailand's market was just a stepping stone for moving beyond it.

Migrant Chinese families dominate the business of all the major cities of Southeast Asia. But most of the big players fit

11

one of two models. Either they are rooted in finance, property, and services (as in Singapore, Hong Kong). Or they work as the investment arm of powerful political interests (as in Indonesia, Malaysia). It is hard to identify firms elsewhere which are rooted in manufacture and which have been quite as *independent, expansive, and successful* as CP.

What has made Thailand's Chinese migrant families distinctive? What has created such powerful conglomerates as CP? And what has made them so outward-looking, so enthusiastic for going global?

Thailand, a potted economic history

Old Siam (the country was renamed Thailand in 1939) was built on trade. From the fifteenth to nineteenth centuries, the capital was a major port on the Asian trade routes running from Japan to Arabia.[3]

The interior of Siam yielded a wide range of valuable trade goods – medicines, spices, dyes, skins, timbers, ores. Chinese traders flocked to Siam to buy. They brought with them Chinese goods which were trans-shipped from Siam to other Asian markets. Siam's port-capital of Ayutthaya became a cosmopolitan city with settlements of Chinese, Europeans, Japanese, Persians, Arabs.

The Siamese kings made their money from trade. The aristocracy included many who had arrived along the trade routes and been welcomed for their mercantile or professional skill.

As the Europeans gradually came to dominate Asian trade, Siam lost its prominence. Ayutthaya was tucked up the "wrong" side of the Malay peninsula. Siam's trade goods had limited appeal in Europe. For the Europeans, other ports such as Malacca and Singapore were more convenient and more lucrative.

Still the colonial era transformed Siam. Colonial rule in other parts of Asia moved people into cities, plantations, mines where they no longer grew their own rice. Siam had large tracts of empty delta swamp which simple drainage works could convert into paddy fields. From the mid-nineteenth century, Siam (and its neighbours of Burma and Indochina) became the rice granary of colonial Asia. Rice exports boomed. Large numbers of Chinese migrated to Siam to provide manpower and commercial expertise for this new economy.

European merchants did a little business in Siam extracting teak, rubber, and tin. But the volumes were small compared to neighbouring colonial territories. The Europeans were more successful at furnishing the growing urban population with imported goods and at providing specialized services such as banking, insurance, shipping, and managing agencies.[4]

On the eve of the Second World War, Thailand's economy was dominated by the rice trade. Four of every five people earned their livelihood from growing, transporting, milling, or trading rice. Paddy supplied 60 percent of all exports. A handful of Chinese-origin rice-barons were the city's new commercial elite. Beyond rice, the economy was little developed and dominated by the Europeans.

Immigrant Chinese

Between the early nineteenth century and 1950, some four million Chinese boarded the ships leaving the ports of southern China bound for Bangkok. Over a million of them stayed on in Siam.[5]

The kings encouraged the migration. They needed labour. They wanted the migrants' trading talents to drive the economy.

The journey to Siam was tough. Most who came were poor and desperate. The main catchment area was the Taejew-speaking region around Swatow. The typical migrant arrived with no more than "one pillow and one mat". Some of them settled on the land. Many more stayed in the city or upcountry towns. They worked as coolies to earn some seed capital, and as soon as possible set up a shop or small trading business. By the 1850s, Chinese petty traders could be found "penetrating every creek".[6]

As China's internal political and economic crisis steadily worsened, the flow of migrants turned into a flood. The

Chinese migrant getting off the boat in Bangkok could find a society of compatriots just a few hundred yards away. By contrast, most Thai peasants had land to till and no interest in going to the city. For them, Bangkok was a foreign sort of place, full of Siamese aristocrats, *farang* businessmen, Chinese merchants and coolies. The Thai peasants stayed in the villages. The Chinese came to dominate urban Siam.

From the final years of the nineteenth century, Siam's rulers worried about the growing numbers, wealth, and confidence of the urban Chinese. Through the first half of the twentieth century, their concern deepened. China's internal politics became more vexed and violent. Some backwash of these politics was imported along with the migrants.

The rulers occasionally took steps to suppress the Chinese. In 1911, the Chinese community leaders called a general strike which paralyzed the city's commerce for five days. The government deported the leaders. The King wrote a tract slating the Chinese as the "Jews of the Orient" – money-grubbing and potentially disloyal, "like so many vampires who steadily suck dry an unfortunate victim's life-blood".[7]

In the 1930s, new nationalist political leaders revived the parallel of the Jews and the Chinese with a fascist tinge. After the Second World War, the government banned travel to Maoist China, threw suspected communist sympathizers in jail, stopped the immigration flow, and harassed leaders of Bangkok's Chinese community.

But this persecution was limited and sporadic. There were no race riots, no pogroms, no mass expulsions. In many other countries of the region, the immigrant Chinese had a rougher ride. Why was Siam more welcoming?

For centuries, Siam had welcomed foreigners who helped to swell the wealth of the kingdom. Many of the great aristocratic mandarin families were descended from such migrants.[8] Until the mid-nineteenth century, these families were active in overseas trade. Later they settled for a simple threefold social division: Thai peasants tilled the land; Thai bureaucrats ran the government; Chinese merchants and labourers ran the urban economy.

The rulers' main concern was about Chinese *politics*. They feared that China's republicanism and communism would flow into Thailand and disturb the social order. They wanted to keep the economic benefits of Chinese immigration but neutralize any political side-effects.

The rulers' strategy was to encourage the migrants to be economically Chinese but politically Thai.

In 1911 they passed a Nationality Act which allowed anyone born in the country, of whatever parentage, to take Siamese nationality. The kings emphasized that "being Thai" was not an ethnic definition but a cultural act. An immigrant who learnt the Thai language, became Buddhist, honoured the king, and *acted like a Thai*, could become a Thai.

The rulers first encouraged and later forced the urban Chinese to put their children through Thai schools where they learnt the Thai language, habits, and attitudes. For many, this was the critical experience.

They were still Chinese but now they were *Siamese Chinese*. In the 1920s, the leading Bangkok merchants formed the *samosorn jin sayam* – the association of Siamese-Chinese. They could not deny their Chinese heritage. But they laid claim to a share in Siamese/Thai nationality, and Siamese nationalism.[9]

Of course it helped that the immigrant Chinese could adopt the dominant local Buddhism and intermarry with local Thai women. But these were details. The critical factor which made integration possible was the attitude of the rulers – who shared with the migrants a Chinese heritage and an orientation to trade.

Nationalism and Profit

In many other Asian countries, nationalists flung out the colonial rulers and then flung out the Chinese (or Indian) migrant merchant communities for collaborating in colonial exploitation. Some countries allowed the Chinese to stay but subjected them to social and economic discrimination.

For a time, Thailand appeared to move in the same direction. In the late 1930s, new nationalist rulers set out to develop "a Thai economy for the Thai people". They reserved certain occupations for Thai labour. They set up state companies to dislodge Chinese merchants from their dominant position in commerce.

But Thailand had no colonial rule. The Chinese merchants were not tainted with colonial collaboration. The nationalist politicians did not have the same sense of mission or the same emotional popular support as the nationalists in colonial territories.

As the Chinese entrepreneurs grew wealthier on the new business opportunities of the 1940s, they became not bigger enemies of the nationalist politicians but more attractive friends. The politicians were easily tempted to tap growing business wealth to bolster their own shaky political power.

The courtship of business and politics began in the late 1930s. The politicians set up state enterprises but then invited leading Chinese businessmen to run them and make them profitable. The relationship deepened through the 1940s. Chinese businesses stacked their boards with Thai politicians and generals. The politicians used the wealth gained from profits and perks to build political war-chests. They repaid their business partners with government contracts, monopolies, and other privileges.[10]

In the second half of the twentieth century, Thailand was unique in having a migrant merchant community relatively unruffled by the strains of decolonization and nationalist rule. In Burma, the Indian and Chinese trading communities were thrown out. In Indochina, most Chinese left in the waves of boat people. In the Philippines, the Chinese were drummed out of the key retail trade. In Indonesia, the Chinese lay low after the pogrom of 1965. In Malaysia, the government discriminated against the Chinese through legislation and patronage. In Thailand, the Chinese merged in and made lots of money.

Shophouse Tycoons: The 1940s Take-Off

Half a century ago, Thailand's urban business was probably smaller and less sophisticated than almost any other country in eastern Asia.

Neighbours like Burma, Malaysia, and Indochina inherited more factories, ministries, proto-technocrats, and educated workers from their departing colonial masters. The Philippines economy was twice Thailand's size. Korea and Taiwan took over heavy industries founded by the colonial Japanese. Taiwan was boosted by expertise, capital, plant, and enterprise transported from Shanghai.

From mid-century onwards, Thailand's economy grew rapidly with hardly a serious break. The growth rate averaged 5 percent a year in the 1950s, 8 percent in the 1960s, and 7 percent in the 1970s. After 1985, it shifted up another gear. The boom was grounded on two generations' accumulation of capital, skills, organizational development, and entrepreneurial talent.

How did it all get started?

Through to the 1940s, Thailand's urban business was overwhelmingly small-scale. A few families had done well in the rice trade but such families were very rare. Many more had been wrecked by the vicious swings of the international rice market.

Even fewer had prospered in industry. Openings for manufacture were limited because the market was small and because foreign agency houses could import most things more cheaply. Only 2 percent of the labour force worked in manufacturing. A cement works, paper mill, tobacco factory, brewery, soap factory, textile mill, and a handful of match factories were the only big manufacturing enterprises. Bangkok was packed with small shops, workshops, and service businesses. Thailand's urban capitalism was stuck at the shophouse stage.

The change came in the 1940s. The war disrupted imports from Europe and wiped out most foreign business. The entrepreneurs who seized the opportunities of this moment became the tycoons of the next generation.

Sukree set up a cloth import business. He became Thailand's textile magnate. The Chirathiwat family set up a grocery store. They went on to build the Central retailing empire. Thiem Chokwatana also started a grocery business. He later moved into manufacture and built the Sahapat consumer goods conglomerate. Wit and Prapha Viriyaprapaikit started a scrap metal business. Their Sahaviriya firm later dominated the steel industry. Thaworn Phornprapha set up a scrap metal dealership and an auto repair shop. He would become the leader of the automotive industry.

Kiat Srifuengfung started banking and insurance businesses. He would later become a leading industrialist with interests across textiles, glass, and chemicals. Uthane Techaphaibun started a liquor wholesaling business which grew into the Sura Maharas distilling empire. Suri Asadathaon began a sugar refinery which became the foundation of the Thai Roong Ruang agribusiness conglomerate.

During the 1940s, most of the entrepreneurs whose companies would dominate Thai business over the next half-century had made their first big decision and the beginnings of their first fortune.[11]

A few of these new entrepreneurs were recent migrants who had stepped off the boats in the last rush of migration in the 1930s. More had been born in Siam of Chinese parentage. Some had grown up in Bangkok but several had been educated partly in Siam and partly in Hong Kong or the mainland. They had one foot in Thailand and the other in a wider Chinese diaspora throughout Southeast Asia.

They used the two usual tactics of migrant enterprise – thrift and cooperation. They joined together in business syndicates. Out of these syndicates came the central institutions of the post-war expansion: the banks.

The Banks

Until the 1940s, trade financing was dominated by the European banks. When these banks closed during the war, it created both a need and an opportunity.

In 1944 nine Taejew merchant families set up a partnership to exploit opportunities in gold dealing, export-import, and banking. They brought in Chin Sophonpanich, a Siam-born and China-educated businessman who was well-known for his facility with finance.

Chin learnt the systems for financing overseas trade which earlier had been monopolized by the European banks. He travelled around the region setting up correspondent relations with banks in all the major export destinations, often tapping relations with kinsmen and clansmen. Chin's Bangkok Bank quickly came to dominate both trade financing and remittance back to mainland China.[12]

In the early 1950s, the government stopped these remittances. In 1962, it passed legislation which made banks more attractive as deposit-holders than the pawnshops which had earlier served the function. The banks began spreading branches upcountry to finance crop trading.

Thousands of Chinese trading families, which had previously kept their savings back in China, in the pawnshop, or under the bed, now deposited them in the banks. The upcountry branch networks funnelled provincial savings back to Bangkok. For two decades, the deposits in the banks accumulated at an average rate of 20 percent a year. Between 1962 and 1981, their deposits multiplied twenty-five times.

Over a third of this amount flowed into Bangkok Bank alone. Much of the rest went into three other banking groups – the Lamsam family's Thai Farmers Bank, the Techaphaibun family's Bangkok Metropolitan Bank, and the Rattanarak family's Bank of Ayudhya.

This aggregation of so many petty savings created stocks of capital available for enterprises of a much bigger scale than the family firm. It also made the major banks the centrepiece of business growth. They acted as much more than just banks. They worked like investment houses, informal chambers of commerce, and business consultancies.

They established lots of their own companies. By 1979, the four major banks had founded a total of 295 companies spread across finance, trade, and manufacture. More importantly, they also financed and promoted the growth of small groups of associated entrepreneurs.

Often these associates were part of the syndicates who had helped form the bank in the 1940s. Others came on board later. For these associates, the banks not only provided finance but facilitated deals, found overseas contacts through their networks in the diaspora, and managed their political relations.[13]

Bankers and Generals

In 1953, the generals who had seized power by coup in 1947 were thinking of setting up a bank to service their growing business interests. Chin Sophonpanich persuaded them not to start a new venture but to join hands with the Bangkok Bank. The generals transferred thirty million baht from the government coffers to the Bank's capital account. Chin put the generals on the board. The generals grew fat on directors' fees, dividends, and presents. Bangkok Bank became the nation's largest bank and never looked back.[14]

Similar marriages of convenience were contracted between the other major banking groups and the generals. These links had to be adjusted from time to time to reflect the fortunes of competing military cliques, but this politico-financial axis dominated until the mid-1970s. The generals skimmed revenue from rising business profits to build their personal fortunes and their political careers. In return, the bankers and their friends obtained privileges and favours which could be critically important in business competition.

These favours could be very simple but highly effective. Government ordered that all taxis should be Nissans. Thaworn Phornprapha, the scrap merchant turned Nissan importer, went on to dominate the automobile industry.[15]

Other favours were more flagrant. In the 1950s, government began to sell off state enterprises. Some favoured businessmen acquired these factories and monopolistic market positions at little or no cost. Uthane Techaphaibun took over the government's monopoly for distilling local whisky and the plant of a government-built brewery.[16]

Other privileges were even more expansive. General Pramarn Adireksarn was a key political contact of the Bangkok Bank. He travelled to Japan in his capacity as commerce minister and helped to negotiate joint-venture deals with Japanese textile makers. Some members of the Bangkok Bank group went on to dominate Thailand's growing textile industry, while Pramarn prospered as a shareholder in many of their ventures.[17]

This marriage of business and politics was formalized in the late 1950s under the regime of General Sarit (1957-63).[18] The US had cultivated the friendship of Thai generals for several years before Sarit came to power. The US encouraged Sarit to adopt a free-world model of development, which meant providing state backing for the growth of private business. Sarit and his henchmen were already sitting on the boards of Thailand's leading firms. They readily agreed.[19]

Helped by US money and expertise, the generals boosted business. With US grants and loans, they built the schools and colleges to train a new workforce. With US expertise, they established the infrastructure to manage a modern urban economy – budget bureau, planning board, upgraded central bank – and trained the technocrats to staff them.

The US advisers and these technocrats restructured the economy in line with the US development model. They scaled back the state enterprises; established tariff protection to protect infant enterprises; introduced incentives for investment; and welcomed in US and other foreign capital to boost local ventures.[20]

With all this assistance, the urban economy began to grow rapidly.

Strategies for Growth

Around this period, the governments of the Four Tigers started to wrench their economies around to manufacturing for export. They recast taxes and tariffs to favour manufactured exports; channelled credit and investment funds towards industries with export potential; sank government money in large-scale industrial projects; helped firms to find the technology and skills needed to compete in world markets.

Thailand's government did none of these things. For both government and business, agriculture promised quicker and surer returns than a difficult leap towards industrialization.

For a century, the Thai economy had been driven by agricultural exports – teak, rubber, and especially rice. In 1960, these three still contributed two-thirds of all exports. In total, agricultural products accounted for almost four-fifths.

The Americans helped build dams and research stations to push the rice economy ahead. They funded new roads out to remote areas where they set up military bases. These roads opened up huge empty areas for growing the crops demanded by world markets.

From around 1950 onwards, world demand for agricultural goods increased, driven by the growth in the economies of Europe and the US. World prices for agricultural goods rose in parallel. The Americans' strategic roads connected this demand to an open land frontier.

The Four Tigers had gone for export manufacture in part because they had few other options. They had little or no spare land. With the American roads, Thailand found it had heaps.

For thirty years, new land was cleared and planted at the rate of over 300,000 hectares a year. Some 2.5 million new farms were created. The total area of farmland doubled. Agricultural exports increased at an average rate of 12 percent a year and powered the economy.

The urban entrepreneurs grew within this framework. Some invested in crop trading, processing, and agribusiness to stimulate the crop expansion and take a healthy profit from it. Others invested in supplying goods to the domestic market rising on the impetus of agrarian exports. At first they imported consumer goods. Then in the 1960s, when government tariffs encouraged import substitution, they moved into manufacture.

Some gradually back-extended into process industries and manufacture of intermediate goods. A few (especially in textiles) began to export some of their product. But these adventures were peripheral to the main thrust of agricultural-export-led growth and import substitution.

Government stimulated this growth of urban enterprise. It held rice prices down so that employers could pay low wages. It offered tax breaks to encourage investment. It provided tariff protection so new industries could charge higher prices. The new urban entrepreneurs were borne upwards by the combination of agricultural growth and indirect government subsidy.

The Conglomerates

Through the 1960s and 1970s a handful of big conglomerates came to dominate this rapid urban growth.

Some had roots way back. The Siam Cement Company had been formed in the 1900s and counted the crown and senior aristocrats among its shareholders. The company extended into heavy engineering, construction materials, and other areas.

A few other firms emerged from the big rice-trading families of the 1930s. The Lamsam moved from rice milling and trading into banking in the 1940s and then onto a range of ventures rooted in finance or agribusiness. The Wanglee, who had been the largest rice-traders, also moved into banking on a smaller scale and into agribusiness on a much larger one.

Many more of the new conglomerates were formed by families which emerged with the new banks in the 1940s. Through the banks, they had access to capital. Through their political friends they secured licences, promotional privileges, government contracts, and other crucial favours. Their strong base and political links in turn made them attractive partners for incoming foreign investors.

The group around the Bangkok Bank was far and away the most prominent: the Sophonpanich family in banking and investment; the Chirathiwat with a base in retailing; the Srifuengfung in glass, chemicals, and engineering joint ventures with the Japanese; Sukree and Saha-Union in textile ventures with the Japanese; the Phornprapha assembling Japanese automobiles and then extending further into companies producing parts and components; the Chiaravanont (CP) family spreading its agribusiness empire out from Thailand to the region; the Techaphaibun in banking, insurance, and liquor.

The leading families drew on the traditions of cooperation and mutual assistance fostered within the immigrant community. They headed up community associations based on clan and origin. They solidified links through marriage alliances which often crossed the usual delimiters of clan and dialect. They took cross-interests in one another's companies. Typically the lead entrepreneur would invite many friends to take a small stake in any new venture. It spread the risk. It shared the gain.

These networks of business and family connections became dense and complex. Journalists and academics sometimes attempted to plot them. The results looked like microchip circuit diagrams and seemed to go on forever.

By the late 1970s, there were around thirty of these conglomerates and their distribution mapped the pattern of urban growth. Six were centred on the banks, with extensions into other financial services and a host of investment companies. Nine were based in agribusiness with their roots in rice, sugar, feedmills, and cassava. Another six were anchored in businesses supplying the domestic consumer market – assembling automobiles and electrical goods, manufacturing pharmaceuticals and other consumer goods. Two specialized in textiles. The remaining seven were in basic process industries – building materials, chemicals, steel, and glass.[21]

Each conglomerate had a cluster of companies grouped around its core interest. Most had extended sideways into related fields. Several had moved into ancillary service businesses such as finance, distribution, insurance, property. Some had branched out into diverse areas through buy-outs or through fathers indulging the business whims of their sons. Altogether the thirty groups had interests in over eight hundred companies.

The leading families looked outwards for expertise and assistance. With their origin overseas and their roots in trading, their horizons extended beyond the limits of Thailand. As late-comers in a developed world, they understood the benefits of profiting from the expertise of those who had developed earlier. They sent their children overseas for education (mainly to the US) and used their learning to upgrade the operations of the family firm. They entered enthusiastically into joint ventures with foreign capital which gave them access to technology, expertise, markets. A quarter of the eight hundred companies were joint ventures.

At first, foreign capital came mainly from the USA. By the early 1970s, Japan had become the largest source. The Japanese invested with the conglomerates in ventures to supply the protected local market and to a lesser extent in textiles for export. Japanese companies explained that they found it easy to do business in Thailand largely because local firms were useful partners. Unlike in many other countries of the region, the local entrepreneurs had good political connections and could operate without serious difficulty.[22]

"Pillow and Mat" Capitalism

"Because we have no social security," said a leading light of the diaspora, "the Overseas Chinese habit is to save a lot and make a lot of friends."[23]

In Thailand they not only saved themselves but also tapped the savings of others through the commercial banks. They made friends not just with one another but also with the generals and the foreign investors. They obtained capital from the banks, technology from their overseas partners, and market privileges from their political contacts. The combination of immigrant enterprise, political security, plentiful capital, and international technology fuelled rapid growth.

From "pillow and mat" migrants, in one or two generations some thirty Chinese-origin families became the commercial dynasts of Bangkok. Government and the banks shaped the environment for the conglomerates to grow.

Government promoted agriculture and used tax, tariff, and pricing policies to transfer a surplus to the urban economy. A large chunk of this surplus accumulated in the banks. The major banks spotted the "winners," the sectors with high growth potential, and allocated funds to their friends to invest in these sectors. Bangkok Bank first financed the rice trade. Then textiles and agribusiness. Then process industries. And later still, petrochemicals and infrastructure.

For two decades, the strategy of agricultural expansion and import substitution worked well for the business leaders. In the late 1970s (see chapter 4), it faltered. The conglomerates put pressure on government to switch to a manufactured-export-led strategy after the pattern of the Four Tigers. For around a decade, the government hesitated about taking a leap into the unknown. Only after the economy faced a major recession in 1984-5, did the government finally relent.

Bangkok's business leaders breathed a sigh of relief. And turned outwards to the world.

3 GOING GLOBAL

Thailand's rising entrepreneurs hailed the age of globalization. But being late-comers in a competi-tive world was hard.

In the mid-1980s, rising currencies and costs in Japan and the Tiger economies made Southeast Asia attractive as a cheap site for export production. Thai entrepreneurs responded quickly. In a few years they were exporting garments, shoes, bags, canned fish, jewellery and plastic goods to the world.

But the multinationals were not far behind. From 1987, foreign capital and companies flooded in to Thailand. Some of the new ventures made cheap-labour goods like garments. Many more invested in medium-tech areas like electronics, electrical goods and automotive parts.

International finance was next in the queue. Between 1990 and 1993 Thailand liberalized its financial market. Fund managers, merchant banks and broking firms set up shop in Bangkok. Thai firms now had access to more funds and cheaper funds than ever before.

But how to use this largesse? Competing against the multinationals in export manufacture grew tougher. Many Thai firms found other openings. Some invested in service industries borne up by booming local demand. Some shifted into heavy industries. In both these areas, local knowledge and political torque conveyed advantages over the foreigners.

Some ventured overseas – into the opening markets of neighbouring countries and, more successfully, into mainland China. Here again, connections counted.

Thailand's entrepreneurs welcomed globalization but sought protection against its realities.

In 1988, Thaksin Shinawatra was running a company which sold IBM computers to government departments. The company was part of Thailand's small and struggling computer-vending industry. It performed a little better than most because of Thaksin's extensive kin and colleague networks in the bureaucracy. He had started the company while a police officer and later resigned to run it full time. But in 1988 computer-vending was not a business likely to generate super-profits.

When Thaksin joined the cabinet in mid-1995, he declared assets worth around seventy billion baht (US$2.8 billion).

Most of this had been accumulated over the previous seven years. Thaksin had ridden the boom both outwards and upwards – outwards across Thailand's borders and upwards into the sky.

From his computer-vending base, Thaksin had expanded into technology-based businesses which rose on growing urban demand – a pay TV service, mobile telephone network, paging system, data transfer facilities. Then in December 1993, he launched Thailand's first communications satellite and placed himself in the driving seat for the expansion of television broadcasting and telecommunications.[1]

At the same time, he spread his businesses into neighbouring countries – Vietnam, Laos, Cambodia, Burma – and began to prospect even further afield – Indonesia, Philippines, India.

Thaksin's success had three foundations: government concessions, off-the-shelf technology, and a spiralling stockmarket.

Thaksin secured his first government concession in September 1989. Over the next two years, he added five more.

He found his technology from all over. The cable TV service relied heavily on US programming. The mobile phones were

Scandinavian. The paging system was Japanese. The Shinawatra satellite was made in the US, mounted on a French rocket, and shot up from South America.

Thaksin used the stock exchange to expand his capital base. After 1988 he floated four companies which by 1995 had a combined capitalization of over 200 billion baht. He used the market deftly. He floated the satellite company just a few days before the rocket launch, allowing punters the thrill of gambling whether it would make it into orbit. It did and the share price followed.

The story of Thaksin's rapid rise to become one of the nation's richest and most high-profile businessmen is astounding in itself. Extending Thaksin's story backwards emphasizes further the extraordinary transformation of these years.

Before the Shinawatra family name became linked to satellites, it was best known for a very traditional product – Thai silk.[2]

At the turn of the century, the Shinawatra family were merchants and tax-farmers in the northern state of Lanna (Chiang Mai). Later they quit tax-farming and concentrated on the cross-border trade between Burma, China, and Siam. Silk became the most lucrative part of the trade.

Like many ex-tax-farmers, the family invested in education and put sons into the bureaucracy and local politics. Several members of the family went into the army. One became an MP, another the local mayor. In 1986, Thaksin's uncle became deputy minister of communications. The next generation went farther afield for their education – to Germany, Japan, and the US. Thaksin took a doctorate in criminology from the US and entered the police. In two generations, the Shinawatra family had hopped from tax-farming to the silk trade, skipped to bureaucrat careers, and jumped up into the heady world of globalized business.

By origin the Shinawatra were provincial businessmen based in one of Thailand's most traditional commodities. In the boom, Thaksin was transformed from computer-vending middleman into mega-rich tycoon. He succeeded by building connections in the bureaucracy, by raising money off the stock market, by buying technology off the markets of the world. In Thailand's boom, this was the recipe for success.

Making for the World

In the mid-1980s, Asia's regional economy went through a revolution. Up to this point, Japan and the Four Tigers had shown the way to export-led growth. But as they prospered, wages and other production costs increased. For a time, these countries managed to stay competitive in world markets by keeping their currencies low. But eventually this resulted in big trade surpluses with the rest of the world and big deficits elsewhere – especially in the US and Europe.

In late 1985, the rest of the world forced Japan to revalue the yen. The other Tiger currencies followed the yen upwards. Thailand had devalued the baht against the dollar a year earlier. Now the baht was linked to the dollar and rode down further against the east Asian currencies.

In four years, the cost of Thai products in terms of yen *halved*. Thailand's small manufacturing sector was suddenly exposed to the tug of world demand and especially demand from booming Japan. The economist-turned-banker, Olarn Chaiprawat, predicted a "golden age" for the Thai economy.[3]

From 1985 to 1990, total exports from Thailand multiplied three times. Exports from Thailand to Japan multiplied four times. And exports of manufactures almost five times.

This export surge was not limited to a small range of products or a handful of firms. Nor at this first stage was it spurred by foreign investment and dominated by foreign firms.

The sharp rise was led by local (and joint-venture) firms in labour-intensive manufacture. Total textile and garment exports from Thailand multiplied eleven times over the 1980s and became the single largest export sector. By 1990, the industry employed almost a million people. Besides this classic cheap-labour sector, the export surge extended to jewellery, shoes, toys, plastic products, furniture, canned and processed foods, leather, rubber goods, and artificial flowers.

As over the last three decades, the big conglomerates led the way. When the boom hit, many of them had spare capacity which could be geared to meet export demand. They made quick profits and reinvested in expansion. Many of the conglomerates also expanded their investments in partnership with inflowing foreign capital. They already had the contacts with the Japanese and other migrant firms. They were still the most attractive partners for incoming investors.

But the conglomerates did not dominate to the extent they had over the past three decades. They could not monopolize export opportunities in the same way they had dominated the local market. They did not have the management resources to expand at the extraordinary rate of the boom.

Many small and medium sized companies were quicker off the mark. Where did they suddenly spring from?

Some were spun out of the conglomerates by the rising generation of the owner families. Many more emerged from the huge base of small trading, service, and manufacturing companies. Several firms which had earlier developed a small business supplying the home market, made windfall profits from exporting during the phase of currency realignment in mid-decade. They then reinvested the profits in expanding their involvement in exports.

Many of these developed export potential from a mix of cheap labour and locally available raw materials. But once they had developed their export expertise, they kept on expanding by processing *imported* raw materials too. They stopped being just local resource-based industries and became significant world players in their sector.

The seafood freezing and canning industry soon moved beyond the diminishing resources of the gulf and other coastal waters. By the end of the decade, it was canning tuna from the Pacific and had become the world's second-largest seafood industry. The leather goods industries developed a high-end segment using Italian and Latin American hides. The jewellery business expanded from cutting and setting (mostly smuggled) stones from Cambodia and Burma, to becoming one of the five major gem centres in the world.[4]

Moving to Thailand

The multinationals were not far behind. From 1987, foreign investment flooded into Thailand.

As the yen and other Asian currencies hardened from 1985 onwards, companies began a race to find cheaper places to site their factories.[5] Thailand was not the immediate choice. Its economy was still reeling from the recession. Only a few foreign investors arrived in 1985-6. But by 1987, Thai exports had turned decisively upwards. Japanese and Taiwanese investors now arrived by the plane-load. Between the middle and end of the decade, the annual net inflow of foreign investment multiplied ten times. The inflow of the last three years of the decade was greater than the total foreign investment of the previous thirty.

Foreign investment transformed upswing into boom. Export growth spurted past 20 percent. Real economic growth lifted into double digits.

While garments and other classic cheap-labour industries were the first products to boom, the surge of foreign investment shifted the emphasis to medium-tech industries, particularly electrical appliances, electronics, and auto parts.[6] Joint ventures which had been set up to supply Thailand's domestic market from inside the tariff walls, were now expanded to produce goods for export.

Japanese parent firms developed complex networks of production spanning several sites across Southeast Asia.

Different units in these networks specialized in producing particular parts and components. By 1990, a Mitsubishi joint-venture in Thailand assembled light trucks for export to North America using parts made in Japan, Thailand, Malaysia, Indonesia, and the Philippines.

To lower their production costs, these Japanese parent firms chivvied their Japanese subcontractors to move overseas. If the subcontractors refused, the parent firms looked for ways to develop new subcontractors in Thailand.

New component factories and process shops mushroomed. Some were wholly local enterprises with technological input from the parent assembler. Some were joint ventures with the migrant subcontract firms. Thailand's industrial structure began to acquire more depth. By the end of the decade, engineering products and other intermediate goods had become some of the fastest growing sectors of both manu-facturing and exports.

Japanese and Taiwanese firms had been assembling electrical appliances in Thailand for the domestic market for several

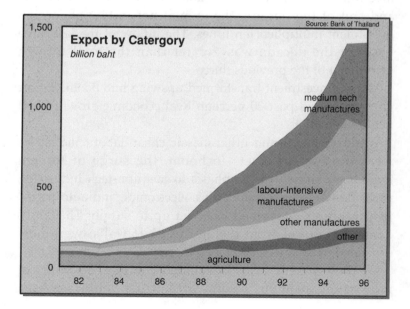

Export by Catergory
billion baht

Source: Bank of Thailand

medium tech manufactures

labour-intensive manufactures

other manufactures

other

agriculture

decades. From the mid-1980s, they geared up these plants for export. Televisions were the lead product. By the 1990s Thailand produced TVs with 70 percent local content and a high degree of international competitiveness.

In the 1980s, several semiconductor companies had set up plants in Thailand but the production was small. Semiconductor companies preferred the EPZs in places like Sri Lanka and Malaysia. But at the end of the decade, Thailand's semiconductor sector began to expand. Between 1989 and 1995, total exports tripled to reach 50 billion baht.

The manufacture of computer parts increased even faster. In the mid-1980s exports were negligible. By the mid-1990s, they were worth over 90 billion baht, more than double the value of rice exports.

The Japanese firm Minebea first came to Thailand to make ball-bearings. By the late 1980s, Minebea had learnt that Thailand was a good site for more sophisticated businesses. It began to shift its computer component businesses from Japan and Taiwan. By the mid 1990s, it had transferred 60 percent of all its production into Thailand, leaving just 20 percent in Japan. It employed twenty-five thousand making printers, keyboards, stepper motors, disk-drive components, and many other parts.

In 1991, Seagate moved a large section of its disk-drive assembly from Singapore to Bangkok. Micropolis, Asahi, Toshiba, Fujitsu, IBM and Read-Rite followed suit. By the mid-1990s, 15 percent of world exports of disk-drives came from Thailand. Seagate alone had six plants, a total workforce of forty-four thousand, and 4 percent of all Thailand's exports. Many smaller local and foreign (mainly Taiwanese) firms set up to supply components and services for the electronics industry.

By the early 1990s, electronics and other medium-tech goods overtook textiles and other labour-intensive goods as Thailand's largest export sector. From 1991 to 1995, they increased at 27 percent a year.

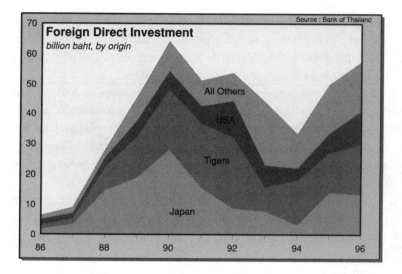

The flow of foreign investment slackened in the early 1990s but then accelerated from 1993 when the yen again began to shift upwards. The Board of Investment set up an office in Osaka to attract migrant Japanese capital. From 1993 to 1996, a new Japanese factory opened in Thailand every three days.

In this "third wave" of relocation, the scale was larger and the technology higher. The main destinations for the foreign inflow were the chemical, petrochemical, electronic, and machinery industries. Samsung announced a huge new semiconductor plant. Toshiba laid plans for a range of electronic component factories. Both Japanese and American firms eyed Thailand as a base for automotive industries.

Since the 1960s, Thailand had encouraged automotive companies to set up assembly plants. Government protected them with high tariffs and hustled them to gradually increase the level of local content. By 1990, fourteen plants produced 240,000 automobiles with 54 to 80 percent local content, and five firms produced 700,000 two-stroke motorcycles with 75 percent local content. Most of the firms were Japanese with Thai partners.

In 1991, government liberalized the auto industry by dropping tariffs and removing other restrictions. Prices fell while incomes rose on the boom. The market exploded.

Imports increased. More strikingly, the main assemblers invested in more capacity and nearly doubled sales in two years. Auto firms now predicted Thailand would be the region's largest market, with a million cars and pick-ups a year by the year 2000. With vehicle tariffs due to drop to 0-5 percent under the ASEAN Free Trade Agreement, the biggest market also made sense as the region's export hub.

Mitsubishi began to export Thai-made pick-ups. Toyota expanded its auto plant to become the company's largest outside Japan and its main platform for exports to Asia and Australia. In 1995, Honda named Thailand as its major production base for worldwide export of automobiles and motorcycles. The Korean firms, Hyundai and Daewoo, established assembly operations. Honda and Toyota chose Thailand to launch new cars designed and priced for the region's booming market of middle-managers. Over 1991-6, exports of vehicles and (mainly) parts grew from 3.7 to 18.8 billion baht.

In 1996, two of the big US auto makers arrived. Chrysler planned to make a hundred thousand cars a year mostly for export within Asia, especially Japan. Ford teamed up with Mazda to make a similar volume of pick-up trucks for export.

These export projects created a secondary wave of investment in parts and inputs. In 1996-7, one hundred new parts firms set up shop. Chrysler had earlier bargained hard for government to scrap the 54 percent local-content policy. But now it expected to use 65 percent local parts. The Ford/Mazda pick-ups would have over 80 percent, including engines and transmissions, from a hundred local suppliers.[7]

At the start of this medium-tech wave, Thai conglomerates and other Thai firms were heavily involved. Joint ventures set up earlier to supply the domestic market were reoriented towards export. Incoming Japanese and Taiwanese firms sought a strong local partner for speed and ease.

Some Thai firms climbed up the technology ladder by watching and copying. When Taiwanese firms set up in Thailand to produce plastic toys, a Thai melamine manufacturer managed to reverse-engineer the process. Within a couple of years, thirty Thai firms were exporting plastic toys.[8]

Many others went out and bought the technology they needed to compete. Most ambitious of all was Alphatec.

The firm was founded by a Thai engineer who had worked in the computer industry in the USA. It bought over the semiconductor plants established by Signetics and National Semiconductor, and an R&D firm in California. In 1995 it launched a project to build Thailand's first silicon wafer plant and a joint venture with TI to make memory chips. It persuaded the government to co-invest in an R&D centre and planned a hi-tech industrial complex around these ventures.[9]

But while Thai firms participated enthusiastically, over time the medium-tech export drive became more of a multinational affair.

Foreign partners increased their share of joint ventures, bought out their local partner, or shifted to a new 100-percent–owned firm. IBM's first disk-drive plant was a partnership with Saha-Union. But its second and much larger unit was wholly owned. Mitsubishi pioneered exporting pickups in cooperation with its old domestic distribution partner but then bought them out.

Within less than a decade, Thailand had been turned first into a typical cheap-labour sweatshop and then into a platform for medium-tech industry. While local firms had been quickest off the mark in the mid-1980s, by the early 1990s they were being overhauled by the multinationals.

More Money from More Places

Because foreign investment was concentrated in the new sectors of the economy, it had an important dynamizing effect. But it was still a relatively small factor. At the peak in 1990, foreign direct investment was sixty-two billion baht, equal to 3 percent of GDP. Total corporate investment, meanwhile, grew six times in five years to reach seven hundred billion baht a year in the early 1990s, equal to around 25 percent of GDP.

Foreign inflows may have sparked the boom. Thai investments made it a big boom.

In the early 1990s, some of the increase in investment was financed by foreign inflows of portfolio capital and bank loans. Some came from household savings mobilized by new financial institutions. But the major contribution throughout the boom was corporate savings – ploughback and reinvestment by local firms. *The volume of saving by private firms jumped seven times between 1985 and 1993.*

The major banks experienced another jolt of rapid expansion, growing their asset base from 714 to 4,605 billion baht between

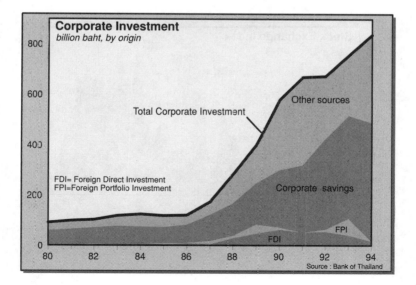

1985 and 1994. Earlier, banks had been the only source of modern business finance. But now more money was available from other sources – from finance companies, stock flotations, and foreign loans. These new sources liberated small and medium firms from dependence on the banks.

Finance companies worked under different rules from banks. They could offer higher rates of deposit and undertake riskier but potentially more profitable types of lending. In the slump of 1983-5, the finance sector came close to collapse. From 1986 on, it boomed. Between 1985 and 1994, total assets increased from 133 to 1,211 billion baht.

By 1991, the sector was so buoyant that the government could sell off companies bankrupted in 1983-5 to investors desperate to get a finance company licence. In the boom, finance companies played a major role in financing the new small and medium firms which did not have the right connections to the banks.

By 1989, the stock exchange offered another new opportunity for raising capital. The Thai stock exchange had been founded in 1975 but had died after the crash of a pyramiding finance company in 1979. In 1987, it came alive again.

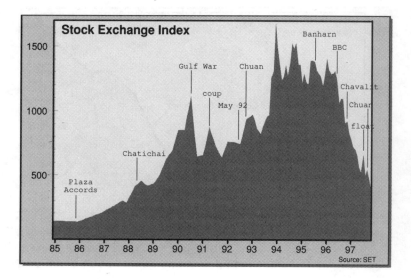

During the recovery from the Black Friday crash of October 1987, speculative portfolio capital from Hong Kong and Taiwan flooded onto the Thai exchange. The market quickly acquired a reputation for being exciting but dangerous. A short-term investment, some said, was one you sold before lunch time. Insider trading was not illegal, it was obligatory.[10]

The stock exchange index rose three times in four years and then doubled again over the next three. The favoured few who had access to the market made quick and easy fortunes.

Some manufactured spectacular asset value by "chain listing" – floating a company, then floating subsidiary companies, with assets and profits transferred along the chain to make each new listing attractive.[11]

When this initial spurt levelled off, a new job of professional stock manipulator was created. These people could be hired to "churn" a share upwards. Other investors chased after knowledge of what shares were in line for "churning". Before long just the rumour that a share was on the list was enough to send it up through secondary speculation.

Entrepreneurs could become fabulously rich overnight simply by being listed on the exchange and selling off shares. The exchange vetted new listings but there were some notorious loopholes. The rules for valuing the assets of property firms, for instance, were famously slippery. The advantages of getting listed (without too careful scrutiny) were so great that influence, political pressure, and money were rumoured to play major roles.

In six years from 1987, market capitalization multiplied twenty-four times from 138 to 3,325 billion baht. Some of the major corporate success stories of the boom era were companies (like Thaksin's) which gained access to the market in this uncontrolled spurt.

The more established Western and Japanese stock-broking firms could no longer ignore the Bangkok exchange. By the early 1990s, foreign financial houses were scrambling to form tie-ups with Thai firms to get access to the market. In Bangkok's bars, the scruffy casualness of the oilie and the tourist gave way to the Armani chic of the young master of the financial universe.

In 1992-3, the government began to control the stock market's more wayward side. It passed a new stock exchange act, set up a supervisory commission, and brought cases against suspected manipulators. Overseas portfolio and institutional investors now felt a little more secure about having a flutter in Bangkok. In 1993, the inward flow of portfolio capital leapt to over ten times the average of the past five years.

The boom also opened up new external sources of capital. After the international stockbrokers and merchant bankers set up shop in Bangkok around 1990, they introduced Thai firms to new sources of finance overseas. Some major Thai domestic firms began to raise funds on the stock and bond markets of London, New York, Tokyo. In 1994, Thailand's banking, finance, telecom, and petrochem firms raised US$ 4 billion on world markets.

In 1992, the government set out to widen the capital market further by breaking down the Thai banks' monopoly. As a first stage, it legalized offshore banking and issued licences to forty-two Thai and foreign banks. Through this window, Thai firms gained another access to outside funds. In 1989 the commercial banks' net borrowing abroad was only fifteen billion baht. In 1994, with the advent of offshore banking, it jumped to 545 billion.

From the 1960s to the 1980s, Bangkok Bank had dominated commercial finance. In 1984, the Bangkok Bank had built a new headquarters on the central stretch of Silom road. The building looked so big in the surrounding landscape of four-story shophouses it was christened the *pla beuk*, after a huge fish native to the Mekong river.

By 1995, the Bangkok Bank HQ was hemmed in by buildings several times its height. The *pla beuk* now looked like a tiddler.

The Bangkok Bank's profile in the economy had changed like the *pla beuk*. The Bank could hardly be called a tiddler, but it no longer dominated the landscape. Businessmen had many new ways to find capital – the finance companies, the stock market, foreign stock and bond markets, the offshore banks.

But where to invest? The multinationals were hogging more of the opportunities in export-led industry. Thai firms looked elsewhere.

Heavying Up

In the 1990s, several Thai conglomerates invested in heavy industries – cement, petrochemicals, steel, power. They were encouraged by the Board of Investment which felt Thailand's industry needed more depth. They were helped by the stockmarket, which liked projects meatier than finance and property. But most of all they were borne along by the spiralling demand for inputs.

The model for these firms was the Siam Cement Group. SCG was one of Thailand's oldest, largest and most established conglomerates (the Crown Property held a major stake). Over the decades it had absorbed several firms which had got into trouble, including a steelworks and paper mill. It had also bought stakes in shipping, tyres, and diesel engines. In the early 1980s, SCG still virtually monopolized Thailand's heavy industry.

In the boom, SCG seemed set to confirm this role. It increased its cement capacity, expanded the steel plant, and widened its range of construction materials. It also moved into petrochemicals under a government plan to exploit newly-found supplies of natural gas.

SCG's progress was grand and stately. The Thai Petroleum Industry group (TPI) offered a total contrast. In a few years of the boom, TPI came from nowhere to rival SCG in heavy industry. The founding family were provincial rice-millers who moved into rice export, fell in with the Bangkok Bank group, and expanded into agribusiness and textiles in the 1960s and

1970s. An engineering-trained son led them tentatively into petrochemicals in 1980. With the onset of the boom, they invested heavily. By the early 1990s, they were the largest force in downstream petrochemicals and were pushing government to let them into the upstream end. They had moved into cement by building a factory right next door to SCG's flagship unit. They had jumped from there to steel and power plants. They were laying plans to build an oil refinery.

A third group also emerged from the Bangkok Bank stable. The group had risen in textiles and now back-extended from synthetic fibres into chemicals and petrochemicals.

The steel ventures under SCG and TPI were mostly geared to supply their own needs. But the boom in construction and in fabrication industries boosted the demand for steel bars and other basic metal products. Two main groups, Siam Steel and Sahaviriya, increased their investments in rolling mills.

With no local sources of coal or iron ore, Thailand had avoided the common temptation to build an upstream steel industry. At least up to this point. But the boom induced fantasies. Construction demand would continue. The automotive industry would consume lots of steel. Sahaviriya announced plans to build an integrated iron and steel plant using imported ore. Siam Steel and TPI pitched in with a joint venture along the same lines.

Demand for electricity doubled between 1986 and 1991 and almost doubled again between 1991 and 1996. From 1995, government looked to private firms to supply much of the expansion. Several of the conglomerates competed in the first round of privatization bids. Textile-based Saha-Union was among the winners.

A handful of the big Thai conglomerates led this plunge into heavy industries. In the export economy, they were being squeezed out by the multinationals. In this new area, they felt more comfortable. They had the political muscle needed for such big projects. Often they were back-extending from their existing businesses. They could buy the technology, much of which came bundled in with plant construction. They could generate the funds from their savings, from their friendly bankers, or from the stock market. TPI became one of the largest non-financial companies on the exchange.

But was this area profitable? By the mid-1990s, the capacity in downstream steel and petrochemicals far exceeded domestic demand. In export markets, Thailand had difficulty competing against countries with their own sources of raw materials.

When government planned to reduce the protective tariff on downstream petrochemicals from 27 to 20 percent, the producers clamoured they would be "left to die".[12] When east European steel imports surged, the local producers clamoured (successfully) for the protection of an anti-dumping tariff.

Built on a mixture of faith and ambition, this sector was heavy but fragile.

Spending It

The profits of growing exports fed back into local pockets. Between 1985 and 1995, real per capita income doubled. Much of this increase was concentrated in the pockets of the urban middle class. They spent this new wealth with glee.

For consumer goods, Thai shoppers could now buy from the world. Many international manufacturers rushed into Thailand. Some were US firms which had virtually ignored Thailand since the Indochina debacle of 1975. P&G set up shop. General Electric laid large expansion plans. Chrysler came in.

But services required more local touch. In some cases foreign participation was restricted by law (land, media) or licensing (telecoms). Here were protected opportunities for local firms. Domestic investment poured into property development, retailing, media, telecoms, and financial services.

The conglomerates played a part. Most had a finance company and a property business. A few dabbled in media. CP and Central dominated expansion in retailing. But much of the drive in the services boom came from a cadre of new entrepreneurs – the *Wunderkinder* of the boom.

Building Fortunes. With new money in their pockets, the new generation of the middle class moved out of the crowded family shophouses in the old centres of the city. They flocked in droves to modern housing developments on the city outskirts. This suburban migration began among the rich but worked its way down to the modestly wealthy.

Business property boomed in parallel. In 1987, Bangkok still had only a handful of high-rise buildings. By the mid-1990s, the skyline was serrated with office blocks, hotels, and condominiums.

Other property sectors opened up in industrial estates, golf courses, recreational second homes, retail developments, and inner-city residential apartments.

In the late 1980s, profits in property came big and easy. Thirty-six property firms were floated on the stock market. Some new exporters quickly sank their first flush of profits into real estate.

But among the huge number of real estate players, a handful of entrepreneurs played bigger. Anant Asvabhokin built his Land & House company on the back of the suburban migration. His family background was in the pawnshop business. His expansion came from the stock market. Capitalized at 62 billion baht by mid-1995, Land & House ranked among the ten largest companies on the exchange. Anant started building upmarket developments out in the swamps and gradually shifted downmarket to cheaper housing and inner-city apartments. He moved into the booming office market, extended into a construction company, and built a golf-course, residential and office condominium "park" in the northern suburbs.

Premature Billionaires. Between 1985 and 1992, the growth of the stock market, liberalization of foreign exchange, and introduction of offshore banking totally transformed the world of finance.

The big banks had grown through straightforward lending to people they knew. The new finance and securities companies played many new and more complex games. They managed and underwrote share flotations, organized takeovers, pieced together financial deals, played the international money markets, dabbled in derivatives. The executives of these firms needed new skills. Most were overseas-educated, smart, and rarely much over thirty. They made money very fast. By the early 1990s, there was an identifiable group of "premature billionaires" scattered through the financial world.

The most prominent was Pin Chakkaphak.[13] He was a member of the Yip In Tsoi family, which was part of the group around the Thai Farmers Bank. The family had begun in the tin-mining industry in the early part of the century and expanded into agribusiness, finance, and manufacturing. From the mid-1980s, Pin built one of the most successful of the new wave of finance companies. He extended sideways into stockbroking, consultancy, and real estate. His success came partly from his extensive contacts in the Thai Farmers Bank group, partly from friendships in the central bank, partly from his skills with the new financial techniques, and partly from an aggressive attitude to financial deal-making. In 1995 he was manoeuvring to buy a brace of medium-sized banks.

Selling News. Until the mid-1980s the media market was dominated by the government and the old conglomerates. Government controlled two TV stations directly and leased the other two to private companies connected to the big banking groups. Virtually all radio stations were controlled by government or the military. The press was more independent but less lucrative. The mass-market daily *Thai Rath* was read by half the urban population. But other newspapers were kept alive for their political purpose more than their profits.

The expansion of the urban population and especially of the new middle class boosted the demand for media. More people bought more papers and watched more TV. The growing consumer culture boosted the advertising industry. From 1985 onwards, total advertising revenues grew at around 25 percent a year, rising to around thirty-six billion baht by 1994. Media became big business. The most buoyant products were business newspapers, news magazines, FM radio, and television.

The business press took off in the second half of the 1980s. Two titles had existed earlier but they were soon overtaken by the meteoric rise of the Manager group. In 1983, Sondhi Limthongkul started *Phujadkan* (Manager) as a business monthly. At first it gained a reputation for muck-raking. Quickly it evolved into a paper which provided the expanding business class with a mix of market information, political news, investigative journalism, and informed commentary. The Manager group expanded to a business daily, a weekly, a monthly, an English-language monthly, and a regional business magazine issued from Hong Kong.

Sondhi attempted (unsuccessfully) to buy up the established but ailing *Siam Rath* daily, joined in ventures to start new television stations, launched ten new magazines ranging from *IT Software* to *Asian Dentist*, bought out the Siam Cement group's communication companies, launched a regional daily newspaper, and laid plans to launch a satellite over Laos.

A similar group evolved around the English-language daily, *The Nation*. The group started a Thai business daily and a clutch of magazines, took stakes in FM radio, ventured into television programming, and in 1996 launched a new TV channel (ITV). The Wattachak group expanded from a minor Thai daily to magazines, radio stations, and an English daily. From 1993, the Crown Property Bureau launched a network of media companies.

Other companies rode the media boom on the software side. The Grammy group began in the music business – staging concerts, recording albums, and managing stars. It branched from there into radio and TV programming, managing radio stations, magazine publishing, retailing, and education ventures.

Into the Sky. From the late 1980s the Thai government opened up new telecommunications projects to privatization. A handful of companies took advantage of these contracts to gain expertise in this new field. They raised the expansion funds through the stock market on which telecoms became a leading sector. They acquired the necessary technology through license or simple purchase from international suppliers. They built up expertise in downstream manufacture, packaging, project management, and service.

The Vilailuck family's Samart company built its first capital base in the 1980s from backyard manufacture of cheap TV aerials for the expanding rural audience. From there it moved into sale and fabrication of satellite dishes and extended sideways into other communications fields including broadcasting. The Jasmine group was started by an ex-employee of the government telephone organization. It built expertise in large-scale fibre-optic networks and expanded downwards into other telecommunication services. The Ucom group began from an agency selling specialized communications equipment to the Thai armed forces. It expanded into supply of other government and semi-government agencies, became the agent for Motorola, and in the late 1980s, began to market Motorola's mobile phones and pagers. The Shinawatra group extended across pay television, paging, mobile phone networks, and its satellite.

Within a couple of years, most of these companies had launched projects in the neighbouring countries of Burma and Indochina. Some had ventured further afield to Indonesia, India, Malaysia, the Philippines. Thaksin Shinawatra claimed, "The opportunities in the year 2000 and onwards will be information technology and electronics, and everyone will have a chance to participate."[14]

In the early 1990s, Charoen Pokphand (CP) formed a new company TelecomAsia to exploit telecoms opportunities in

Thailand. The firm won the major contract for expanding Bangkok's telephone system, floated several related tele-communications projects and ventured into other countries of the region.

CP also applied the principles of business integration which had been the foundation of its success in agribusiness. Under the cover of its contract to install two million new telephone lines in Bangkok, it laid fibre-optic cabling. This network could carry communications services which extended far beyond simple telephone transmission. CP started planning to supply cable TV, video phones, and other data services. It also took a 20 per cent share in a company building a global fibre-optic network; opened negotiations with Samsung for a joint venture in ICs and other electronic components; and tightened its relations with Nynex through a strategic cooperation agreement.

Exporting Capital

Thailand's success in exporting goods was followed rapidly by export of capital and expertise. Businessmen were drawn to the opportunities in less developed regions only a little beyond the country's borders.

In 1986, Vietnam announced *doi moi* or economic liberal-ization. Two years later, the Thai prime minister (Chatichai) proposed to "turn battlefields into market-places", to stop treating Indochina as an enemy and start treating it as an economic opportunity. Thai businessmen immediately became lyrical about *suwannaphum* (golden land), an old fantasy of Southeast Asia as a land of prosperity focused on Siam.

Chatichai's government (1988-91) pioneered closer diplomatic and commercial links with Vietnam and founded a project to build the first bridge across the Mekong into Laos. Across the western border, it began a policy of "constructive engagement" with Burma. This meant resisting international calls to outlaw the military dictatorship in order to foster trading links.

Anand's government (1991-2) continued this outward-looking trend by pushing the idea of an ASEAN Free Trade Area. Chuan (1992-5) joined in the new enthusiasm for "growth geometry" – forming new zones of economic cooperation which spanned the region's international boundary lines. Chuan personally led a large delegation of Thai businessmen to visit Yunnan in southern China and gave keynote addresses at conferences on growth circles, triangles, squares, and hexagons.

The businessmen who moved most rapidly across the newly porous borders specialized in some of Thailand's less savoury but more profitable ventures – logging, smuggling, massage parlours, beauty contests. Even without the effect of this advance guard, Thailand's neighbours were understandably leery of Thailand's economic intentions. Taiwan, Malaysia, and Singapore emerged as much more acceptable and prominent players in the opening markets of Indochina and Burma.

Yet the total flow of Thai investment abroad advanced rapidly after 1988. Some flowed to the West. Thai hotel chains took their acknowledged expertise in the service business and opened ventures in the US. The Dusit Thani group purchased the German-owned Kempinski hotel chain and two hotels in London. The Imperial hotel group bought properties in London and New York.

Some Thai investment went to ASEAN and Hong Kong. Increasing amounts flowed to Indochina, Burma, and China. In 1993, the outflow was one-sixth of the inflow of foreign direct investment. In 1994-5, it rose to one-third.

Among the front ranks of overseas investors were the new service companies which had come up like rockets on Thailand's consumption boom. The telecoms companies secured contracts in Cambodia, Laos, India and the Philippines. Sondhi's Manager group launched newspaper ventures and hotel projects in China and Vietnam. Grammy founded a company in Taiwan and planned to expand its music-based businesses across the region.

But business overseas was not easy. Shinawatra's India venture was embroiled in a corruption scandal. Its projects in Laos and Cambodia were bounced around by local politics. A company bought in Eastern Europe turned out to be involved in gun-running.

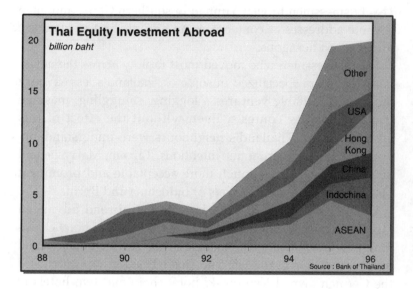

The conglomerates fared a little better. SCG went into plastics and construction materials in China, Indonesia, Philippines and Vietnam, and into petrochemicals in India. TPI followed suit with cement and petrochem ventures in India and Laos.[2]

Some of the conglomerates drew on their family links back to the mainland. The Saha-Union founder sent his son off to Shanghai after his own mother-in-law rose to a high post in the municipal administration. Saha-Union launched ten power generation projects in China, before it ventured into the power business in Thailand.[15]

The most bullish investor in China was CP.

CP founded its first agribusiness project in China in 1979. By the mid-1980s it diversified into new areas including automotive manufacture, bicycles, oil refining and distribution, petrochemicals, beer brewing, property, industrial estates, electronics, power plants, and retailing. By the mid-1990s, CP had around 130 ventures in China, spread across twenty-seven of the thirty provinces and was reckoned one of the single largest foreign investors. In 1997, CP opened a US$100 million headquarters in Shanghai.

CP became Thailand's unofficial economic commission to China, acting as "big brother" for Thai companies investing in China such as Boonrawd, Siam Cement, and Thai Gypsum.[16] A Singapore brewery also ventured into Shanghai under CP's wing "because they have unbeatable connections".[17]

To fund this expansion, CP tapped the stock markets in Tokyo, New York, Shanghai, London, Taipei, Hong Kong, Jakarta, and Bangkok. By 1994, the group had 250 companies with 100,000 employees and revenues of US$7.6 billion spread across twenty countries. Its expansion plans covered India, Latin America, and the US. Dhanin Chiaravanont, the CP chairman, said, "We are really going to go global in the future."[18]

Kiat and the globe

Kiat Srifuengfung's biography shows how Thailand's "mat and pillow" capitalists became players in a global economy. He came from a Chinese family. He prospered in one generation by building connections across the world. Finally he took those connections back into China.[19]

Kiat's background was typical of the entrepreneurs who built the Thai conglomerates. His father emigrated from Swatow in the 1920s. He set up a tailoring business in a shophouse in the market of Suphanburi. He became a pillar of the local community.

Kiat's education introduced him to the world. He studied at Thai schools but was then sent off, like many immigrant boys in this generation, to finish his education in China. He studied in Swatow, Hong Kong, and Canton where he was caught up in the Second World War. He joined an air squadron which the US Air Force sent off to Texas for training.

After the armistice, Kiat returned to Bangkok to set up a branch of the Bank of Canton. In Mao's revolution, the parent bank was dissolved. But Kiat used the banking licence as his ticket into the charmed circle of fellow Swatownese clustered around the Bangkok Bank. Kiat became part of the group which General Pramarn helped to establish in textile joint ventures with the Japanese.

Kiat's textile venture did not prosper. But over the next few years Kiat used the Japanese connection to find the technology for a series of other ventures. He set up a glass factory in partnership with Asahi and back-extended into a string of process plants making basic chemicals. Along the way, he also established the insurance, finance, property, and trading companies typical of the conglomerates of this period.

Kiat remained very much a son of China. When the mainland opened up in the 1980s, he returned, equipped with the contacts built up over a long and wide-ranging business career. He talked to Chinese friends he had made during his early days in Canton to get the licences. He drew on his experience working with the Japanese to get the know-how. He brought in his Texan colleagues from the USAF to get the latest technology. With all this, he set up China's first modern glass factory and planted a Thai flag on top of it.

Going Global, Maybe

These Thai firms could launch out into the world so quickly because the nature of the world economy was changing so fast. The dynamism of Asia, and especially the opening of China, meant that all the good opportunities were close at hand. The liberalization and globalization of financial markets gave ambitious firms unprecedented access to sources of capital.

The market for technology had also changed. Against the background of the West's prolonged recession, firms were increasingly ready to sell their technology off the shelf or enter into non-equity joint ventures.

Chai-Anan Samudavanija, a prominent political scientist and public intellectual since the 1970s, coined the word *lokanuwat* to translate "globalization".[20]

He drew attention to the increasingly porous state of Thailand's economic and political borders. Capital flowed in and out with apparent ease. Thai workers migrated off to the Middle East, while a million Chinese, Laotians, and Burmese leaked in over the land boundaries. Economic planners merrily drew growth circles and triangles which crossed the political boundaries. Thai consumer goods flowed (illegally) out across these borders, while supplies of gems and logs flowed in. Information flowed in and out by satellite broadcast, by fax, by e-mail, by Internet.

Increasingly, Chai-Anan argued, Thailand was becoming part of a global economy, controlled more by the forces of global markets than by the regulation of its own economic managers.

The word *lokanuwat* quickly became a catch-phrase, a fad. It became a routine part of everything from the titles of seminars to the patter of television comedians. The Royal Institute complained that Chai-Anan's coinage was wrong. *Lokanuwat* meant "turning with the world", and *lokapiwat*, "extending across the world", would be better. The fascination with the word suggested that many Thais saw globalization as an opportunity.

The relocation of capital and production from Japan and the Tigers was a global shift – passing backwards along the echelon of Asian flying geese. Why did Thailand come to play such a large role – in comparison to other countries and in comparison to its earlier role?

Of course Thailand had cheaper labour than the north Asian economies. But its infrastructure and investment incentives were far inferior to Malaysia; its labour price and resource base less attractive than Indonesia; its labour supplies less abundant than China and South Asia; and its traffic jams more daunting than almost anywhere.

Japanese firms which migrated to Thailand after 1985 told a survey that wage rates had been important in their choice but not decisive. More importantly, Thailand was a good place to do business. The government was pro-business. There were no racial complications. Thai companies were good partners and responsive suppliers. Many Japanese firms had a generation of experience in Thailand and close links with Thai companies.[21]

The strength of Thai firms and the openness of the economy created a virtuous circle. Most Thai firms felt no need to pressure government for protection against foreign competitors. The government understood that Thai firms could look after themselves and so placed few restrictions on capital inflow. Foreign investment created opportunities for Thai firms to grow even stronger – through joint ventures, through access to funds, technology, and expertise, through opportunities for copying or emulation.

Thai firms seized the opportunities of the age of globalization. They multiplied corporate investment six times in six years by ploughing back profits and exploiting new financial markets. They raided the stock markets of the world. They bought the newly unbundled technology off the shelf. They sucked in marginal labour across Thailand's porous borders and sent goods, services, and investment back the other way.

In 1995, eleven of Thailand's business families made it to *Forbes* magazine's list of dollar billionaires. A handful of years earlier, none had. The eleven mapped the changing pattern of business success across the past three generations. One family (the owners of Boonrawd brewery) descended from the handful of businesses which pre-dated the 1940s change. Three others were heirs of the four biggest banking groups which emerged in the 1950s and 1960s. One (CP) was in agribusiness, the boom sector of the 1970s. The remaining six were in sectors which has spurted in the boom – two in telecoms, two in real estate, one in construction, and one in petrochem.[22]

But there was a growing paradox. The Thai economy was booming on manufactured exports. But only two of these leading business dynasties were significant players in that area. The rest were focused on industry and services supplying domestic demand.

Globalization was a great idea. But in the short term, local opportunities were more protected, more profitable.

4 RAISING A TIGERCUB

The government shaped an environment in which private business could flourish.

In the rapid growth phases of Japan and the Tigers, governments played an active role. They drew up sophisticated plans, invested in technology, controlled credit markets, told firms what to do.

Thailand did not seem to fit this pattern. It was a "soft state". Its economic management was "passive". In the 1970s and 1980s, it was easy for economists to correlate the Tigers' greater success with their more assertive government policies.

In the mid-1990s, after Thailand had been booming for almost a decade, economists began to notice some different facts. In the second oil crisis, the Thai economy had not slumped as low as its neighbours. On the upswing, it had taken off quicker. Through four years of careering double-digit growth, it had not slid off the rails. Thailand was doing rather well. Now Thailand's passive economic management was described as "prudent". Now the government's limited role was seen as a tribute to laisser-faire.

Hardly. Government has always played a large role in shaping the economy. In the 1960s and 1970s, it looked "passive" to economists interested in urban growth because it was concentrating on something else – namely agriculture. Since the early 1980s, the government has learned very quickly how to manage export industrialization and has played a large role in shaping the transition.

*Thailand's economic management has not been the same
as in the Tigers. But the variation has a lot more to do with
sequence and timing than with differences in intent.*

Thailand and the Tigers

Most economists now recognize that the spectacular economic
growth of the Asian Tigers owed a lot to their governments.
Korea, Taiwan, and Singapore were run by dictatorial rulers
who made development a nationalist crusade. They set up
powerful economic ministries and planning boards to plot
their economies' growth. They staffed these institutions with
skilled technocrats. They cajoled and bullied private
entrepreneurs to invest, to expand, to export – to catch up with
the more advanced economies of the world.[1]

Economists debated which of these policies were really
successful. Still, it seemed that in the competitive, developed
world, economic success needed the drive and singular vision
of a committed and powerful government.

Thailand has sometimes been pictured as a contrast to these
development-oriented countries. It had a "soft" state. It let the
economy muddle along without much discipline or direction,
rather like the Bangkok traffic. This softness "explained" why
Thailand lagged behind the Tigers' surge into export-oriented
industrialization.

But in the early stages of the post-war era of development,
Thailand was more like the Tigers than different. Thailand also
made development a national crusade. Thailand also installed
a technocracy and an institutional base to make it happen.

The core of this institutional base was the Bank of Thailand.
The Bank was established in the early 1940s to protect the
economy from the worst depredations of the occupying
Japanese. From the start, the Bank felt it had a mission to
nurture the economy and to keep itself as independent as
possible from political influence.

Around 1960, the US helped to set up the rest of the infrastructure for modern economic management: a Board of Investment (BoI) which offered incentives to local and foreign entrepreneurs; a Development Board (NESDB) which wrote five-year plans; a Budget Bureau to handle the government accounts. A new cadre of technocrats in the Bank of Thailand, the Development Board, and the Finance Ministry self-consciously formed a golden triangle to control economic management.

In the Tigers, governments trumpeted economic development as a nationalistic crusade in the face of external threats – Korea from the north, Taiwan from the mainland, Singapore from bigger neighbours. Similarly, Thailand was a frontline state in the Indochina conflict. General Sarit (prime minister 1958-63) touted *phatthana* (development) as part of the nationalist mission to save Thailand from communism.[2]

Yet in the 1960s, the direction and style of policy-making in Thailand and the Tigers evolved very differently. Three major factors contributed to this divide.

First and foremost, the raw materials the technocrats had to work with were very different. None of the Tigers had much land. For them, growth had to come from the urban economy. By contrast, Thailand had lots of unused land and lots of people to work it. Over four-fifths of the population lived in the villages. The government saw it had the opportunity – and the duty to its large peasant population – to grow by pumping up agriculture.

Second, the new technocrats studied differing schools of economics. In Korea, as in Japan, top policy-makers read the French and German economists who worked out how to industrialize by *copying* from the pioneer example of Britain. These economists showed how government could speed up the process by identifying the sectors with high growth potential and concentrating resources there.[3]

Thailand's new technocrats, by contrast, imbibed their economics from Wisconsin, Cornell, LSE, and attachments at the IMF and World Bank. Their teachers stressed that economies worked best if markets were left to work by natural laws. Government attempts to take charge of allocating resources smacked of communism and were doomed to failure.

Third, these differences in economic ideology and material base dictated different policies towards the capital market. In order to allocate resources to sectors with high potential for industrial growth, the Tiger governments took control of the banks. In Korea and Taiwan, they nationalized them. In Singapore, they left them in private hands but told them what to do. This control over capital funds made it possible for the Tiger governments to convert economic plan into business reality.

By contrast, the Thai policy-makers considered the capital market one of the markets that worked best if left on its own. In 1962, government formally promised not to nationalize the Thai banks.

The Thai technocrats wrote five-year plans identifying growth sectors with just as much foresight and elegance as their Tiger counterparts. But to translate these plans into reality, they had a more limited toolkit – tax and tariff incentives, licence allocations, some limited credit subsidies.

The Thai pattern meant that the private sector played a very large part in the way economic plans were implemented. First, the banks played the role, which governments played in the Tigers, of allocating funds to high-potential sectors. With an eye on their own profits, they spotted growth areas and financed their business friends to exploit them.

Second, the businessmen manipulated the government's other policy-making tools. The administration of incentive policies, licence allocations, credit subsidies was scattered across many government bodies. The businessmen invested time and money in gaining access to the bureaucrats who administered these tools.

Third, over time the businessmen became better and better at lobbying for government to change or adjust policies to suit their interests.[4]

In Thailand *policy-as-implemented* differed substantially from policy-as-written in the five-year plans. It evolved from a subtle mixture of government vision and business ambition. From the mid-1950s onwards, this mixture committed Thailand to a strategy of agricultural-export-led growth.

Agricultural-Export-Led Growth . . .

At the heart of Thailand's economic policy-making there is one long-term constant. The policy-makers believe that Thailand must *grow through trade*. In part this belief has been shaped by history. Old Siam was a major force in Asian trade. From the mid-nineteenth century, expansion was driven by rice exports. But the belief also has a modern rationale. As a small economy and a late developer, Thailand must increase exports in order to buy goods, technology, and expertise from the outside world.

In the late 1950s, Thailand launched into development on a strategy of *agricultural-export-led growth*. It pursued the strategy with just as much enthusiasm as the Tigers showed for export-led industrialization.

The policy evolved through a blend of public and private initiatives. Government invested in the infrastructure needed to unlock the countryside's spare capacity. It built a massive system to stabilize and extend irrigation in the main rice-growing area of the Chaophraya delta. It set up research stations to improve crop strains. More importantly, it accepted US funds to build strategic roads into the more remote and still forested areas of the uplands. These roads opened up a new land frontier. Government taxes on rice exports encouraged farmers to move into the uplands to grow non-rice crops with export opportunity ("getting the prices wrong").

The private sector spotted the emerging opportunity. The leading banks channelled funds towards agribusiness. The businessmen tapped the government's investment incentives to found crop export companies, feedmills, sugar mills, cassava yards, fish farms, rubber plantations, sugar factories, livestock businesses, and ancillary enterprises like insurance, gunny sacks, trucking, silos, warehouses. They entered into joint ventures to get the foreign technology needed for new undertakings such as fruit, poultry, fish-farming, dairy.

Government soon became dependent on the export earnings of agricultural growth and added new policies to boost growth further. It increased the volume of institutional credit for farmers from almost nil in 1950 to nineteen billion baht in 1979. It provided special credit windows and other facilities for agricultural exporters.

This was hardly a "passive" role.

The results were impressive. In three decades, the land under cultivation tripled. Rice yields in the Chaophraya delta increased by 50 percent. Crop exports expanded at a cumulative rate of 12 percent a year. The total economy grew at 7-8 percent a year, driven largely by these agricultural exports.

... and Import Substitution

From the 1930s to the early 1950s, nationalist politicians had argued – just like their counterparts in the Tigers – that the state would have to take an active part in developing the urban economy. The government had invested in factories, distribution companies, and export enterprises.

The results were not good. Some of the enterprises were simply badly managed. Others were just a device for looting public funds. The losses fell on the public budget.

In the 1950s, US advisers argued that such state capitalism was dangerously socialist. The new technocrats saw that government and enterprise was a very dangerous mix because politicians and businessmen simply colluded to make quick profits.[5]

After 1957, most of the state enterprises except for infrastructure companies were closed down or sold off. Instead, government resolved to support the growth of private business through import-substituting industrialization. But this strategy was very secondary to the main emphasis on agricultural exports.

In Latin America in the same era, import substitution was the main strategy. Powerful business groups lobbied hard for government to protect them from foreign competition. Governments responded by excluding foreign capital and boosting domestic business through subsidies and protection.

In Thailand the pattern was different. The lobby in favour of protection was not so powerful. Import substitution was never a goal in the five-year plans. The government drifted into it almost by accident.

By the 1950s the Finance Ministry was already heavily dependent on revenue from trade tariffs. To fund the infrastructure programmes, it raised these tariffs even higher. To reduce the impact on domestic industries, the Ministry was persuaded to lower the rates on capital goods and industrial inputs. The Board of Investment offered further reductions as part of its incentive packages.

The tariff wall and differentiated tariff rates encouraged firms to invest in manufacturing for the home market. The firms which responded to these incentives included basic process industries such as cement, glass, and steel; simple manufactures like textiles; and assemblies of automobiles, electrical, and other consumer goods from imported parts.

The tariff walls were lower than in most of Thailand's neighbouring states and much lower than in the fortress economies of Latin America. The government granted protection to foreign and domestic capital on more or less equal terms. The World Bank classified three-quarters of developing countries as "inward-looking" but put Thailand in its category of "moderately outward oriented". Over the period 1960 to 1972, only 8 percent of manufacturing growth could be attributed to import substitution. Almost four-fifths came from the expansion of the domestic market, driven by the motor of agrarian exports.[6]

The development strategy shaped the way the government managed the economy. The Bank of Thailand and Budget Bureau became expert in macro-management geared to keeping agricultural exports in a healthy state (see below). The Development Board planned the infrastructure projects critical to extending the agricultural base and made projections which enabled the macro-managers to work effectively. These bodies worked very differently from their counterparts in Tiger countries where industrialization was the major goal and where control over capital was a major tool of development policy.

In the Tracks of the Tigers

By the 1970s, many of Thailand's technocrats were worried about the limitations of the agriculture-led strategy. Most of the growth came from simply expanding the cultivated area. At some point this physically had to come to a stop. It would be impossible to raise productivity per head in agriculture to the same levels attainable in industry.

These concerns were deepened by two other factors. First, from the mid-1970s, world prices of agricultural goods, which had been trending upwards for two decades, began to slip downwards. Second, the Tiger economies swept past Thailand. Mass prosperity in the West sparked a boom for the products of cheap industrial labour in the East. In the bigger Tiger economies of Korea and Taiwan, the governments encouraged local entrepreneurs to produce for export. In the smaller island economies of Hong Kong and Singapore, governments set up export-processing zones to attract footloose capital from the more advanced nations. The Tigers flooded the world with cars, cameras, clothes, and electronics.

In Thailand, manufactured exports grew but much more slowly. By 1980, 30 percent of exports were classified as manufactures but the figure is misleading. Most of these were agricultural goods with a little processing.

Some Japanese and Taiwanese capital shifted to Thailand to produce textiles for export. Some Japanese and US capital came in to set up semiconductor factories. But most domestic and foreign business interests were happy to plunder the opportunities in agriculture and import substitution. The government took no interest in attracting footloose foreign capital looking for new platforms for export manufacture.

As with any strategy, Thailand's commitment to agriculture-led growth nurtured a coalition interested in keeping the strategy in place. At the head of this coalition came the Finance Ministry which became hooked on the proceeds of the tariffs. Behind that came the BoI and other pockets of officialdom which lived off the grant of licences and privileges, and the perks such grants could earn. Behind that came the businessmen who profited from protection and had no wish it should end. Behind them came the generals making a bit on the side.

Maintaining the agriculture-led strategy created barriers against any move towards Tiger-style expansion of manufacturing exports. High protective tariffs on inputs added to the cost of manufactured exports. Export procedures for manufactures were smothered in red tape. The taxation system had been designed for a trading economy and tended to penalize manufacturers. The credit facilities for industrial exporters were no match for those available in competitor countries.[7]

Most of all, the baht was overvalued. Thailand's economic managers believed that for agricultural exports to grow smoothly it was vital that its export customers saw that the

Thai currency was "stable". To achieve that stability, Thailand linked the baht to the US dollar. From the late 1970s, the dollar rose in value and carried the baht upwards, making Thailand's manufactured exports more expensive and less competitive.

From the early 1970s, many technocrats pushed for measures to promote export-oriented industrialization. The Development Board wrote promotion of manufactured exports into the five-year plans. The Board of Investment revised its incentives to favour firms which exported.

In the early 1980s, the World Bank also urged Thailand to follow the Tiger strategy. Thailand had to go cap-in-hand to the World Bank for loans to tide over the second oil crisis. The Bank wrote a sheaf of reports urging Thailand to follow Korea's model. The Bank made its loans conditional on a package of "export push" reforms.[8]

Businessmen added their weight. When the underlying momentum of agricultural growth wavered in the late 1970s, Bangkok's businessmen began to look for new frontiers in export. When they found the difficulties facing them, they complained to government.

The banks were uniquely sensitive to the trends of the urban economy. They were the first businesses to put pressure on government to provide more assistance for manufactured exports. Next came textile firms, who were already the leading exporters of manufactures. The textile magnates went directly to the Bank of Thailand and asked for an export financing scheme. When the Bank agreed, gem exporters asked for similar help.

Then in the late 1970s, the Association of Thai Industries began to lobby for export promotion. In the early 1980s the government set up a consultative board to listen to the business lobby. The businessmen used the forum to push for reforms to help exports. They went along to one meeting with a vast chart showing the obstacle race for export paperwork.[9]

But despite the pressure from the technocrats, the businessmen, and the World Bank, the structure of the economy changed little. As long as the economy was going well, the main policy-makers saw no reason to switch strategy. As the economy became more unstable from the mid-1970s on, they became even more reluctant to take risks.

The technocrats' advocacy was largely ignored. The Planning Board was left with stacks of unread copies of the export-oriented fourth five-year plan.[10] Most of the World Bank's proposals were buried in committees and feasibility studies. The government did respond to the business lobby by starting to sort out the red tape and by pulling down some tariffs. But the big changes still did not come.

Through to the early 1980s, the government's policies still favoured agriculture and import substitution. The Ministry of Finance went on *raising* tariffs and trade controls as part of its management of recession. The Board of Investment was allowed to impose further protective surcharges. The average level of effective protection *doubled* between 1970 and 1980 and grew by *half again* over the next seven years. The baht went on zooming up with the dollar. In 1978, 100 baht cost 1040 yen. By mid-1982 it had gone up to 1180 yen. Government devalued the baht in 1981 but not by enough to stem this upward trend.[11]

The big break came in late 1984. By clinging to its old agriculture-led strategy as agricultural growth slowed, Thailand eventually ran out of reserves and creditors. By attempting to stabilize the economy through rigid deflation, the government eventually provoked a major business crisis.

High interest rates caused a shake-out in the financial market. One bank crashed. Three others had to be bailed out. Out of 127 finance companies, twenty-two went out of business and another twenty-five had to be rescued by a "lifeboat" scheme. Even the big conglomerates faced plummeting profits and financial difficulties. Thousands of lesser companies went bankrupt. Many thousands more small entrepreneurs found themselves in court for issuing bounced checks. Some went to jail. Some fled. Some succumbed to pyramid scam schemes which promised to make them rich again overnight.

Only in the eye of this crisis was the government prepared to cut loose from the old strategy. In November 1984, it devalued the baht by 14.8 percent. This was a traumatic move because a stable baht was so much a pillar of the technocracy's religion of economic management. But eventually it was inevitable because there was nothing left in the reserves and no prospect that the economy would revive without a change of direction.

The devaluation would stabilize the economy only if it stimulated exports. Since agricultural exports were on a long-term slide, this had to mean manufactures. The government had finally bet on manufactured-export-led growth. Now it started to bring in reforms to make it work.

Thailand's technocrats had studied with admiration how their counterparts in the Tigers managed export industrialization. After the shock of the crisis and the devaluation, they were called in to work the magic necessary to get the economy moving again.

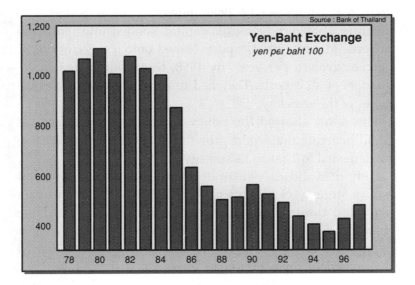

Source : Bank of Thailand

Yen-Baht Exchange
yen per baht 100

The BoI brought in new promotional rules, drafted under World Bank sponsorship, which favoured exporters. The Bank of Thailand's scheme of subsidized credit for agri-exports was opened up to industrial exporters. Foreign firms were allowed 100 percent ownership as long as they exported all their output. The Commerce Ministry set up a Department of Export Promotion which ran trade fairs and mediated contacts between foreign buyers and Thai entrepreneurs. The moves to scythe down the red tape quickened. The business tax was simplified. The baht was managed downwards even further against the mark, the yen, and other East Asian currencies.[12]

The technocrats were still not sure the economy would respond.[13] Most of the World Bank's proposals for a strategy of "export push" still lay on the shelf. The technocrats did what they could to make export of manufactures easier without undoing too much of the old strategy. Then they held their breath. . . .

Over the next couple of years, the revaluation of the yen and other Asian currencies multiplied the impact of the baht devaluation. The 100 baht which had cost 1180 yen in 1982 was going for just 508 yen by 1988. Industries began to shift from Japan to Thailand. Domestic capital flooded into industrial projects. Manufactured exports leaped onto a trajectory of 30 percent growth per year. By 1990, they contributed three-quarters of all exports. They had replaced crop exports as the motor of the economy.

This spurt showed the policy-makers that manufactures could generate the export growth which they considered so fundamental to Thailand's strategy.

Only then did they institute many reforms in the World Bank's strategy of "export push". The business lobby again provided the impetus and the technocrats supplied the techniques. In 1988-9, Chatichai's business-dominated cabinet approved a first major round of tariff reductions and started the process of replacing the business tax with VAT. In 1991, Anand's cabinet of technocrats and businessmen pulled down the tariffs again, introduced VAT, swept away many trade controls, and reformed the corporate and income tax structures. In 1994, the Finance Ministry under the banker Tarrin Nimmanhaeminda pulled down tariffs again.

More importantly, government now managed the currency to promote manufactured exports. In the mid-1980s, the baht was effectively re-attached to the dollar. As the dollar continued to slip down against the yen, the baht grew steadily cheaper for Japanese traders and investors. From 1988 to 1995, the cost of 100 baht fell from 508 to 388 yen.

In parallel there were major changes in foreign policy, education, financial policies, labour policies to gear the country for the new economic strategy. Old traditions of macro-management were altered to suit the new circumstances (see following section).

Again this was hardly a passive government role.

The dramatic changes faced little opposition. Delaying the major policy shifts until the boom was well under way undermined the objections of the major defendants of the old strategy. The Ministry of Finance was awash in revenue and no longer felt reliant on high tariff levels. The businessmen enjoying protection had time for a soft landing. Some made the shift into export. Others survived on the property boom. A few struggled but not enough to make a noise.

In sum: over the long term, the Thai economy is geared to growth from exports. From 1870, the export good was rice. From the Sarit era, this expanded into a range of crops. In the 1980s, it switched to labour-intensive manufactures.

In the Sarit era, a strategy of import-substituting indus-trialization was grafted onto the export orientation – a by-product of the expanding domestic demand created by crop exports. But this was a secondary strategy. It was not a nationalistic import-substitution programme driven by a powerful domestic business lobby. It was not allowed (except briefly in the confusions of the early 1980s) to get in the way of the long-run commitment to growth from trade. Hence the tariff barriers were never pushed up too high. And did not remain in existence for too long.

The move to follow the Tigers into export of manufactures was advocated by technocrats and international advisers from the early 1970s. But ultimately it was driven by the business lobby. The growth of manufactured exports was not really engineered by a programme of "export push". Most of the programme was implemented *after* the technocrats felt confident that manufactured exports had *already become* the motor of the economy. The crucial elements in the changeover were the agrarian decline, which induced business to look elsewhere for growth; and the currency realignments of 1984-6, which utterly transformed Thailand's competitive advantage.

Macro-management for an Open Trading Economy

Thailand developed a tradition of consistently conservative macro-economic management. While macro-management was conservative, it was not static. Macro policies evolved with the changing nature of the economy. From the mid-nineteenth century to the boom, there were four distinct phases.

The first phase covered the century in which the economy depended largely on the rice-export trade. Through this era, the government learnt that the best way to promote this trade was simply *to keep the currency stable*. It linked the baht to an external standard of value (gold, later sterling, later the dollar). Then it concentrated on keeping both the trade gap and budget gap under close control.

The trade gap was quite easy. In Siam's simple economy, imports tended to follow exports. If the rice market dropped, people became poorer and bought fewer imports. The budget gap was more difficult. If government's expenditure rose, Siam could not take the obvious route of increasing revenue through tariffs because of restrictions in colonial treaties. Even short-term deficits created problems. As a small country with no colonial patron, Siam had difficulty raising loans in the international money markets.

This meant Siam had to keep its budget in balance by controlling government spending. By the early twentieth century, Siam had established the institutions and the traditions for this. Balancing the budget became a religious commitment.

After the Second World War, macro-management entered a second phase. Thailand began to import large amounts of oil and consumer goods. Imports no longer obediently followed exports. If the rice market slumped, the current account tended towards deficit. Balancing the budget also became more difficult because of higher government spending on infrastructure, on soldiers, and on growing numbers of bureaucrats.

The macro-managers adjusted to the new circumstances but remained devoutly conservative. They still saw a stable currency as a main objective. So they focused on avoiding inflation at all costs.

They could no longer always avoid budget deficits. But they managed them in ways least likely to cause inflation. Here American inflows of aid and loans came to the rescue. Through the 1960s these flows financed most of the deficit. The remainder was met by borrowing from the local money market. Only when the US flows declined after 1975 did the government resort more to borrowing overseas. And only very, very rarely did it resort to printing money.

To manage the more wayward trade gap, the authorities ventured cautiously into counter-cyclical demand management. On the economic upswing, the Bank of Thailand manipulated interest rates and credit volumes to suppress demand and choke off excess imports. These policies were probably not very effective. But the budget account helped by exerting "fiscal drag". The upswing tended to increase government revenues faster than the bureaucrats could spend them, pushing the budget towards surplus, and hence depressing demand.[14]

Thailand still had inflation but it was low. From 1961 to 1991, the annual average was 5.6 percent. The comparable figure for *all* developing countries was 61.8 percent.[15] Moreover, most of Thailand's inflation was *imported* – caused by rises in international prices for the oil, rice, and other goods which Thailand traded. Very little was attributable to deficits in Thailand's budget or trading account.[16] The baht remained stable against the dollar.

The macro-managers clung to this style of conservative management because it was straightforward and seemed to work. Others found it rather unambitious. The economist Ammar Siamwalla called it a "behaviour pattern" and quipped that "to use . . . the more purposive term 'policy' . . . would be altogether too flattering".[17] It did not require the government to invest much effort in understanding the working of the economy or in developing more sophisticated tools to control it.

Businessmen occasionally complained that the government should be more growth-oriented. Some economists advocated the techniques of demand-stimulated growth popular in current development economics. But the authorities resisted. This way worked – why take higher risks? The macro-managers viewed attempts to use deficit-financing or similar fiscal trickery to stimulate the economy rather like using drugs to stimulate an athlete – cheating, wrong, and ultimately foolish.

This conservative strategy did not "work" because it was somehow intrinsically superior. Rather it worked *because Thailand's large rural sector took most of the strain.*

To overcome the long-term problems caused by rising imports, the macro-managers relied on the countryside to deliver up rising revenues from crop exports. To overcome short-term crises, the macro-managers depended on the village to act as a cushion. In economies which imported their food, balance-of-payments crises commonly resulted in shortages, inflation, and disorder. But Thailand was self-sufficient in food. Most of the people still lived on the land and grew their own rice. Many in the cities retained links to the village. If deflationary strategies depressed the urban economy, they could still go back home and share in the family rice bowl.

In the 1970s, macro-management entered a third phase of uneasy adjustment. The old strategy of economic management became less successful for one key reason: the rural economy ceased to play its critical role. International crop prices turned downwards. The land left to bring into cultivation was more remote, less fertile. The growth of agricultural exports slowed.

This underlying problem was magnified by the growing instability in the international economy, especially the oil crises.

Thailand weathered the first oil crisis of 1973 quite well. Rising world prices for Thailand's agricultural exports blunted the impact of the oil price hike. The government hoped to overcome the residual effects using the old methods. In the short term, it hid the impact of the oil price hike in the accounts of some state enterprises. In the longer term, it planned to substitute oil imports with local energy resources and to increase agricultural exports to cover the higher import bill.[18]

But the value of agricultural exports grew too slowly. To add to the problems, the US withdrawal from Indochina cut off the flows of aid and loans which had been so useful in financing short-term deficits. By the late 1970s the balance-of-payments was looking very sick. As the economy decelerated, the urban business lobby pressed government to abandon its conservative approach to macro-management and instead try pumping up the urban economy.

Government instead looked for new ways to restore export growth. It promoted service exports such as tourism and migrant labour in the Middle East. It attracted more Japanese investment. These tactics were quite successful. But not successful enough.

Until 1975 Thailand's overseas debts were negligible. After 1975 they rose rapidly. Thailand borrowed to pay for the investments in local energy sources, to pay for the arms the military wanted after the Americans left, and to cover the

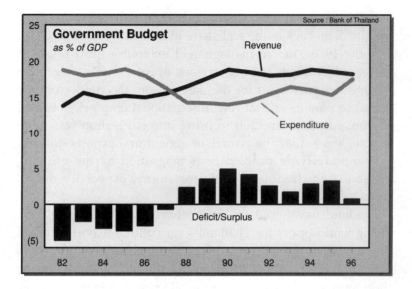

growing budget deficit resulting mainly from the oil debts hidden in the state enterprises.

The second oil price hike turned this growing debt problem into a debt crisis. Between 1978 and 1981, the oil import bill tripled. The current account deficit went from 2 to 5 percent of GDP. The government's external debt multiplied eight times in six years. Debt service climbed from insignificant levels to a peak of 23 percent of GDP. The urban economy slumped into recession. Businessmen hounded the technocrats to use deficit-financing and other tools to keep the economy moving.

Yet the crisis was much less traumatic for Thailand than for most of its neighbours and for most other developing countries. Debt peaked at 39 percent of GDP (compared to 50 percent in the Philippines, 49 percent in Korea). Inflation peaked at 20 percent. Growth fell no lower than 3.2 percent, while in Malaysia and Singapore the economies actually shrunk.

The economy performed relatively well through the recession because the technocrats exercised their usual commitment to conservative macro-management. They blamed the crisis squarely on politicians and businessmen who had departed from the hallowed traditions. These hotheads had driven the government to try deficit financing and to borrow too much abroad. The technocrats called for a return to fiscal discipline.

The government set out to bring the external debt back to manageable levels and to pull the budget back into balance. It imposed a legal upper limit on the level of foreign debt. It slashed its own expenditures to get public debt within the limit. It imposed credit controls, tax hikes, and tariff increases to bring down private borrowing.

As before, the government's strategy was to rely on the rural economy to take most of the strain. Under the deflationary regime, many in the countryside became poorer. In four years (1981-5), all the previous decade's gains in poverty alleviation were wiped out.[19] But as before, the strategy worked. There was no political upsurge to convert debt crisis into political crisis.

This time the urban economy could not escape. The financial crisis of 1984-5 was worse than earlier shocks. But the economy never lost its full momentum. And it bounced back rapidly after 1985 when international circumstances changed.

The return to rapid growth began a fourth phase. The macro-managers were no longer pestered by business politicians wanting deficit-financing to boost the economy. They could again rely on the upward trend of exports to smooth away balance-of-payments problems in the medium term. They could return to what they knew best. For an industrializing country, the macro-managers soon realized, controlling inflation was at least as important as it had been when exporting crops. Low inflation helped to make export goods competitive and helped to build foreign confidence in Thailand's economy.

But the task was not easy. The sudden acceleration from 1986 onwards made the economy unstable. The macro-managers reacted with the techniques they had honed over the last two decades. They tried to rein in a growing trade deficit by suppressing demand through credit squeezes, budget cuts, and tax hikes.[20]

But 1986 had begun a change in the whole economic structure which made these old techniques inadequate.

First, the external exposure of the Thai economy had increased sharply. Total trade (exports plus imports) rose from 54 percent of GDP in 1982 to 89 percent in 1994. International trends, out of the macro-managers' control, would now have a bigger and quicker impact.

Second, the surge of investment sharply increased imports of capital goods. Total imports doubled in two years. The current account balance lurched from an even balance in 1986 to a deficit equivalent to 8.5 percent of GDP four years later. Old methods to control import growth by suppressing demand had no effect. Between 1989 and 1992, government abandoned many of the interest-rate controls which it had been using to manipulate demand.

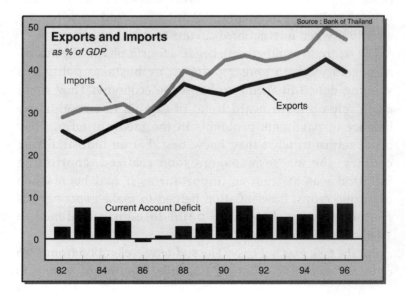

Third, the economy now depended on growth in manufactured exports, and this growth in turn depended on a low
baht. The macro-managers dragged the baht's value
downwards and then had to find new ways to manage the
inflationary consequences.

Fourth, foreign money poured in. Between 1985 and 1990,
the inflow of private capital increased ten times. This was even
more of a shock to the economy than an oil-price hike. The
urban economy was awash with money. The property market
went mad. The stock market shot up.

This had all the markings of an inflationary bubble. The
macro-managers were not used to this and they reacted slowly.
But Thailand's fiscal drag was more fast-acting and more
effective. The rapid increase in trade and business activity
doubled government revenues between 1985 and 1989. The
bureaucracy simply could not spend this windfall fast enough.
It used some to pay off the backlog of foreign debt. But still
there was more. The budget went from a slight deficit in 1987
to a surplus equivalent to almost 5 percent of GDP in 1991.

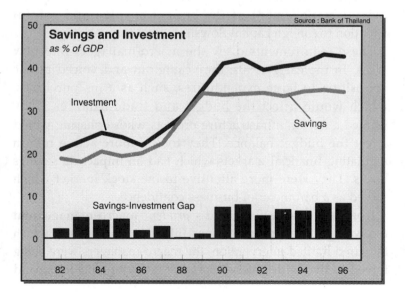

The budget surplus drained away much of the excess demand. Business also helped by saving hard to reinvest in growth. Total savings rose from 22 percent of GDP in 1986 to 34 percent in 1991. Government introduced new controls on money supply and credit to further constrain demand. By 1991, the economy had calmed down. But now the main tool for regulating the economy in the boom had become the budget surplus. Through the early 1990s, the surplus ran at 2-3 percent of GDP.

The job of managing the macro-economy had totally changed. Just minimizing the budget and trade gaps and dabbling in demand management were no longer enough. In effect, the old concept of "stability" had gone out the window. Thailand now had an artificially low baht countered by high interest rate levels and monetary controls; and a structural current account deficit countered by large foreign inflows and a budget surplus. The era of stability had been succeeded by an era of managed instability.

In the long run, preventing instability deteriorating into crisis meant reducing the current account deficit and reducing the dependence on foreign money. In the short run, it required careful management of the budget surplus and careful attention to foreign capital flows.

These requirements drew the macro-managers into new areas. In the early 1990s, they came out and voiced public opposition to large expenditures, such as arms purchases, which would affect the budget and trade balances. They wanted a say on infrastructure projects whose phasing would affect the budget balance. They took a more active role in regulating financial markets which had an impact on savings levels. They were more attentive to the stock market which served as a barometer of business confidence.

Ironically just as Thailand's *prudent* macro-management received praise from institutions (like the World Bank) which favoured limited intervention, the macro-managers were being forced to live with a very *imprudent* situation and to expand their role. The liberalization of the financial market in 1991-3 tipped the macro-managers into a new era in which all these problems would get worse (see chapter 5).

Nurturing Firms

In Japan, export growth was led by the *sogo shosha*, the massive trading companies and their associated business groups. In Korea, five *chaebol* came to generate over half of total GDP.

This concentration was not a matter of chance. In Japan and some of the Tigers (especially Korea and Singapore), governments fostered the growth of a few large firms. They believed that big firms would compete more successfully in the world to achieve national economic strength. Often too, these governments found it simpler to apply policy through a few large firms rather than through many smaller ones. And often too, there were strong personal links between the politicians, the technocrats, and the owners of these large firms.

These governments boosted favoured firms by providing tax breaks, by supplying cheap credit, by policing competition, by encouraging mergers, by subsidizing their technology development, and by bailing them out of trouble. Nowhere were these policies more explicit than in Korea. The Korean government set export targets for firms; rewarded those that achieved the targets with cheap loans and other bonuses; punished the failures by sending in the tax auditors, removing the bank credit, and even cutting off the electricity supply.

In the 1960s, Thailand's technocrats were not seduced by the idea that big firms were needed to achieve big growth. In part this was simply a rational view of the market. In Japan and Korea, export firms were setting out to compete against established Western firms and needed scale to survive. In Thailand, firms were engaged mainly in agribusiness or in import substitution. In part it reflected the technocrats' trust in the market principle. They had been trained to believe in "perfect competition". They tended to view big firms as greedy, predatory, and potentially over-powerful.

The government's overt policy towards business was to provide the same forms of assistance for all and to encourage market competition in order to minimize monopoly profiteering and rent-seeking.

The Board of Investment (BoI) did not try to police competition by offering its investment incentives to only one or two firms in each sector. Rather it preferred to offer incentives to several firms and let them fight it out.

Beyond these incentives, the government played little role in promoting the fortunes of individual firms. It made no attempt to provide cheap discretionary credit. It gave no subsidies for technological development. It offered no rewards for performance. It took no joint equity in large prestige projects.

It even made little effort to favour domestic capital over foreign. Except in a few sectors where foreigners were barred (notably banking), foreign firms were allowed 100 percent ownership and access to the same investment promotional privileges as the locals. Over four-fifths of the European and US firms which set up in Thailand in the 1950s and 1960s were wholly foreign-owned.[21]

Even so, large conglomerates dominated Thailand's domestic business growth from the 1950s to the 1980s (see chapter 3). Two factors were largely responsible. First, even if government did not ration credit, the few big banks did. The handfuls of firms clustered around the major banks dominated business expansion because of access to scarce funds.

Second, while government offered no special favours to individual companies through the front door, it was a very different story at the back. The clusters of firms around the major banks functioned as powerful lobbies for all forms of useful government assistance.

Increasingly the bankers' friends were also the firms which benefited most from the packages of promotional incentives. Often too they happened to be awarded the big government contracts. Because of their good standing with both banks and generals, they were easily the most attractive partners for incoming foreign investors. Of course they had to share some of these benefits with the generals. But within little more than a decade of development, thirty or so conglomerates had come to dominate the urban economy.

In the 1970s, the relationship between government and the big firms shifted. With the opening up of parliament, leading businessmen rushed to get better access to government through seats in parliament and cabinet or through influence over parties and political leaders.[22] As the urban economy decelerated, the businessmen used this new political torque to press government for more protection and more favours. For a time they were quite successful in this strategy. It appeared as if Thailand might be moving towards something like the Japan-Korea pattern.

Business urged government to discriminate more between foreign and domestic players. In 1970, a big Japanese petrochemical investor was "persuaded" reluctantly to accept a 50-50 joint venture. Soon after, government changed the rules to force many existing firms to convert into joint ventures and to allow only Thai-majority JVs for new projects. Only US firms were exempted, in recognition of the USA's generous aid.[23]

Some conglomerates convinced the government to protect them from increased competition, either local or foreign. Established firms in steel and glass got the BoI to withhold privileges from new competitors on grounds that these sectors were already saturated. In the automobile industry, the existing firms persuaded government not to allow any new entrants, any increase in capacity, or any imports. In banking, government was dissuaded from issuing any new licences. In the sugar industry, the major firms induced government to help them form a cartel to fix prices, allocate export quotas, and exclude competition.[24]

The BoI now made *scale* a condition for investment promotion. It rejected projects floated by new and smaller competitors of the conglomerates. The Ministry of Industry, whose minister from 1976 onwards came from one of the big business parties, regularly refused licences to potential new rivals of established firms.

Following these successes, the conglomerates tried to institutionalize government favouritism for selected big firms. Around 1980, several businessmen became interested in the Japanese and Korean models of development. The World Bank encouraged this trend by trumpeting Korea's spectacular success in the 1970s as a model for Thailand's future. Several businessmen and technocrats visited Korea. A few of the conglomerates set up trading companies in the hope these might be the germs of Thailand's own *chaebol* or *sogo shosha*.

Business leaders activated associations of industry, banking and commerce to act as lobbies for government support. These three associations set up an umbrella group consciously modelled on the *keidanren*, the Japanese business group which acted as the main channel of negotiation with government.[25]

Boonchu Rojanastien, who progressed from Bangkok Bank to the cabinet, drummed up support for "Thailand Inc". The phrase was based on the title of a popular book which attributed Japan's success to the close cooperation between government and major firms. As a minister, Boonchu tried to set himself up as "economic czar" on the model of Japan's minister of trade and industry or Korea's head of economic planning.[26]

The technocrats were still nervous of an open embrace with big business. Boonchu's political career ran into a brick wall. But the government did establish formal machinery for allowing the leaders of the business associations to influence economic policy. Through the mid-1980s, business politicians, many of them closely tied to the major conglomerates, were increasingly successful at using direct political influence to favour specific corporate interests.

The advent of the boom disrupted these moves towards a more Korea-like pattern of business-government relations.

First, the heads of the conglomerates were distracted by the boom. They stopped trying to cuddle up to government and concentrated their energies on the new global opportunities. Some simply had less time for political ventures. Others (see chapter 9) were pushed out by a new wave of provincial businessmen.

Second, the technocrats grew stronger. The slump of 1983-5, the shock of the devaluation, and the leap into the new and unknown world of export-oriented industrialization made politicians and businessmen rely more on the technocrats who could manage these traumatic changes.

The technocrats, with their spiritual centre still in the Bank of Thailand, decided that two main policies were needed to achieve the leap into Tigerdom. First, keep the macro-economy as stable as before so trade could grow smoothly. Second, liberalize the financial markets so that business could easily diversify. This second policy would undercut the financial oligopoly at the core of the conglomerates' domination of the economy.

The technocrats had long been worried about the power of the major banks. In 1979 the Bank of Thailand tried to reduce their dominance through legislation. It also licensed finance companies under rules which gave them advantages against the banks in industrial lending. The policy had been tripped up by the 1983-5 recession. Now it worked. The finance companies boomed.

From the late 1980s through the mid 1990s, the technocrats continued opening up the financial market. In 1987 they kick-started the stock market. In 1992 they improved regulation to make it more attractive for investors. In 1993 they licensed mutual fund companies. In 1994, they urged finance companies to extend operations into the provinces.

Between 1989 and 1992 they scrapped interest rate controls. In 1990-1 they abolished exchange controls. In 1991-2 they broadened the areas of business activity open to banks and finance companies. In 1993 they inaugurated offshore banking and issued licences to forty-two Thai and foreign banks. In 1994, they announced plans to issue full banking licences to five foreign banks and began urging finance companies to upgrade to full bank status. At the start of 1995, the finance minister said that a major ministry objective was to liberalize the financial sector even further in order to destroy old monopolies.

During the boom, the technocrats also swept away most of the restrictions on competition which had built up through the 1970s and 1980s. In successive waves of reform beginning in 1988, most import restrictions were removed and tariff rates were brought down. In sectors like automobiles, steel, and glass, the restrictions on new entrants were taken off.

The possibility that the conglomerates clustered around the banks could seduce government into a Korea-Japan style project of cooperation had been blown away. In the boom, the numbers of firms multiplied. The prominence of the banks was qualified. The domination of the conglomerates diminished. The technocrats scrapped many of the systems for favouring individual firms. Thailand moved away from *chaebol*ization rather than towards it.

But government stopped some way short of full liberalization. Entry into the banking industry was still regulated by licences. The booming telecoms sector was parcelled out in concessions. Petrochem investments depended on contracts with the upstream state enterprises.

Firms like Shinawatra and CP which spurted ahead in the boom quickly understood the new situation. They started buying up technocrats. Shinawatra hired the managing director of the telephone organization (TOT) and a departmental director of the communications authority. CP took on board the former head of the petroleum authority. Ucom lured a permanent secretary of the Communications Ministry and a former head of the central bank. Sahaviriya signed up the former head of the stock exchange. Bangkok Bank hired the ex-deputy-head of the Development Board and raided one of the central bank's rising young stars.

In part these firms simply needed to find managerial talent quickly. In part they depended heavily on government licences and contracts, and needed friends who knew how the technocracy worked. In part they were seeking ways to sustain the crucial links between business and government in a new era. "Connections are always important," confessed the head of Ucom, "people open their doors to us when we knock."[27]

In sum, the Thai government had no policy like that of the Tigers to build selected firms as world-class competitors. But, as in so much of the Thailand development story, it is often important to look at the lines of force leading from business to government rather than those running in the opposite direction. Big firms sought privileged assistance from government, first through the generals, later through the parliament, and later still through technocrats.

Eastern Seaboard: industrial push Thai-style

Government launched the Eastern Seaboard Project (ESB) in 1981 to maximize benefits from the natural gas found in the Gulf of Thailand. The project included an integrated petrochemical complex, soda ash plant, fertilizer plant, and steel complex. Big investments in port and other infrastructure would turn the surrounding area into Thailand's industrial hub. Government investment in the project would drive the economy towards the twenty-first century.[28]

Around this time, many technocrats, businessmen, and foreign advisers were urging Thailand to follow Korea's development path. The ESB would be Thailand's version of Korea's HCI (Heavy and Chemical Industries) project. It would be the first surge of public investment since the 1940s. It would transform the Development Board from a back-room function to MITI-like status.

In the early 1980s recession, this grandiose scheme came apart. The Finance Ministry and central bank ganged up against it. They argued that the recession meant the whole scheme was

---

probably unprofitable. The investment costs would make the country's debt problems even worse.

In 1985, the steel complex and soda ash plant were dropped. In 1986, the fertilizer project was shelved. Much of the infrastructure was deleted or delayed. The petrochem complex was whittled back to single upstream olefins plant as a public-private joint venture.

The container port opened but did little business because there were no new roads or rail links to serve it. The industrial estates opened but struggled to find custom because water supplies were inadequate, infrastructure poor.

Thailand's industrial "big bang" had been reduced to a sputter. To make sure the petrochem plant prospered the government resorted to extreme measures. It banned competition, erected protective tariffs, herded the downstream customers into a cosy cartel, and forced them to accept fail-proof prices.

After 1987, the boom changed all the cost equations. Home demand soared. The queries about profitability disappeared. The fears of external debt evaporated.

But government reacted slowly. The Development Board which had earlier championed the project was in retreat. Other agencies had no interest in restoring the project to its original grandeur. Only the petrochemical segment of the project regained its old momentum. Two further upstream plants were built with majority state ownership.

The private sector was much nippier. The small group of existing downstream petrochem firms laid ambitious expansion plans. Some of the big conglomerates piled into the project. With its experience in heavy process industries, the Siam Cement Group was keen to move into petrochem. With its long record of "picking winners", the Bangkok Bank was interested in the sector. The TPI conglomerate, which had originally emerged from a rice-trading firm backed by the Bangkok Bank in the 1950s, became the most aggressive of the downstream firms.

In the early stage of the ESB, many powerful interests had speculated in land around the zone. Now they too helped to urge the project ahead. Some thirty private industrial estates appeared. Property firms like the Ban Chang group developed the housing, hotels, commercial centres, and other infrastructure to make the zone grow.

In the mid-1990s, the government again took an interest in the ESB. It accelerated many of the delayed infrastructure projects. It restarted some shelved projects like the fertilizer plant.

But government had to accept that the nature of the project had changed from the original plan. The public sector was no longer the driving force. Private business had seized the initiative.

Demand for upstream products was running rapidly ahead of the output of the government plants. World prices for upstream products were falling below what the government was forcing the Thai downstream private producers to pay. Led by TPI, the downstream producers pushed government to remove protection from the government's upstream plants and allow the private sector to invest here too.

Under pressure, government agreed to lift the restrictions from 1997. The Bangkok Bank and Siam Cement promptly launched projects to compete with the government plants. TPI and other petrochem firms started a host of new projects including downstream units, power generation, cement manufacture, and oil refining. More industrial estates appeared and filled up with factories and service industries of all kinds.

The ESB was restored to something like the scale of the original plan. But with different owners. When the state petroleum authority announced plans to resurrect the concept of a public-sector integrated up-downstream petrochem complex, the private entrepreneurs howled that this would be unfair competition. The head of TPI called it "communist style economics" and advised: "The best thing is to allow private firms to compete freely."[29] The petroleum authority backed away from the project.

In 1995-7, all the major groups began major expansion projects which would mature over 1998-2000. And now more foreign firms took part. Esso and Chevron launched plans to establish aromatics plants. Dow, Mitsubishi, and Phillips came in on joint ventures. Total capacity would expand from 4.1 million tons in 1995 to 18.6 in 2000 and exports were projected to grow from 1.1 to 3.9 million tons over the same period.

Raising a Tigercub

In the 1950s, both Thailand and the Tigers created new cadres of technocrats who saw development as a nationalistic goal. The Tigers sought growth through industry and had to compete with the advanced countries of the world. But their business groups were relatively weak after the experience of colonialism. The technocrats studied how European countries had competed against a more advanced Britain. They took on the responsibility of deciding what had to be done, telling the businessmen to do it, and providing them with the funds. They took charge of banking and funnelled capital into sectors with high potential for growth.

Thailand's path differed from the Tigers in two main ways. First, Thailand could take an easier option because of its generous natural resource base. The economy grew on the basis of agriculture without the need for a Tiger-like command structure. Government concentrated on managing the macroeconomy. Business in reality made much of the remaining economic policy.

Second, Thailand's entrepreneurs did not need so much attention. They expanded rapidly from the time of colonial retreat in the 1940s onwards. By the time Thailand made the shift to industry, the banks and conglomerates had become strong and sophisticated. They had taken on the role of channelling resources to growth sectors. They did not need to be bullied to follow policies which aligned so well with their own self interests. They had become politically powerful enough to defy such bullying. Over a few short years in the late 1980s, they led a massive shift of resources from agriculture to industry, from import substitution to export orientation. The principle of concentrating resources in high-potential areas was the same as in the Tigers. The way it was carried out was different.

In Thailand, economic policy-making often appears less purposive and decisive than in the Tigers because two different forces are involved – the technocrats and the business lobby – and because they work on different agendas.

The mind-set of the technocrats was framed by two influences. First, most of them were trained in the US and absorbed a Cold-War version of development theory. They viewed "planning" as a dangerous socialist device and believed devoutly in the laws of the market. Second, their first role in the government was to sweep away Thailand's disastrous experiment in state capitalism.

They saw their role as creating the environment in which private business could grow, *not* helping individual business-men. They concentrated on managing macro-economic stability and investments in infrastructure. They argued that other forms of government intervention were wrong. State investments outside infrastructure were risky. Priming the pump with aggressive fiscal policies was foolhardy. Nurturing the growth of favoured firms would be biased.

In public they kept a mandarin aloofness from business (whatever was going on at the back door). In setting out systems for promoting enterprise, they encouraged com-petition and resisted attempts to skew favours to specific groups. Later during the boom, they joyfully swept away the panoply of restrictions and favours which had built up over the past decade.

The rise of the banks presented the technocrats with a dilemma. They recognized that the banks played a huge role in the economy – not just raising capital but channelling it to growth sectors. From the 1960s to the 1990s, the government protected the banks from foreign competition. Yet equally the technocrats saw the banks as an over-powerful, distorting force in the economy. From the 1970s they tried tentatively to bring them under control. During the boom they placed a big emphasis on liberalizing the financial markets to undermine the major banks' over-mighty role.

While the technocrats worked on a model of competitive markets and equal opportunities, businessmen sought always to create special advantages. In the 1950s and 1960s they snuggled up to the generals to get favours. In the 1970s they sought access through political parties. In the 1990s, they hired technocrats with celestial connections.

Individual firms exploit these links to gain privileged market positions which deliver high profits. Some business leaders have pushed further to institutionalize government favours to major firms on the Korean model. Occasionally they try to adjust the macro-managers' crisis management to help business.

The relative weights of the technocrats and the business lobby see-saw over time. In periods of rapid growth and change, the technocrats have more influence. Businessmen rely on the technocrats' expertise to handle these difficult transitions. And anyway at such periods the businessmen are too distracted by making money. In the move to rapid agriculture-led growth in the 1960s, and then again in the first five years of the spurt to export-oriented manufacture, the technocrats were dominant.

But when growth slows, the business lobby becomes more insistent. During the uneasy transition of 1975-85 they pushed for more aggressive macro-management to pump up the urban economy; more direct access to policy-making; and more government favouritism for leading firms.

Yet the struggle between technocrat and businessman has been played out within narrow limits. In the long run their interests converge. If exports grow fast, both are happy. If exports slump, the macro-managers' conservative methods have proved the most efficient way to get them moving again.

Until recently, this cosy alignment was underwritten by the countryside. The economy barrelled along at 7-8 percent a year because of the growth of crop exports. Urban business grew rich on the surplus extracted from the countryside. The strict fiscal and monetary management worked because the countryside absorbed the short-term shocks. The government did not have to worry about distribution because the land frontier acted as a social safety valve.

The urban boom introduced new complications. First, the increased external exposure made macro-management more complex. Second, with the decline in agriculture and the shift of population from village to city, the countryside would no longer serve as such a compliant and effective shock-absorber in times of crisis. In future, old-style conservative crisis management will fall more sharply on the city.

As the tigercub starts to grow up, he gets more difficult and more dangerous to handle.

5 BUBBLING OVER

Export growth had driven the boom. Through 1996, it petered away to nothing. With it went confidence in the future of the Thai economy.

Thailand had fallen a pace behind in the export race. New countries like China and Vietnam were taking the market for cheap textiles, shoes, and toys. Thailand's exports of electronics and auto parts were growing but not fast enough.

Since 1989, foreign money had been flooding into Thailand. From 1992, the export economy was weakening but the money inflows were getting bigger. More funds went into inefficient investments, into luxury consumption, and into gambles on the future of property and stocks.

Government denied there was a problem. But in 1996, the export slump and a spectacular bank crash set confidence on a downward slide. The floodtide of money went into rapid reverse. The gambles turned very bad indeed.

The stockmarket dived. The finance sector collapsed. The baht was hammered by speculators. The government fled into the icy arms of the IMF. Shock waves battered other economies in the region. Was this, some asked, the end of the Asian miracle?

Rather, this was a cyclical trade downturn, overlain with a finance-stock-property bubble pumped up by huge foreign inflows. Many had seen it coming for some time. But little had been done. Economic policy-making and financial controls had lagged behind the changes in the nature and pace of the economy. Politics had got in the way.

There would be no easy solutions. The ending of the
boom was a reality check, signalling the need for change.

The Export Slump

In the first quarter of 1996, exports grew 7 percent compared to
24 percent in the same period a year earlier. Olarn Chaiprawat,
the banker who had foretold the "golden age" in 1984,
pronounced "our luck is running out".[1]

By the end of 1996, export growth was zero, down from a
23.6 percent increase in 1995 and a trend of 21 percent over the
past decade. Like a stampeding lemming, Thailand's exports
had suddenly reached the cliff edge and plunged vertically
down.

Maybe not quite. Since VAT was introduced in 1990, tricky
businessmen had been faking exports to claim VAT refunds.
Containers were shipped empty. Or the "exports" existed only
in the paperwork. Textile "exports" from Thailand to one
Middle East destination were eighty times the value recorded
as imported at the other end. By 1995, this fraud may have
boosted the export statistics by a hundred billion baht,
exaggerating the growth then and the decline later. Exports
had probably grown 21 percent in 1995 and 8 percent in 1996.
The break was still very sharp.

From the late 1980s, pundits and economists had predicted
that Thailand's export boom would not last. Costs would rise.
Thailand did not have the skills or the infrastructure to move
up from cheap-labour products. Other countries would offer
even cheaper labour.

But Thailand managed to move into medium-tech areas
more quickly than expected. Exports went on surging through
the turn of the decade. In the post-coup dip in 1992-3, analysts
again predicted the end. But exports surged yet again, driven
by computer parts and other electronics.

Yet behind the year-to-year flux, there was a longer-term

trend (see graph). Export growth was gradually slowing. Three main factors were behind the trend – increasing competition, the weakening of the yen, and under-investment.

Until 1990, new industries pulled labour out of the villages at low cost. Real wages remained flat. But then the flow slackened. From 1991 real wages grew at 8 percent a year to attract the extra labour. The impact on many cheap-labour industries was probably less than this, as they used a lot of casual workers and illegal immigrants. But certainly the labour market tightened and costs rose.

More importantly, new competitors appeared in the export markets. China, Vietnam, Indonesia, and India had all gone through free-market reforms in the late 1980s and were now breaking into exports. These countries had backgrounds of extreme poverty and firm political controls. Their labour costs were a quarter or fifth of Thailand's level – far lower than Thailand *before* the export boom and wage inflation. In cheap garments, shoes, plastic goods, Thailand could no longer compete. Exports of these items dropped 30 percent in 1996. "We didn't anticipate that growth in China, Indochina, India would be so rapid," said a financial analyst, "and that they would be competing head-to-head with us in so many key areas."[2]

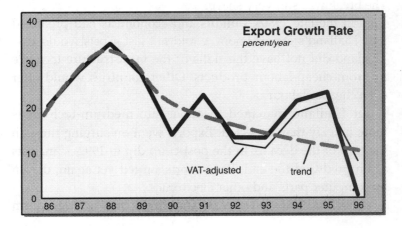

Next, the yen made a U-turn. Since 1984, the yen had risen against the dollar and the dollar-linked baht, keeping Thai goods cheap for the Japanese. In 1995, the yen was weakened by the long recession in the Japanese economy, while the dollar strengthened as the US prospered. In mid 1995, a Japanese buyer paid 341 yen for 100 baht of Thai goods. By early 1997, he paid 476 yen or 40 percent more.

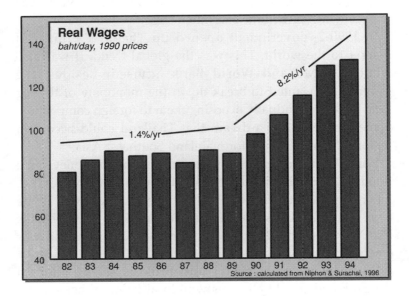

Real Wages
baht/day, 1990 prices

1.4%/yr

8.2%/yr

Source : calculated from Niphon & Surachai, 1996

Growth in Thailand's exports to Japan shrunk to 1 percent in 1996. Investment from Japan fell by a third. The yen's U-turn also caused a ripple across Asia. Thailand's trade with the rest of the region fell. Exports of ICs and other goods linked to the regional electronic industry showed no growth in 1996.

Finally, Thailand had not invested enough in upgrading export industries to stay ahead of competition. In particular, more domestic capital had been lured into property and other service industries which delivered higher short-term profit, or into heavy industries which had a sense of grandeur.

The export slump was not a surprise. It had been predicted for years. It was a matter of simple arithmetic – on the changing value of the yen, the gap in wage rates between Thailand and its new competitors, and the allocation of capital resources.

Finance: From Fad to Panic

The export slump signalled the end of the boom. But it was finance which turned the end into a crisis.

In 1990-2, government opened up Thailand's financial market to the world. This was the global trend. It was also what the IMF and World Bank advised. Besides, the government wanted to break down the monopoly of the big local banks by gradually exposing them to foreign competition. Some ministers had a dream that Thailand could become a regional financial centre for mainland Southeast Asia.

When Thailand opened the door, the foreign money came flooding through. Financial markets in the West were dull. Emerging markets were where the action was. Asia was all the rage. Staid old banks like Barings were packing young bloods like Nick Leeson off to exotic oriental places. Thailand was emerging, Asian and *new*.

Western merchant banks and brokers set up shop in Bangkok and sought alliances with local financial houses. Big institutional investors began to buy shares on the Bangkok stock market. Thai corporations and finance companies sought loans from Western and Asian markets. Eurodollar loans flowed into the Thai market through the new offshore banking window (BIBF). Hot money parked in Thailand overnight in search of margin gains on interest and exchange rates.

The new foreign entrants scrambled to establish themselves as significant players. They competed to extend their loan portfolios, build up their presence on the stock market, win market share. The foreign banks in BIBF built business fast in the hope of winning the race to be awarded a full banking licence.[3]

Suddenly parachuted into this new and strange market, the foreign finance houses were desperate for knowledge. They offered jobs to long-term *farang* residents. They yanked lecturers out of the universities to set up research departments. They hired young Thais fresh back from an overseas MA or MBA – not so much for their knowledge as their language skills and their social networks. Finance industry salaries rocketed. Performance bonuses ran up to twenty-four or thirty-six months. By 1994-5, a Thai with one year's experience in finance commanded the same salary as an incoming expat with ten.

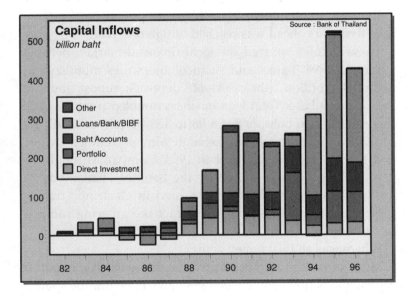

For Thailand's finance industry, this inflow was like a dose of amphetamine. The industry spun much faster. In 1993, inflow of foreign portfolio investment jumped from 14 to 123 billion baht. In 1994, the inflow of bank loans went from a zero average to 350 billion baht (though some of this was a transfer of direct corporate lending into the BIBF). Then in 1995, things really took off. The World Bank announced that Thailand had been the world's fastest-growing economy in the past decade.

The Economist published projections of Thailand as the world's seventh largest economy by 2020. Merrill Lynch predicted Thailand would be "one of the fastest-growing economies in the region" and that "liberalization . . . will make foreign inflows through the banking sector easier".[4] Buoyed by all this enthusiasm, net foreign inflows jumped 69 percent. *In one year, more money flowed in than over the whole decade of the 1980s.*

Between 1992 and 1995, the total annual inflow of foreign funds doubled from 237 to 516 billion baht or from 8 to 11 percent of GDP. The total external debt roughly doubled from forty to eighty billion US dollars. The inflow exceeded even the enthusiasts' expectations. Merrill Lynch's projection of external debt five years ahead was reached within one year.

These inflows spurred the local financial market. Between 1992 and 1996, banks and finance companies mobilized an extra 2,000 billion baht in private deposits, almost doubling their deposit base. Total loan business doubled from 2.7 to 5.5 thousand billion baht, or from 96 to 133 percent of GDP. The capitalization of the stock exchange almost doubled in 1992 and then more than doubled in 1993. Companies fought for new broking licences offered by the Bank of Thailand at 300 million baht apiece. Brokers invested in electronic trading rooms like big video-games to attract the growing ranks of retail investors.

Where was all this money going?

Much of it went into productive investments. The import of capital goods doubled between 1992 and 1995. But the spurt in 1994-6 was exceptional. With money so easy to come by, entrepreneurs became less careful, more ambitious. Many big industrial projects were started which might not have passed a feasibility check in tougher times. Many local entrepreneurs sunk money in heavy industry because government provided encouragement and some protection from foreign competition. These sectors were quickly overcrowded, and returns low.

The finance industry had difficulty placing all the funds flooding in. Less and less went into project finance, more and more into hire-purchase loans, property development, and margin loans for stock traders.

The stockmarket index soared upwards from 600 after the 1991 coup to a peak of 1750 in January 1994. Stock prices lost any contact with the reality of company profits. The average price-earnings ratio rose from sixteen in 1992 to twenty-six in 1993. For the blue chips, the ratio was airborne above thirty.

From here, there was nowhere to go but down. But the descent was uneven. The foreign funds stayed away from firms which made or sold things, firms in the "real economy". Future earnings were predictable and would never justify the bloated P/E ratios. Instead, they put some anchor money into a few "safe" stocks, including the big banks and famous companies like Siam Cement. Then they put the ambitious money into the speculative side of the market – into property, finance, telecoms – where booms might deliver a windfall capital gain. By 1996, just eight stocks accounted for a third of market capitalization. Some 57 percent of all transactions were in banks and finance and another 22 percent in property and telecoms.

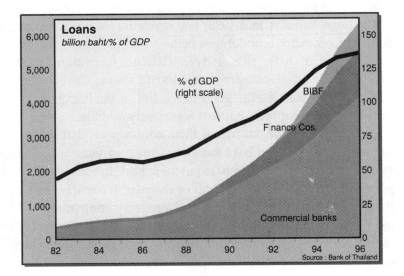

The inflow generated its own logic based on inflating asset values. "No one wanted to upgrade textiles exports," commented an analyst later, "when more money could be made selling condominiums and betting in the stock market."[5]

Some twenty to thirty stocks attracted all the market activity. From early 1994, most of the other 380 went into slow decline, first miring the retail investors in 140 billion baht of margin loans, and then driving many of them out of the market. In November 1995, a hysterical retail investor shot and wounded himself in the stock exchange building (shown live on TV). Government threw thirty billion baht into a support package which did little to deflect the trend.

Finance firms outside Thailand began to warn clients that the market was overloaded. But those that had set up shop in Bangkok were committed. They wanted growth and good news. Almost every day a Bangkok-based researcher or executive of an international financial firm would tell the press that the fundamentals were good, the long-term prospects were still sound, the market downtrend was reversible. In early 1996, foreign firms were still the most active on the Thai stock market. In March, the British merchant bank BZW paid 600 million baht for a Bangkok firm to get access to the market.

The break came in mid-1996. The revelation of the Bangkok Bank of Commerce scandal (see below) was the psychological turning point. After this, it was difficult to pretend that Thailand's financial industry was in terrific shape. The boosters still kept broadcasting the good news. But in the background, the hiss of air escaping a balloon was clearly audible.

Foreign players began to sell their holdings of Thai stocks, unloading fifty billion baht between June and year end. The stocks which the foreign investors had favoured now plummeted. Over the second half of the year, the market lost a third of its total value. Finance and property companies had led the way up. Now they spearheaded the plunge. Some saw their stock price cut to one-hundredth of their peak value. One commentator noted that some Thai stocks were now worth less than *patongo*, the Chinese breakfast snack that cost five baht for two pieces. Soon share certificates, he predicted, would replace used newspapers as the raw material for paper-bag manufacture.[6]

Foreign sources also began to pull back their loans to local banks and finance companies. From June 1996 onwards, the gush through the BIBF slowed to a trickle. Short-term funds slipped away. The overseas analysts now wrote scathingly about Thailand with phrases like "the decade of easy money", the "asset bubble" and the "manic honeymoon".

Local bankers and politicians talked of the need to restore confidence in the Thai economy and reverse the accelerating outflow of funds. The election in November brought a moment of hope. Maybe the return of the Democrats with an economic team headed by two financial figures would have a magic effect. When the Democrats lost by a hair, the stock index took another lurch down. By the end of 1996, nobody talked about confidence any more. The phrase "financial crisis" crept into the daily vocabulary.

The finance companies had been shaped by the stream of incoming money and the resulting escalation of asset values. They grew and prospered by leveraging as heavily as they could. But when the money stream reversed and asset prices plunged, they were quickly beached. Their balance sheets were destroyed by the fall of the stock index. Their cashflows wrecked by defaults on property loans and by the withdrawal of foreign funding.

In early 1997, Finance One collapsed. For a decade, Finance One had been the most swashbuckling and most successful of the finance groups. It had grown by leveraged takeovers of six other finance companies in the late 1980s and early 1990s. Its asset base was larger than several banks. Only a couple of years earlier, it had been trying to take over two of them.

But Finance One's success had depended a lot on the illusions which flourish in a rising market. Many of its assets were overvalued. Too much of its business was in property and hire purchase. Too many of its loans had gone bad. Its profits had been padded with gains from trading in the shares of its own subsidiaries. It was "purely a capital market animal, dependent on liquidity and market sentiment". The top executives had been preparing for disaster for about a year by gradually selling their own holdings.[7]

The head of Finance One, Pin Chakkaphak, had been a symbol of the boom – a new man who came up through networking, skill, drive, and ambition. At the peak, he was said to be worth ninety billion baht. Now he was a symbol of the bust. "He built his empire on the simple mathematics of asset expansion" – buy something, boost its value, borrow against it, buy something bigger.[8] Government tried to arrange a shotgun marriage with a bank Pin had recently been trying to buy. But the suitor found that the dowry was a mountain of bad debt.

The foreign analysts and rating agencies now dug down hard to find how bad the mess really was. How much had been lent to the property market? Estimates climbed up to 800 billion baht. How much was tied up in projects in trouble? Maybe a third. What was the total extent of non-performing loans? Estimates started out around 7-800 billion baht in late 1996, and a year later had climbed to 1,360 billion baht – a fifth of all lending by banks, and a third of all by finance companies.[9]

In June 1997, the central bank told sixteen finance companies to stop operating and in July suspended forty-two more. In December, fifty-six of these were closed, leaving only thirty-five open. Several laid plans to merge for greater strength. Rumours circulated that five of the fifteen local banks were also in trouble. Deposits migrated to the bigger banks.

In 1995, the Thai finance industry had paid a consultant to teach them how to keep foreign firms out of their preserve. Now many finance companies touted for foreign buyers or partners to stay afloat. Finance and securities licences, which had commanded large bids a few years earlier, were on the slab at fire-sale prices

Financial liberalization is attractive, commented the heir-apparent of Bangkok Bank, but "the truth on the darker side has not been clearly revealed until recently".[10]

Liberalization was only part of the problem. The wayward behaviour of the international finance market was the other. In the early 1990s, international finance had become enthusiastic about emerging markets, about Asia, and finally about Thailand. Foreign banks and fund managers stuffed money in, without a lot of caution. The Thai authorities did not try to stop them. The local finance industry revelled in the resulting frenzy. But the real economy was already decelerating. No efforts were made to channel the flow towards export growth. Too much ended up in doubtful projects. Too much was borrowed short and lent long. Too much was bet on the prospect that asset values would rise and rise.

Then the mood of the international market changed. The Mexican peso crisis in late 1994 made international finance firms rather thoughtful about the kind of dangerous instability they themselves could create in emerging markets. The Nick Leeson affair made western finance houses more wary of sending bright young things out east with lots of money. The BBC crash raised doubts about Thailand's finance industry and government supervision. The strengthening of currencies and stock markets in the west persuaded a lot of money to return to base.

Financial markets tend to be driven by fads and panics. In 1992-5, Bangkok was fad. In 1997, panic.

The BBC Crash

On 8 May 1996, the Democrat MP Suthep Thuagsuban rose in the parliament to make his contribution to a no-confidence debate. He would talk, he said, about the Bangkok Bank of Commerce (BBC). Everyone knew the bank was in trouble.

Few knew quite how badly. "The bank could collapse in the next one to two days", Suthep concluded.

Suthep's speech focused on BBC loans to cabinet ministers for suspect land deals and share manipulation. A fuller picture emerged in the press over the next few days – an eighty billion baht fraud involving bankers, government ministers, an international arms trader, dodgy land deals, and shady finance companies from Moscow to the Cayman Islands. Estimates of the rescue costs climbed to 178 billion baht. In comparison, the recent Barings crash was rather modest.

What's more, Suthep said, the central bank had known about this for years. His information was based on the bank's own documents. The central bank had already charged BBC with malpractice. But shareholders, customers, and the public were still being told BBC was not a big problem.

Within a few weeks, a run on deposits had brought the bank crashing down. A mastermind had fled to Vancouver. The deputy finance and interior ministers had been forced to resign. The head of the central bank followed soon after.

As the full story emerged over the remainder of 1996, it seemed like a metaphor for the whole bubble economy. Too much easy money. Too little supervision. Too much cosy self-interested camaraderie among those with power. Too much greed.

BBC ranked ninth among Thai banks. Like some others in this size-range, it had been founded to service family business interests (those of an aristocratic group including the Pramoj family). Also like others, it got into trouble in the slump of 1984-5. One of the family, Krirk-kiat Jalichandra, was pulled away from his job in the Bank of Thailand to sort things out.

BBC meandered through the late-1980s boom without much improvement. In 1992, it still had bad debts of nine billion. But in the bubble, lots of people could find uses for a dull bank with good political connections.

Enter Rakesh Saxena, an Indian with an uncertain past who pitched up in Bangkok in the 1980s. He worked as a journalist and consultant, and acquired a reputation as a financial expert. Saxena suggested to Krirk-kiat that the way to pull BBC out of its hole was to rack up the share price. He contacted Sia Song who specialized in "churning" shares upwards. But then the two fell out when Song threatened to gain control. Krirk-kiat had to buy shares back or be forced out. Song was arraigned by the Stock Exchange Commission for malpractice (but got off). Krirk-kiat retained control but at the cost of an additional 2-4 billion baht in debt.

Next enter Group 16, a bunch of young and ambitious politicians who got together in 1992. Some of them sat on a parliamentary committee which investigated the BBC/Song affair. They saw secret documents on the bank. Rather than advising closer public controls, they set out to exploit BBC's vulnerability for private gain.

Over the next three years, some members of Group 16[11] worked with Krirk-kiat and Saxena on a range of pyramid money-making schemes using BBC funds.

They took loans from BBC to buy land; had the land revalued outrageously (times forty in some cases); then used it as collateral to take out much larger loans from BBC.

They set up paper companies which borrowed from BBC; then set up more companies which borrowed more loans to buy up the original companies; and so on. Eventually ninety-seven such paper companies were traced.

They took unsecured loans to buy up listed firms, then used further loan money to fan up their share prices in the hope of realising a quick profit.

They set up companies in offshore havens such as the Cayman Islands. These companies took loans from the BBC to buy up the group's existing holdings of shares and companies at inflated prices.

Next enter some raffish characters from the flightier edges of international finance. The arms-dealer, Adnan Khashoggi. The wheeler-dealer Rajen Pillai, who had tried to gut Nabisco and faced an arrest warrant in India. Plus a smattering of funny finance companies in Moscow, Australia, Tianjin, and Canada. They presumably got wind of BBC from the ramps in the offshore havens. They too wanted to join in. Khashoggi used BBC funds to make takeover bids for three listed Thai companies.

These pyramid schemes were outrageous. But at the time, plenty of people were making money simply by holding assets which inflated in value ridiculously fast. Krirk-kiat and friends were just helping the process along. For four years, nobody rumbled them. They bought a yacht and a corporate jet. They swanned off to Europe. Many of their political and banking friends joined in this revelry.

BBC's bad debts were steadily rising – from nine billion in 1992, to eleven in 1993, nineteen in 1994. But Krirk-kiat and Saxena took care to doctor the bank's books into the black.

In 1994, the central bank's investigators noted there were too many doubtful loans. In early 1995, the central bank ticked Krirk-kiat off for breaking some banking laws, and insisted on an expansion of capital to cover doubtful debts. Krirk-kiat easily complied by lending friends BBC money to buy the extra shares.

But once figures like Khashoggi appeared in the plot, some alarm bells began to ring. The central bank halted loans for leveraged takeovers and launched a bigger investigation. By mid-1995, the regulators knew the scale of the mess.

But Vijit Supinit, the governor of the central bank, still held off. Reportedly he took personal charge of the confidential reports and kept them in his drawer. Instead of charging Krirk-kiat, he mobilized over fifty billion baht of funds to help the BBC out. Some came from the Rehabilitation Fund amassed from a tax on bank profits. Some came from the assets of the Government Savings Bank, which were mostly savings of kids and the aged. These funds were poured into the hole which BBC had become. And disappeared.[12]

Later many would speculate on Vijit's action. Was he somehow involved? Did he just feel bound to help Krirk-kiat, his old central bank colleague? Was he under political pressure to keep things quiet? The opposition alleged BBC had helped finance the 1995 election success of Banharn's Chat Thai party.

At the end of 1995, the regulators reported to Vijit that BBC was technically bankrupt, fraud was unquestionable, and the management was liable to prosecution. Still the affair was kept under wraps. Papers were passed onto the police but without much sense of cooperation. Nobody, it seemed, wanted to take the lid off.

But other commercial bankers were fed up with paying money into the Rehabilitation Fund only to see it flow out and down the BBC hole. Rumours began to circulate about the extent of the BBC problem. Saxena responded with full-page press ads ranting about an evil smear campaign against a respectable financial institution.

Finally someone leaked the Bank of Thailand's confidential documents to Suthep. The contents were published in the parliament and then in the press. The news was out.

The figures were staggering. BBC had lent some seventy-eight billion baht of suspect loans. Sixty-four billion had no collateral at all and much of the rest was backed by over-valued land and other assets. Thirty-six billion had gone to Krirk-kiat and associates, eighteen billion to Saxena, twenty-five billion in the offshore schemes, and ten billion to Group 16 politicians. Saxena fled to Canada, surrounded himself with lawyers, and threatened to implicate many other people unless he was left alone. Krirk-kiat gave himself up. Group 16 members went very quiet.

The scandal was far larger than anything the regulators had dealt with before. At first, they tried to get new investors to take over the crippled bank. But as the bad news was still compounding, interested suitors soon drifted away. Eventually, the central bank foisted BBC on the IFCT, a lacklustre government-owned finance arm which did not have the power to refuse.

Attempts to prosecute were equally hobbled. In February

1997, the Attorney-General cancelled the main case against Krirk-kiat and others on grounds the police had not finalized charges within the statutory one year allowed. The controversy which followed suggested the police had barely known how to proceed and the central bank had not been enthusiastic in helping them out.[13]

The story was better than most novels of international financial skulduggery. The cast of characters spanned the monied elite – from royal-related aristocracy to adventurers like Rakesh; from the summit of the technocracy to the sharpest new business politicians. The central theme was not so much greed as the corrupting belief that something could be made out of nothing. In the bubble years, many people made money simply by holding assets which inflated in value. Many, many more made careers by joining companies (finance houses, stockbrokers, property dealers) which lived off this asset inflation. A new business press emerged which specialized in lionizing the heroes of this world. Financiers often stated openly that it was right and proper that finance made more money than manufacture. They liked to tell self-conscious jokes about "people in the real economy who, you know, make things with their hands".

Crane City

In 1988, Thailand had a small handful of golf courses. When a new club opened on Bangkok's northern outskirts, the value of its land plots and membership fees went up by eight times in one year. This looked like a good business. By 1996, Thailand had over two hundred golf courses. Only a few were making any money. Weekday golfers could easily believe they were playing at their own private club. This was elegant but no longer a good business.

The same story was repeated across the property market from retail malls to mountain resorts.

In the first bubble of 1988-90, basic instinct led many families to put their first new wealth in land. Tens of thousands quit the shophouse home in the old city centre and joined a mass trek to the new suburbs. On the eastern fringe of the city, large tracts of swamp land were filled and colonized with amazing speed. Beside a newly cut road to the west (Buddha Monthon), orchards and coconut groves disappeared under concrete. Along the first 20-30 kilometres of all the city's radial roads, housing estates sprouted in paddy fields.

Driven by this sudden spurt, the property market grew red hot. In 1988-90, prices of prime land in the city centre and suburbs soared up to ten times. Over the next few years, this inflation rippled out along the city radials, set off mini-booms in resort areas of hill and coast, and gradually took in the provincial towns.

Commercial property was pulled into a similar spiral. With the boost in the urban economy and the influx of foreign firms, Bangkok quickly ran out of office space. The craze for shopping created demand for retail projects. The influx of factories required land for industrial estates. Projects were floated in the last years of the decade and started to come on stream in the early 1990s.

Many people made fast and extravagant fortunes by selling or developing old family landholdings. Others got rich by deft buying and selling. These early successes provoked a huge second wave with a wide array of players. Most of the big banks and finance groups launched a property arm. So did several non-bank conglomerates. Old property hands from Hong Kong, Singapore and Malaysia set up joint ventures, usually with local financial interests.

Many, many others plunged in on a smaller scale. Firms which had made money in the first surge of export manufacture diversified into property because it seemed such easy money. When competition in export markets increased in the early 1990s, some switched completely into property. At the peak, fifty new real estate projects were launched each week.

While thousands of small companies entered the property market, a handful of big ones dominated. Most were families which had built up stocks of land in a previous generation. The Karnchanapas family had bought up large areas when prices slumped after the US withdrawal in 1975. Others had old family holdings on the outskirts which suddenly became valuable as the city expanded.

For almost a decade, these big property interests were borne up by the twin forces of asset inflation and credit availability. In the 1988-90 boom, their landholdings soared in value. With the stock exchange also zooming up in the bubble, developers floated companies to raise more capital. At this stage, the exchange was not too careful at monitoring flotations. Property companies used various tricks to boost their share prices. The Somprasong company, according to allegations by its own employees, cooked the books to show a rise in profit from 78 to 174 million just before the flotation.[14] Tanayong launched a clutch of new housing projects at giveaway prices and went into the market bathed in the euphoria of the inevitable sell-out. Other companies simply over-valued their land holdings.

In the early 1990s, it became more difficult to raise money for property development on the exchange. But a new source of credit was available. Jardine-Fleming and other foreign finance companies suggested the big property firms should tap cheap funds from Europe. They put together roadshows and trooped off to London. With his youth, good looks, Oxford education, and famous surname, the Thai managing director of Jardine-Fleming symbolized the dynamism and promise of booming Thailand. The Europeans lined up to invest. In 1992-4, led by the top developer Land & House, six major property companies raised twelve billion baht in dollar loans. Tanayong raised over three billion baht in debentures.

Over the next two years, the property companies found another lake of credit – the foreign and local funds flooding into Bangkok's banks and finance houses. Compared to other investments, property still seemed to promise high returns. It also had the extra comfort of land as collateral. In early 1995, the authorities sensed the beginning of a bubble and restricted bank lending to property. But finance companies faced no such limitation. They liked property loans because it was their only chance to demand collateral, because it looked safer than lending to the decelerating export economy, and because they did not have to compete against banks with cheaper sources of funding.

As more money poured into the finance industry, more poured out to the property market. It barely mattered if the developer could not repay the interest. The value of the land collateral could be increased and the unpaid interest rolled into the loan. Between 1991 and 1994, bank lending to property firms doubled from 200 to 400 billion baht or 10 percent of all their loans. By 1996, finance companies had lent 350 billion baht to property, almost a quarter of their total loan business.

With so much credit available, success depended not on selling homes, shops and offices, but on acquiring more and more assets which could be used as collateral for more and more loans.

In most countries, the real estate and construction cycle is a bit behind the business cycle and a bit more wayward. In booming Thailand this was very much the case. Partly this was simply because the market was a mystery. Entrepreneurs had little data to help them plan ahead. Projects had to be registered but the details filed were often vague or inaccurate. No agency collated and published these data. Besides, there was no trend data on which to mount projections. In the past, Thailand did not have the suburban estates, office condos, shopping malls, golf courses, and resorts which were now being built. There was no intelligent way to project demand. And no sure method to check supply. Property was, by definition, a punt.

And until 1994, a pretty good punt. Office rents increased

and new buildings filled up on pent-up demand. Housing projects spread out from the new middle-class city suburbs to medium-income groups and provincial towns. Condos and golf courses captured speculators. The big property developers walked tall. The lifestyle magazines asked them about their business success and philosophy of life. The home magazines displayed their palatial homes and extravagant penthouses.

Bangkok had become a city of cranes.

But in 1995, the cracks began to appear. The supply from so many parallel developers began to scoot ahead of the demand that none of them could gauge. Buildings, as one major developer noted, started to come up in the wrong places. Housing projects in remote fields. Luxury condos in undesirable areas. And a seemingly unending stream of new golf courses.

At the fringes of the market, small developers began to go under. Many projects just disappeared. Others stopped half way leaving angry buyers in the lurch. In the eighteen months from January 1995, 350 small property companies applied for bankruptcy.

By early 1996, the supply of credit had started to drop. The big guys also felt the pinch. The largest developer, Land & House, sold its flagship North Park project before the market slid too far. A few months later, the Ban Chang group sold off shareholdings to boost its cash flow. Four big Bangkok buildings changed hands.

Modelled on Hong Kong's satellite cities and sold with the country's biggest-ever advertising budget, Muang Thong Thani had been the largest of all the projects. But Bangkok was not Hong Kong. Thais were not yet used to living in high-rise and factories did not need to be stacked on top of one another. Only a few of the units were sold and even fewer occupied. Muang Thong became an eerily empty canyon of concrete. The developer, Bangkok Land, was said to be carrying thirty-three billion baht of debt.

For salvation, Bangkok Land looked to its political contacts.

It won the contract to develop the site for the 1998 Asian Games. It made 1.5 billion from selling offices to the Defence Ministry and was working on similar deals for the police, telephone organization, and Foreign Ministry. It also hoped to make three billion baht as the site for a temporary new parliament building but the press and opposition cried foul.[15]

In October 1996, the Somprasong company defaulted on the interest payments on its European loans. The company's own employees told police that the owner had been adjusting the books to cover up the widening hole in its accounts. The owner was arrested for fraud.

Through late 1996, analysts unravelled just how bad the problem was. In 1996, office space had grown by 0.7 to 5.6 million square metres and occupancy was still relatively good at 83 percent. But projects still climbing their way into the sky would add over a million square metres a year over the next three years, about double the trend of demand. In the retail market, supply was similarly at the point of racing ahead of demand. Condo units already under construction would absorb current demand for the *next ten years*. In the dispersed housing market, the picture was bad but unclear. Some said 120,000 units were unsold, some 300,000, and some even more.[16]

Banks and finance companies had lent a total of 800 billion or 13 percent of loan portfolios to the property market. Some believed more was hidden under other loan categories.

The cranes now perched lifeless over Bangkok like the skeletons of some petrified life-form.

Macro Blues

Thai technocrats were proud of their reputation for careful management of the economy. But the boom, and especially the financial liberalization, changed what had to be managed. From 1992 onwards, the macro-managers were wrestling to understand and control the impact of foreign money flows. From 1995 onwards, their efforts were complicated by politics.

In 1990-2, the Thai authorities liberalized the financial system (see chapter 3) but stopped short of liberalizing the exchange rate.

The IMF advised that in a liberalized financial market, a floating currency worked as a regulatory valve. If too much money flowed in to buy baht, the price would go up and the inflow would slacken.

Since 1984, the Bank of Thailand had pegged the baht to a basket of currencies dominated by the US dollar. The stable baht had become an article of faith. It made Thailand attractive for investors and trading partners. Besides, Thailand did not have the institutions and experience for dealing with open currency speculation. The managed baht had worked well for Thailand in the past. Better to stick with it.

But financial liberalization changed the nature of the money inflows. Less now came as direct investment. More came as portfolio investment into the stockmarket or loans to banks and companies. And some came as short-term hot money, parked in safe stable-currency Thailand for a few days, hours, seconds until something better came up.

With no flexibility on the exchange rate, the macro-managers had to use interest rates to control these flows. But they were also in the habit of using interest rates, along with the budget surplus, to keep the domestic economy stable. They were now in a bind. Using interest rates for both at once was tricky.

Since 1988, money inflows had tended to make the economy overheat. Some pressure could be drained off with bond issues but the authorities had not managed to develop a proper bond market. Running a budget surplus countered overheating very well but it was not a very flexible or fast-acting tool. Tight money policies had never worked very well. Now they barely worked at all. If money flowed in and stoked up the economy, raising interest rates tended to make things worse by attracting even more inflow. Capping bank credit just diverted borrowers to overseas sources.

The macro-managers were about to discover that they were waging a new hi-tech war with some very rusty old weapons.

From 1993 onwards, the economy began to overheat on rising inflows of foreign money. Inflation edged upwards. Economists talked of "macro stress". The Democrat government reacted by raising interest rates, capping credit, and soaking up some excess money with bond issues. It also planned to replace the inflows by raising local savings but these schemes would take time.

In early 1995, on the backflow of the Mexican peso crisis, international speculators mounted an attack on the baht. They saw that Thailand, like Mexico, had rising foreign debts with a high proportion in short-term money. They thought they could easily induce the short-term money to flee, bringing the baht crashing down. But at this point, the Thai economy still seemed moderately strong. Foreign reserves were equivalent to six months of exports. The short-term money stayed put. The speculators turned their attention back to Latin America.

Immediately after, the Bank changed some rules to reduce the flows of short-term money. But the bigger problem remained. The total inflow surged in 1995, well beyond anybody's projections. The money supply grew by 23 percent in fifteen months. Inflation crept towards 6 percent. Excess cash poured into suspect investments, a consumption boom, and the bloated property market. The current account deficit shot up from just over 5 percent of GDP between 1992 and 1994 to 8.1 percent in 1995. Foreign inflows were encouraging Thailand to live beyond its means.

In July 1996, the IMF again urged Thailand to allow the baht to float. Technocrats debated schemes to release it gradually. But again the final decision was not to change. Rather, the central bank combated rising inflation and current account deficit with the usual strategy of high interest rates and credit limits. The high interest rates hurt local small businessmen who depended on local sources of credit. But the inflows continued and the current account deficit widened further to 8.2 percent of GDP in 1996.

For the technocrats, adjusting to financial liberalization was tough enough. From 1995 onwards, they faced an even tougher challenge: politics.

Technocrats and Politicians

In the past, Thailand's technocrats had kept a firm grip on economic management. Their commitment to fiscal discipline, currency stability, and careful management had carried Thailand through previous crises. Now it seemed that things were spinning out of their control.

As a whole, the technocracy had been weakened by the boom. The middle ranks had been lured away by the pay-cheques and excitement in the private sector. The NESDB had been sidelined in the late 1980s. Prime ministers chose flexible friends as finance ministers.

The Bank of Thailand had also lost many top personnel. Three governors of the Bank had been dismissed within twelve years. A tradition of collegial teamwork had been replaced by competition among the key executives. The Bank governor, Vijit Supinit, had risen from temple boy to top technocrat by sheer ability. But he did not appear to have the support from his colleagues, nor the wider network in the power elite, to deal with political pressure from the cabinet.

The technocrats could not escape contagion from the get-rich-quick world of Bangkok finance. Many of the bankers they were supposed to regulate were old friends and colleagues. Vintage wine had become the currency of social networking. Technocrats enjoyed it too. Easy money could be made as an insider on the stock market. Vijit was found to have bought some finance shares at par value, making an instant capital gain. It was not technically illegal but certainly looked unethical.[17]

The technocrats had grown weaker, while the politicians had grown stronger.

The Banharn government installed in July 1995 had little understanding of the workings of the economy. Banharn also needed to pay back his friends and supporters. For finance minister, he first selected Surakiart Sathirathai, an academic lawyer with some experience in trade negotiations. Later he replaced him with Bodi Chunnananda, a budget bureau official who had reportedly helped channel large allocations to Banharn's constituency. Neither had any experience in macro-management or any base of political support. Both were dependent on their master. In perfect times, the finance minister and central bank governor worked together to manage the economy. But these times were not perfect.

Since 1988, the budget surplus had acted as a counter-weight to overheating. Between 1993 and 1995, the surplus rose from 55 to 136 billion baht, helping to counterbalance the surge in money inflows. But in 1996, the surplus melted away.

Almost the first act of the Banharn government was to increase planned budget expenditure by ten percent, mostly for road construction. Even in its dying days between resignation and election, the cabinet approved hundreds of spending projects.

To a lesser extent, the Banharn cabinet also undermined revenues. It reduced tariffs on many luxury goods on the extraordinary grounds this would save the foreign exchange which Thai consumers would spend travelling abroad to buy the same merchandise.

By late 1996, the budget was careering towards deficit. Fearing that the government would soon impose cuts, many departments spent their allocations faster than usual. The successor Chavalit government found it difficult to combat the deficit, because so much budget funding had already been committed. "Politicians want to spend money" commented one technocrat, "to help the people who elect them. You cannot expect them to put stability ahead of all else."[18]

On Christmas Day 1995, the head of the Stock Exchange Commission was fired for revealing sensitive information. He was known to be professional if a little indiscreet. The evidence against him, based in part on wire taps, smelled of political victimization. He had reportedly resisted political pressures and possibly been rude about Banharn. He had also been a rival of the Bank of Thailand governor, Vijit Supinit, who executed the dismissal. Both the firing and Vijit's involvement showed how the technocracy had become entwined with politics.[19]

The collapse of the BBC confirmed this. Behind the collapse lurked politicians and financial tricksters inflating asset values, seizing land, and cooking documents. The Bank of Thailand had known about it but kept quiet.

As economic problems mounted in late 1996, the Bank of Thailand seemed to fall in with the politicians' strategy to deny the problem and ramp up confidence. It published optimistic projections of economic performance. It down-played the disaster potential of the financial sector's exposure to the property market. It insisted that the current account deficit would be no more than 7.1 percent of GDP but later had to publish the disastrous figure of 8.2 percent. The IMF issued a formal caution about the strain on the exchange rate. The Bank of Thailand countered with a paper insisting the strain could be managed.

In July 1996 Vijit was replaced. But his successor immediately promised a "soft landing in '96" with a positive budget surplus, export growth, and a significant drop in the current account deficit. In January 1997, after none of this had come true, he still insisted that the economy was bottoming out, that the BBC mess would be cleared up in three months, and that growth in 1997 would be strong.[20]

The move towards financial liberalization had been based on the idea that free markets worked better. But how free was

Thailand's financial market? Regulators had been bullied by politicians. Banks had been manipulated and looted by powerful figures. Good data were hard to come by. Leading financial companies had been playing pyramid schemes. Property companies had inflated land values and cooked the books. With so much "influence" and "non-transparency", how well could the market operate?

Burst

A few weeks after the BBC crash in May 1996, Thammasat University economists published an open letter announcing "the economy is sick", policies were contradictory, and the Bank of Thailand was dangerously subject to "political pressures". Chulalongkorn University published a survey of businessmen and officials who complained that "politicians increasingly interfere with the day-to-day operations of the Bank of Thailand".[21] The association of stockmarket investors called on the government to resign. The Bankers Association demanded the "depoliticization" of economic management. A senior technocrat urged that macro-management "is so urgent and technical it cannot be left to the politicians".[22] A foreign finance house noted: "We felt very comfortable viewing the central bank as a lifeboat for the economy but this sort of thing [BBC] has put people off."[23]

But among all these panicky voices, the finance industry was the loudest. If we go down, the financiers threatened, then everything goes with us. Look at Japan.

In public, financial analysts dominated the debate on what should be done. In the background, bankers lobbied for their own interests. Right up to the eve of Finance One's collapse, Pin Chakkaphak was offering his analysis of the economy. In the throes of the finale, Chatri Sophonpanich, the head of Bangkok Bank, emerged to give the government public advice to protect the finance and banking industry.[24] After the IMF came in, finance houses lobbied frantically to change bailout policies.

At the general elections in November 1996, both major parties fielded economic teams staffed by bankers. Amnuay Virawan, who became finance minister and chief economic policy-maker, had been an executive of Bangkok Bank. The policy programme he announced on taking office focused exclusively on the finance industry. He presented it to serried ranks of bankers who nodded in approval.[25]

For six months, the government and central bank threw money and ideas at the finance and property crisis. They provided some cheap finance to officials for buying homes. They announced a scheme to buy out stalled property projects to improve the developers' balance sheets. They poured fifty billion into Finance One, following the twenty billion already sunk in BBC and sixty billion in the stockmarket. They quietly allowed the wrecked finance companies to borrow a staggering 430 billion from the central bank's Rehabilitation Fund.

But with confidence plummeting, most of these funds flowed straight out of the country. Foreign investments had begun to leach away. The balance-of-payments slipped into deficit from November 1996 onwards. Liquidity in the market dried up like a puddle in the hot season. "I don't know where all the money has gone", lamented a banker.

Devaluation, warned many economists, was now inevitable. But banks, finance companies, property developers, and big corporations were carrying over US$60 billion dollars of foreign loans. They lobbied against a devaluation which would wreck their profits and balance sheets.

The significance of the high-interest rate policy changed. Before, the high rates had been introduced to cool down the economy. Now they were retained to dissuade foreign funds from flowing out and undermining the baht and the finance firms. What had first been a tranquillizer had become an addiction.

With leaks appearing everywhere, the bubble began

deflating fast. Property companies defaulted on overseas loans. Finance One collapsed. Moodys down-graded Thailand's sovereign debt rating. The baht again came under fierce attack in the international currency markets. The stockmarket crashed down through 800, 700, 600, 500. The leading electronics company fell into financial trouble.

The Concerned Citizens for the Survival of the Thai Economy, including many high-profile businessmen and socialites, called for cuts in private and public spending to stave off "national bankruptcy".[26]

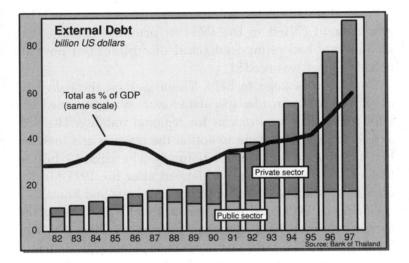

From mid-1996 onwards, one after another of the nation's macro-economists spoke out for unpegging the baht and allowing it to depreciate.[27] At first, they could barely be heard above the boosterism of ministers and central bankers and the baying of the finance industry. But through early 1997, these other voices softened in the face of reality. The advice of the economists began to break through. But by now it was too late.

The currency speculators returned to the attack. The economy was now much weaker than in the post-Mexico skirmish and the speculators more determined. After three rounds, the central bank had committed US$23.4 billion in the battle of the reserves and could not predict how much it would get back. To maintain this fight and to hold up the finance industry, it had been forced to commit the cardinal macroeconomic sin of printing money.[28] There was no choice. On 2 July 1997, the Bank of Thailand threw away the peg and floated the baht. The currency plunged from twenty-six to the US dollar to below fifty. The financial industry teetered. Some smaller banks and finance houses were hit by short-term runs on deposits.

With no reserves left for defence of baht or banks, the Thai government called in the IMF. In previous crises, Thai technocrats had reimposed fiscal discipline. But now an outside agency was needed.

The IMF was keen to help. The attack on the baht had developed into a broader speculative war on Asian currencies, with frightening implications for regional stability. The IMF agreed to a standby credit to bolster the reserves and took the hat round Asia for additional funds. The US$17.2 billion bailout was the IMF's second-largest after the 1995 Mexico crisis (soon surpassed by bailouts for Indonesia and Korea).

Under the IMF conditions, government had to bring the current account balance down to 5 percent of GDP in 1997 and 3 percent in 1998; raise taxes and cut spending to deliver a budget surplus of 1 percent of GDP in 1998; and accept guidance on financial restructuring.

But capital continued to leak away. The falling baht wrecked balance sheets. The suspension of fifty-eight finance firms created seizure in the money market. In late 1997, the economy contracted much more sharply than the IMF expected. GDP growth sank to near-zero. The target for the current account balance was overshot. But the target for a budget surplus became more difficult as government revenues shrank. In November, the IMF accepted some easing of conditions, particularly an increase in government overseas borrowing to ease the liquidity crunch.

At the core of the crisis was the crippled finance industry. By one estimate, 286 billion baht, or 4.5 percent of GDP, would be needed to write off bad debts and rebuild the capital base.[29] Where had all this money gone? Some was tied up in un-wanted concrete. Some, the BBC case suggested, had just been stolen and some looted for political investments. Much had been siphoned off in the super-profits of the bubble. The 286 billion baht was roughly equivalent to the industry's profits of the previous three years. Pin Chakkaphak was reputedly putting finishing touches to a 600 million baht house.

The bust brought home how much investment of recent years had been based on nothing firmer than the hope that growth would continue, assets would go on inflating, the good times would roll. Many big projects crashed or were put on hold. Alphatec's ambitious vision for the electronics industry collapsed. TPI shelved plans for a refinery, power plant, cement works, ethylene cracker, and three overseas projects. CP announced it would locate its wafer fab in Hong Kong or China. Seagate shifted its expansion plans to Indonesia and the Philippines. The Manager media empire began to crumble. Plans for new banks were quietly forgotten.

The heavy and service industries which since 1990 had attracted the more ambitious Thai investors (see chapter 3) were stopped in their tracks by the rapid slowdown and the disappearance of credit. The head of Bangkok Bank predicted that two-thirds of Thai business tycoons would be wiped out. Bust. Bankrupt. Bought over.

Bubbling Over

The boom made Thailand famous. In one week, seven major international publications ran a lead story on the economic crisis.

Manufactured exports had driven the boom. From the early 1990s, growth faltered. New and cheaper competitors had entered the market. Demand from Japan had slackened. Too little had been invested in improving productivity. By 1996, export growth had dwindled away.

But this was a downturn. Finance made it a crisis.

From 1993, foreign money had poured in, attracted by the lure of Asian fortunes. The inflow obscured the export slowdown and pumped up a bubble economy of inflated assets, overbuilt property, excess spending, and incautious investment. The bursting of this bubble made the downturn sharp, fast, and deep.

But bursting bubbles are common features of the final stages of a cycle. Thailand's 1997 crisis was worse than elsewhere, worse than before.

The technocrat institutions which had built such a reputation for careful management failed to cope. They were weakened by the loss of people to the private sector. They were infected by the contagious bullishness of the bubbly finance sector. They were tempted and intimidated into collusion with the world of crony politics. And finally they seemed to panic: losing the reserves on gambles against the hedge funds, pouring 10-15 percent of GDP into the black holes forming in the finance industry, and finally printing an unknown amount of money. The bubble burst in long strings of zeroes.

The end of Thailand's boom, someone commented, was like watching a car crash in slow motion. Perhaps a better metaphor lies in the agonizingly slow movements of Thai classical drama:[30] on left stage, the troops of Thai exporters, circling in a dance of decelerating tempo; centre-stage, the fattened-up bird of finance miming a slow-motion plunge from heaven to earth; and at right, the princes and nobles of the Thai technocracy, ancient weapons raised, frozen into a stock-still tableau.

6 Manpower and Womanpower

From 1984 to 1996, Thailand mobilized three million people to work in manufacturing and another four million for other urban jobs. But it was a scramble.

In the classic view, Asian industrialization is just the result of mixing together international capital and large supplies of cheap labour. But in the last decade of the twentieth century, the chemistry is not quite so simple.

On the one hand, Thailand's pool of cheap labour turned out to be neither as deep nor as accessible as supposed.

On the other, the firms which migrated to Thailand (and the local ones which copied them) were relatively sophisticated. They did not downgrade their technology when they shifted location. They might like cheap labour. But they needed skilled and educated labour to handle the technology.

Thailand's labour force was not at all prepared for industrialization. The educational system was geared for a society of peasants and bureaucrats. In the early '80s few were schooled beyond a minimal primary level. The universities were oriented to producing government administrators.

Besides, the expanding land frontier kept most people in the villages. Bangkok had grown rather modestly. It was not a typical third world city, bloated with surplus supplies of labour.

Finding the workers and the skills for the boom was not easy. In the short term, Thailand scrambled to get by. But by the 1990s, real wages had begun to rise. Labour was

> *becoming restive. And the shortage of skills had become a*
> *heavy constraint.*

For the boom to happen, many working lives had to change. Over less than two decades, the whole pattern of employment shifted. In the early 1980s, 70 percent of working people were in agriculture. Over the next decade, all the additional recruits to the labour force went into urban jobs.[1]

Around 1980, the urban labour supply ebbed and flowed on the rhythms of the agricultural economy. When the rains stopped, over a million people came to the city. When the rains started again, the people left for the villages. By the early 1990s, this seasonal fluctuation had been sharply reduced. More people stayed in the city.

Around 1980, most employed women were part-time workers in agriculture. From 1986 onwards, female labour became the mainstay of the labour-intensive industries driving the boom.

Around 1980, four-fifths of working people had four years of education or less. As long as agriculture was the mainstay of the economy, government thought it wasteful if not dangerous to invest any more in education. Between 1987 and 1994, the numbers going on to secondary education increased by one million.

Around 1980, the higher education system was still geared to staffing the bureaucracy. Over the next decade, the numbers working in white-collar jobs in the private sector grew four times.

Few people were ready for these changes. Over the last generation, the urban labour force had grown quite slowly. Never had it been subject to the sudden increase in demand which came from 1986 onwards. None of the projections of the educational planners forecast that the demand for skilled and educated workers would increase so fast. In the early 1980s, human resource planners were still worried about *over*production of educated people and about growing *un*employment.

New lives

Fon left school immediately after completing the four years of compulsory primary. The nearest secondary school was twenty kilometres away from the village, and anyway, mother wanted her to help around the house and to earn some wages. Fon transplanted rice seedlings, cut sugarcane, and minded buffalo for the richer neighbours.

When Fon was fourteen, her father died. The family needed a new source of income. Fon took the bus and went to join her cousin in Bangkok. She found a job working in a garment factory. She was paid piece-rate. By working long hours and every day, she could make about 1,700 baht a month.

One day a woman stopped her outside the factory and offered her a job in a bar. She would get two thousand baht a month and could earn more from tips. She tried it for six months. But she kept having her salary cut for arriving late. She was not pretty enough to attract the bar-goers. And she grew scared about AIDS.

By chance she met a friend from the garment factory. The friend was now working as a golf caddy. The pay was less than the bar. But being outdoors was better than being cooped up in a bar or factory. And she still managed to send back a thousand baht a month to her mother.

Jiew left his northeastern village after the cassava crop failed. In the early 1970s, when his family first cleared the land, the yield was good. But four years later, it was hopeless. Jiew had heard about the firms in the nearby town which recruited workers for the Middle East. A month later, he was in Saudi.

He worked as a driver for a construction crew. For the first six months all his earnings went to pay off his debt to the job agency. After that he saved fast. There was nothing much to waste money on in Saudi. He found he had a knack for repairing the trucks and other machines, which earned him more. Within two years he had saved a hundred thousand baht and decided to go home.

He spent most of the money building a house in the village. Then he went to Bangkok. With his Saudi experience, he easily found a job in a Japanese factory assembling trucks. After a six-month trial, the firm sent him to Osaka for training. He worked there for six months and managed to learn a little Japanese. On his return to Bangkok, he was made a supervisor.

Prasit studied at one of Bangkok's most prestigious schools. In the annual nationwide examinations for university places, he just failed to make the grade. His merchant father dug into his pockets and sent him off to a private university in the American midwest.

He came back three years later with a degree and a drawl. His father found him a job in a bank which paid nine thousand baht. After a year he left to work in a finance company which paid him double. With his American English, the company put him to work looking after its *farang* clients. He got to know some young expats. Through them he met Dan who had just arrived from New York to set up the branch of a broking firm. Dan needed local staff with some financial experience. He hired Prasit, paid him double again, and put him on an incentive scheme.

Prasit had to look after overseas investors who wanted to place money on the Thai stock exchange. In the first year, the company doubled its business. Prasit got twelve months bonus and a raise of fifty percent. One day his father called him up and asked him to leave the brokerage and help him run the family trading business. Prasit refused. But two years later, when the finance industry crashed, he decided to be a good son.

From Village to City

In many parts of the developing world, the first signs of urban growth prompted a stampede to the city. In Latin America in the 1960s, north Asia in the 1970s, and China in the 1990s, masses of peasants opted for hope in the city.

Thailand's villagers did not immediately rush off to the city in this way. In 1970, the population of Bangkok was around three million. Outside Bangkok, urban growth was negligible. Most upcountry centres were little more than big villages.

In the past, Siam had been a labour-short country. The population was small. The expansion of rice exports pulled people away to the agrarian frontier. The rulers had to import poor Chinese to work in the city. But between the world wars, this shortage disappeared. Falling death rates drove population growth up to 3 percent. Bad rains and bad prices forced peasants to look for work in the city. From the 1950s onwards, the rapid commercialization of agriculture split the peasantry into winners and losers – and forced the losers to look elsewhere for work.

But the trickle into the city was slow compared to other countries and often only temporary. While some peasants quit the village and moved to the city for good, many more just went to the city to work for a short time. During the dry season, there was nothing to do in the rice fields. Villagers would go off for three to six months to work on a construction site, drive a taxi, serve in a restaurant, sell noodles on a street corner, even work in a textile factory. This flow grew steadily.[2] By the 1980s, the non-agricultural workforce grew by over a million people in each dry season.[3]

Others went to the city for a little longer but still temporarily. Many village boys had traditionally travelled for a couple of years in search of knowledge and experience before settling down to work the family land. Now more and more this rustic "grand tour" was routed through the city.

And more and more village girls joined in. They could find work in the city at least as well as the boys. They laboured on construction sites, in shops and restaurants, as house maids, and in the mushrooming sexual services trade. In the 1960s, forty thousand US troops were stationed in Thailand and thousands more visited on the R&R programme. The sexual services industry, which was already large, became larger still.

When the Americans left, the excess capacity was marketed to visitors from the oil-rich Middle East and to package tourists from the West.[4]

This special demand helped to establish a high female showing in the rural-urban migration. Most estimates found a little over half of all migrants were female. From the 1970s, the female migrants were also pulled more into factory work – into the assemblies for electrical and electronic goods and into the textile plants.

Still most of these migrants went home again after a couple of years. Some came and went between village and city several times. This flow created its own infrastructure. Local entrepreneurs set up bus services to handle the regular movement of people between the city and remote villages. Some early migrants stayed on in the city and set up hostels to house the temporary migrants. Localities developed specialization in certain trades (housemaids, taxi-driving) and the old hands passed on training to the new recruits. Many Bangkokians in the 1980s met taxi-drivers who haggled the fare with skill and conviction but then drove off with only a vague idea of the route.

Why did they not stay on in the city?

Many reasons. Most still had some family land. They still saw land, house, family, and village as their long-term source of livelihood and social security. They were used to the independence of a peasant cultivator and often took badly to working for others. They preferred the culture and ways of the village to those of a city which had been built by aristocrats, *farang*, and Chinese. Compared to the numbers going to the city, many more migrated to work in other parts of the countryside which were not so strange.

On top of all this, they were not equipped to succeed. Only a fifth of the rural workforce had more than the legal minimum of four years primary education (raised to six years with practical effect from the early 1980s).

Until the 1960s, even the primary school network did not reach out to the remoter areas. American aid cured that. But secondary schooling went no deeper than the provincial towns. For village kids to get more than the four years was expensive and difficult. That did not matter so much as long as they stayed in the village. But in the city it was a disadvantage. It limited their choice of job and their chances of earning.

Through the 1980s, the boom accelerated the demand for urban labour. Over the decade, the urban population grew by around four million people. From 1984 to 1996, the numbers working in manufacturing grew from 2 million to 4.8 million.

Where did these people come from?

The growth of the total workforce was slowing down. From the 1970s, family planning helped reduce population growth from its 3 percent peak. By the late 1980s, the population of working age was expanding at 1.5 percent a year.

But agriculture was slowing down even more. And government now put a brake on the expansion of land under cultivation (see chapter 8). The decline of agriculture helped to push the workers out of the villages to meet expanding urban demand. In the 1970s, three out of every five new entrants to the workforce went to agriculture. From the early 1980s, all the additional entrants went to urban jobs.

In the 1970s, the biggest flows to Bangkok came from the nearby provinces in the central region. By the 1980s, most came from the more distant but poorer northeast where the agrarian decline hit hardest. Between 1980 and 1990, 1.1 million people from the 15-30 age range disappeared from the northeast, mostly headed for Bangkok.[5]

More people came more permanently. The numbers moving to the city just for the dry season actually declined from 1987 onwards. Most of the short-term migrants now were men. Many women made a more permanent shift. Slums and temporary settlements appeared in every nook and cranny of the city. By 1990, Greater Bangkok had 1,404 slum settlements housing over 1.2 million people.

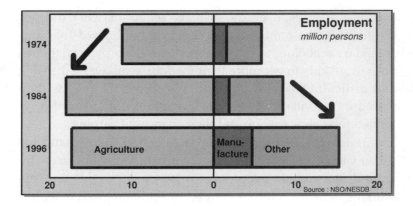

Over half the longer-term migrants to the city were women. *In seven out of the ten leading export industries, 80 percent of the workforce was female.* Women also dominated employment in service industries such as tourism. They were valued for their nimble fingers and their service charm – but also for their readiness to accept a lower wage rate. On average women in manufacturing earned three-quarters of the male wage.[6]

The flow grew to a stream but still not to a flood. The links to land and village still held many people back. And there was a new disincentive – the growing horror of Bangkok. The poor were specially vulnerable to the growing pollution, poor infrastructure, and constant traffic jams. They were specially shocked by the contrast with the village. "They want us to go and die in Bangkok's pollution," complained one migrant who fled back to the village.[7] "The city is full of mosquitoes, the water reeks of chlorine, and it's hot," remarked another, "Only fun for a visit, not to live there permanently. Living in the village is better."[8]

A migration study in 1992 recorded 1.5 million people moving *back* from city to village. They had stayed on average five years. They were fed up with the bad air, bad water, bad traffic, bad housing, stress, and unfriendliness of the city.[9]

Some had probably worked in the labour-intensive industries and then been discarded in favour of younger, more productive workers. Some were target workers who had saved up the nest-egg to start a small business back in the provinces. In the villages and upcountry towns, the mid-1990s saw a spread of small trading and servicing businesses hatched from the nest-eggs of returned migrants.

Industry had to move towards the workforce. In 1980, nearly all of Thailand's modern industry was concentrated around Bangkok. For ten years government had run schemes to disperse industry into the provinces. But the incentives could not compete with the benefits of being near the port, the airport, the government offices, the best infrastructure. After 1986, the first wave of new factories were mostly built in and around Bangkok.

But by 1988-9, it was difficult to get enough labour near the city. The factories spread farther and farther out along Bangkok's main radial roads. Many companies set up bus services (or canal boat services) to ferry workers between the factory and villages up to a hundred kilometres away. Then new industrial areas started to spring up outside towns about fifty kilometres from the capital: Ayutthaya, Nakhon Pathom,

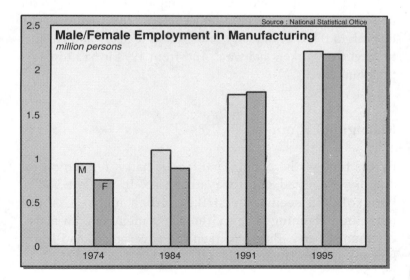

Bang Pakong, Chachoengsao. Next, entrepreneurs started building industrial estates in regional centres with high concentrations of population – in the Chiang Mai valley, in the heart of the northeast around Korat and Khon Kaen. To attract tenants, the industrial estates advertised their "plentiful supplies of local labour".

Several sectors such as garments and gem-cutting developed putting-out and subcontracting systems to reduce their plant and permanent labour costs. At first, these sub-contractors recruited labour from households and sweatshops in the city suburbs. But by the end of the decade, they too reached out into the countryside. Villages around Chiang Mai became centres of garment-sewing. Some villagers who had migrated to the city went back to their homes and set up subcontracting businesses supplying their old city employers.

Around 1989, the labour market tightened. Over the previous seven years, real earnings in non-agricultural jobs had increased very slowly, at 1.4 percent a year. But now firms had to pay more to drag extra labour out of the villages. Over the next five years, the increase jumped to 8.2 percent a year.[10] In some advanced industries, it averaged 10-15 percent.

The countryside responded to the rapidly rising demand for unskilled factory labour. But rather reluctantly. There was still no rush to the city. Industry often found it easier and cheaper to meet the workers halfway. And from 1990 it had to pay a premium.

Managing Labour

By the time of the boom, Thai labour had a reputation for docility. This had not always been so. In the late 1940s, Bangkok had seen large strikes, urban mobs, a labour federation claiming seventy thousand members, an active communist party. But since then the government had learnt how to suppress labour politics.[11]

It used many tactics. Much of the trouble in the 1940s was caused by workers in state enterprises such as the port, tramways, and especially the railways. These workforces ran into several thousands. Many of the workers were skilled and permanent. They could hold the public to ransom for their demands. They had become steadily more radical from the 1920s onwards.

After the 1947 coup, the military took control of the state-enterprise unions. It ran their radical leaders out of town and set about turning the workers into a docile and cooperative labour aristocracy. It pushed up their wages to almost double the private-sector average. It granted them welfare and legal protection equivalent to minor civil servants. In return, the state-enterprise workers tempered their political radicalism. Occasionally they took to the streets to support the generals in times of political crisis.

Private-sector workers were left to the mercy of the market. Employers tended to fish in the migrant stream for recruits and to trade off a high labour turnover against a low price. From the late 1940s, workers pressed for legislation of a basic labour code of rights but were bitterly opposed by the military rulers. A Labour Act was passed in 1955 but immediately revoked following the coup in 1957. Another Act was passed in 1975 but then shredded in implementation after the coup of 1976.

The military rulers suppressed labour unions for most of the time and took care to isolate labour issues from politics. The labour acts banned unions from playing a political role. The authorities reacted sharply to any sign of political radicalism. They banned the communist party in 1933 after the appearance of a handful of scrappy pamphlets. They passed an anti-communist law in 1952 broad enough to use against any form of radicalism. They met the upsurges of left-wing politics in 1945-8 and 1973-6 with concerted violence – bombs thrown into rallies, mass arrests, leaders assassinated, books burned.

With no legal code, no organization, no political torque, and little strength at the workplace, private-sector workers were highly vulnerable. Some large employers practised enlightened labour management, providing their workers with training and welfare in order to limit turnover. But many smaller enterprises used threats, thugs, and the ultimate backup of the government.

Labour was ground down into silence for most of the time. But in the mid-1970s, the frustrations boiled over. A wave of strikes helped to bring down the military rulers and to drive radical changes in politics. The epicentre was in the textile industry but the tremors spread into all kinds of manufacturing and service business. In four years, there were 1,232 strikes involving 384,000 workers and over two million man-days lost.[12]

After 1976, the military rulers opened the door for employers to reimpose control through threat and force. Labour activists were weeded out by dismissals. Many workers were transferred onto casual status to evade the provisions of the labour law. The 1970s upsurge quickly became a distant memory. Labour unions were allowed to exist only under stringent conditions. The umbrella labour federations were controlled by the military's men. Any attempt at a strike was likely to result in mass sackings, thug tactics, or even military intervention.[13]

This dreary history hung over labour politics during the boom. The urban labour force expanded and the urban economy's dependence on it increased. But labour was not able to leverage this growing power. Only 5 percent of the manufacturing workforce was unionized. Until 1991, there was little labour agitation. Suppression by now had been institutionalized.

In the boom years government made moves to regularize labour management. Since the early 1970s, the modern business lobby and technocrats had supported schemes to bring government in to regularize the rough-and-ready labour management in the private sector. Joint labour-employer-government ("tripartite") bodies were set up to run workers compensation schemes, fix minimum wages, arbitrate disputes, draft safety standards. Through the boom, government pushed up the minimum wage slightly faster than the inflation rate. In 1989 it introduced a Social Security Act which laid down basic

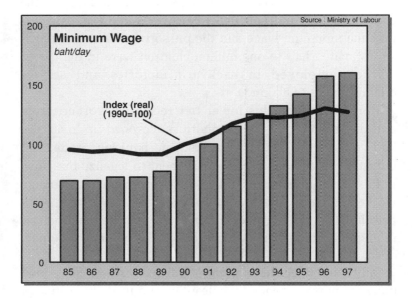

systems for health, maternity, insurance, and superannuation. In 1994, the Labour Department was upgraded into a ministry to reflect its growing role.

In effect, government managed labour during the boom with a two-tier strategy. In the upper tier, government took a larger role in regulating wages and conditions with the aim of maintaining the flow of new recruits and preempting labour discontent. In parallel, government tacitly allowed the development of a second tier where wages were lower, conditions worse, and regulation absent.

The second tier was large. Many major industries avoided the minimum wage and other labour laws by using subcontract or casual labour. Most of the 800,000 workers in the garment industry were employed on subcontract. Surveys of major factories in Bangkok found around a quarter of the workforces treated as casual or temporary employees.[14]

For the mass of small-scale businesses, the government's labour laws simply did not apply. The labour department had only a handful of inspectors for enforcing regulations on wages and conditions in over 200,000 registered workplaces. In the early 1990s, around half the urban workforce was paid less than the minimum wage and the proportion was increasing.[15] An estimated half to one million children were in the labour market, employed in backyard factories and service establishments of all kinds.

More and more, this lower tier recruited workers from outside Thailand. By 1994, authorities reckoned up to 400,000 had crossed the porous borders. The banking, trade, and industry associations urged government to legalize this flow. In June 1995, government did. In forty-three provinces, foreign workers already present could register for a two-year work permit. Officially many restrictions were imposed and no *new* immigrants could apply. But in effect, the borders were now open.

Only 370,000 registered in the stipulated three-month period but government extended the deadline and made little attempt to punish errant employers. Middlemen did good business trucking new arrivals from border crossing to work site. Official numbers rose to 800,000 and informed estimates to 1.3 million. Around 80 percent were from Burma, with other large numbers from Cambodia, China, Laos, and Vietnam. They worked in construction, fishing, rubber plantations, small factories, housework, tourist industries, and the sex trade. They were paid around 50-60 percent of local wage levels.[16]

For several years, this dualistic policy was an apparent success. The urban labour force increased rapidly in line with demand. Even when real wages increased from 1990, small, medium, and start-up enterprises could still recruit cheaply from the clearing ground of the migrant, immigrant, and child labour markets.

As the organized labour market tightened in the late 1980s, labour protest tentatively re-emerged. Public-sector workers protested against privatization schemes which would undermine their privileged position in the labour market. In 1988-9, dock-workers successfully opposed plans to privatize the operations of the new Eastern Seaboard ports.

Flush with this success, the state-enterprise labour leaders projected themselves as leaders of the labour movement as a whole. They organized support for the social security bill. They opposed the growing trend to use casual, subcontract, and illegal workers outside the provisions of the labour law. They publicly led support for other labour causes.

In 1991, government reacted by banning the state-enterprise unions. One of their prominent leaders disappeared without trace. The ban stifled the opposition to privatization and cut off the state-enterprise labour leaders' ambition to lead a strengthened labour movement.[17]

But as politics eased after 1992, labour became more assertive. Through 1993 and 1994, the number of strikes and labour protests increased seriously for the first time since the 1976 suppression. Labour leaders protested bitterly about the policy to admit foreign workers. In late 1995, the two biggest labour organizations (LCT and TTUC) tried to merge into a federation representing 300,000 workers. In 1997, public-sector workers again flexed their muscles to block privatization plans, this time in electricity generation.[18]

In the private sector, labour organization was still stifled by legal impediment. But workers could form associations within individual plants. They received some help from non-governmental organizations (NGOs) and from informal guerilla-style "labour clubs". In the early 1990s, labour in established industries such as textiles rankled at their slow progress in pay and conditions in contrast to the rapid enrichment of the urban middle class.

In 1993, the workers of Thai Durable Textiles protested against management plans to retrench workers as part of a

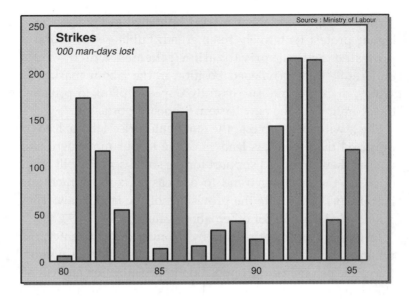

Strikes
'000 man-days lost

Source : Ministry of Labour

programme of technical upgrading. The largely female workforce organized under the leadership of a woman with nearly thirty years service in the firm. Through NGO help, they made their protest a public issue and forced the management to rescind the plan.

In early 1996, a major dispute broke out in the Thai Suzuki motorcycle plant. The firm had expanded rapidly in the 1990-5 boom and now had a workforce of 1,890. Management liked to handle workers in a paternalistic way under the slogan "we are the same family". It opposed unionization and two attempts at forming unions had crumbled. When 890 workers petitioned for increases in pay and allowances, mostly to offset inflation, negotiations came to nothing. The company decided to lock out the protesting workers.

Emotions rose. The protesters camped outside the factory gates. The company sacked 241 for desertion and disorder and sued fifty for causing damage. The workers' camp was harassed with gunshots and molotov cocktails. The dispute dragged on for eighty-three days before being resolved in a compromise. The company had lost three billion baht worth of production.[19]

As the economy slowed in late 1996, fears of labour unrest rose. In December, a warehouse and office at a Sanyo factory were burnt down after two thousand workers demonstrated about low bonuses. The firm had a union but the management again preferred a paternalist style. The workforce was unsettled by a plan to relocate the factory. Since 1987, bonuses had run at 5-6 months and most workers understood this to be a regular part of the remuneration. Management cut the bonus to three months but failed to make the workers understand why.[20]

Many employers braced for a wave of trouble. Two senior officials rushed to Japan to apologize. Some other companies hurriedly revised their bonus payments. But Suzuki and Sanyo turned out to be the exceptions rather than the rule.

In 1997, as the economy slid into crisis, the labour market loosened. Economists predicted up to 3 million would be laid off from the urban economy. As firms went under, the workers melted back into the villages or the informal sector. In some firms, workers agreed to share a lower workload and remuneration. Bigger firms used the opportunity to streamline their workforce. In May 1997, two big textile firms, Thai American and Thai Melon, closed down for two weeks, then reopened and announced they planned to shed five thousand workers. The first batch dismissed were mostly aged over forty.

Much of the rationalization came in the white-collar workforce, particularly in the bloated financial sector. Four big banks announced plans to downsize by a total of thirty thousand people. Many more expected to lose their jobs in finance companies. Some would take the traditional route and start their own business.

In sum: long before the boom, the government had learnt how to suppress labour – by practising divide and rule, by denying legal protection to unions, by isolating labour issues from politics, by ruthlessly suppressing radicalism. During the boom, government operated a dual policy. At the bottom end, it allowed employers virtually free rein to recruit foreigners and children, to evade labour laws, to pay and practice what an unprotected market could stand. At the upper end, it intervened more and more in labour management – to regulate wages, arbitrate disputes, provide welfare. These policies allowed employers to be rather careless about labour management. As the boom faltered, some suffered the consequences.

Skilled and Educated

The nature of Thailand's industrialization as a late developer boosted demand for skilled and white-collar labour even faster than blue-collar.

Although many firms moved to Thailand in search of cheap manual labour, they still required a cadre of local executives and managers. Much of the technology imported along with foreign investment was relatively sophisticated and the capital-intensity of Thailand's emerging industrial sector was quite high. Technicians and managers were needed. In 1960, there were just half a million people in white-collar jobs. By 1991, this figure had multiplied nine times to 4.5 million.

The foreign firms relocating to Thailand after 1985 quickly hit shortages in the supply of skilled labour. The pool of workers with industrial experience was small. The number with secondary education was limited.

Several hundred thousand Thai workers had migrated to work in the Middle East after the second oil-price hike. As world oil prices slumped, many returned home in mid-decade. Some had picked up enough language skill, technical ability, and work experience to take up skilled industrial jobs.

For the rest, firms got by. They poached from other firms. They introduced on-the-job training schemes. They sent workers to extension courses organized by the government.

They transferred workers to the parent company in Taiwan or Japan where they got on-the-job training and provided a cheap source of labour at the same time.[21]

From 1991, government responded to the skills shortage. It increased the provision of extension courses. It launched a crash programme to extend secondary schooling. Between 1987 and 1994, the proportion staying on from primary to secondary rose from 33 to 63 percent. Government planned to boost the figure to 95 percent by the turn of the century. In 1995 government launched a cheap loans scheme designed to encourage private investors to build more schools faster than the government could. It followed this up with a student loan scheme to encourage more students to stay at school longer.

Government also tried to interest firms in contributing to a major expansion in its skill-training schemes. The big firms refused. Most had already set up their own in-house schemes or contracted help directly from universities. They suggested instead that the government should subsidize these schemes.

Tertiary education was similarly ill-prepared for the upsurge in demand.[22] Until the 1970s, Thailand's tertiary education was geared to staffing the government. The first university, Chulalongkorn, had evolved from the college which trained administrators inside the palace. The second, Thammasat, had been formed after the 1932 revolution to turn out bureaucrats of a less royalist stripe. Kasetsart, Mahidol, and Silpakorn Universities were formed in the 1960s to staff the government's growing involvement in agriculture, health, and culture respectively. These universities focused on the skills needed by the bureaucracy. Many studied public administration. Rather few studied engineering.

In 1970, only some 120,000 had a tertiary degree, and the greater part of these worked for the government.

The US aid effort of the 1960s placed a high emphasis on tertiary education and in the 1970s this began to bear fruit. The first three provincial universities opened, followed by the Ramkhamhaeng open university.

Places were still limited and the demand for higher education among the growing ranks of the prosperous overflowed into teachers' colleges, vocational schools, and universities overseas. From 1970 to 1980, the numbers of those with university or other tertiary degrees multiplied four times from 180,000 to 720,000.

The big expansion in the bureaucracy absorbed much of this increase. But in the early 1980s, the expansion was over. The annual growth of the numbers of government servants skidded down from 10 to 2 percent. After 1985, the demand for white-collar recruits boomed. The stream of graduates was rapidly redirected away from the bureaucracy to business.

Government responded to the demand by building more universities but also, more significantly, by opening up tertiary education to the private sector. By 1994, there were twenty-six private universities and technical colleges with a total of over 125,000 students. Several other private universities were in various stages of construction. The numbers of tertiary educated in the workforce multiplied ten times between 1970

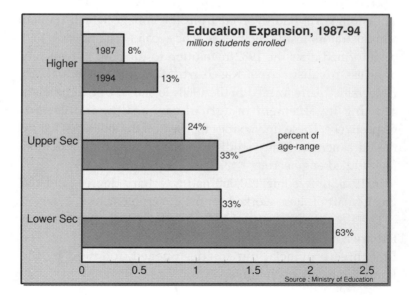

and 1991. Between 1987 and 1994, the total enrolled in higher education (excluding open universities) grew from 364,000 to 659,000.[23]

But the content and quality of higher education changed less quickly than the numbers. It was impossible to generate large numbers of scientists and engineers without the labs, the teachers, the equipment. Government increased the number of overseas scholarships. Many others went overseas privately for at least the last 2-3 years of their education. But in key sectors, demand leapt ahead of supply.

White-collar salaries soared. Engineers were in especially short supply. By 1997, 15,000 engineers were at work and another 27,000 urgently needed over the next few years.[24] The explosion of the finance sector induced firms to pay unprecedented salaries and bonuses to attract the right talents. The bureaucracy suffered a brain drain, especially from the ranks of university teachers and from the trained staff in technical departments.

The boom pulled back educated Thais who had settled overseas. Many Thai architects who had settled in Hong Kong and Singapore returned to work on the property boom. Some of the large community of Thai doctors and dentists in the US packed their bags and returned home.

To meet the rapidly rising demand for new and specialized skills, the government relaxed the rules for expatriate workers. Between 1991 and 1994, the number of new work permits issued to foreigners doubled. By 1994 the total number of foreigners with work permits reached 160,000.[25] Possibly as many again were reckoned to be working illegally on tourist visas. Thailand pulled in scientists, engineers, and skilled workers especially from China, the Philippines, and Eastern Europe.

The City Remade

Thailand found the workers for the boom. But it was a scramble. The decline of agriculture pushed people out of the villages towards the city. But the flow never became a flood. Firms had to move towards the workforce, mobilize female workers on a large scale, bus in villagers, put out work, entice illegal workers across the borders, and recruit children. The return of migrants from the Middle East provided a core of skilled workers. But firms had to supplement by setting up crash training schemes, sending workers off overseas, poaching from each other, stealing skilled workers from the government. The pool of white-collar workers had to be supplemented by rapid expansion of private education, import of expatriates, return of Thais from overseas, and a drain of talent from the public sector.

No-one had been planning for such a boom. The education system had not been geared up for an industrializing society. Although government began to make rapid changes from around 1990 onwards, it would take many years for these changes to work through. The state of Thailand's human capital at the onset of the boom had several longer-term effects.

The unskilled end of the urban labour supply remained very unstable. Many of those drawn into factory and service jobs still treated urban work as a passing phase. With so little education, they could see no long-term career in the city. They kept one foot in the village. They worked to save a nest-egg and return home. The rapid turnover created an artificial tightness in the labour market. Lower-end firms responded by recruiting illegal migrants.

For firms at the more organized end of the market, wages rose rather steeply. By the early 1990s, firms were moving away from labour-intensive activities which depended on a supply of cheap labour. The fastest growing sectors were electrical and electronic industries. Much of the work was still of an assembly nature but it required a more sophisticated workforce.

This expansion faced problems. Workers needed secondary education as a basis for acquiring the necessary skills. But even with the rapid gearing up of secondary education, by the year 2000 over 70 percent of the workforce would still have no more than six years of primary education.

These changes in the labour market generated major tensions. For the early years of the boom, the tensions were contained by two methods which government had perfected over many years. It eased labour supply problems by winking at illegal immigration. It deterred labour protest by suppressing labour organization. But by the mid 1990s, these strategies were running into difficulty. Labour protests were on the rise. Health and safety at work had become a growing problem. The import of foreign workers carried major risks. Thai workers objected strongly, particularly when employment demand weakened in the slowdown. Social workers noted the immigrants brought in diseases (elephantiasis, stubborn forms of malaria, tuberculosis). Local tensions could easily revive the old Thai-Burmese rivalry.

The transformation of the labour force had enormous social consequences for the longer term. First, Thailand suddenly acquired a large new urban middle class with new work patterns, new aspirations, new values, new wealth, and new needs. Second, income differences grew very rapidly wider. At the top end, salaries for the skilled and educated adjusted to international levels. At the bottom, the migrant with low education earned five dollars a day in an organized factory respecting the minimum wage, and less in the second-tier market. Third, many people now flowed back and forth between city and village. They donated their labour power to the urban economy and brought back to the village new skills, new knowledge, and new attitudes.

In the boom, many working lives changed. And collectively these changes transformed the city, the village, and the relations between them.

Men, women, and work

The roles of men and women in the economy present something of a paradox to those whose expectations have been formed in the West. Thai women are not excluded from work and confined to the family. Almost as many women work as men. In the nineteenth century, foreign observers were surprised to find that "the women are the workers of the country".[26] Now seven out of the ten major export industries powering economic growth are staffed overwhelmingly by women.

Yet among the ranks of the politicians, the bureaucrats, and the corporate leaders, women are a rare sight.

This situation has been shaped by some separate and often conflicting traditions – in particular the contrast between rural and urban influences.

The traditional rural household revolved around its women. Men were too unreliable. They were constantly going off to hunt, to serve in the army, to perform forced labour – with no guarantee of safe return. The family property was passed down through the females. The matriarch was not only the ruler of the family but often also the manager of the family farm. In an extreme view, the traditional rural family was a female-run enterprise which contracted in men.

The decline in hunting and forced labour and the regularization of military service modified this ideal model. Males became more settled members of the household, assumed leadership roles, demanded shares in the inheritance. But the female role continued to reflect the tradition. Women participated fully in work. Often they controlled the household purse. There was no move to force them into a life of household management or decorative leisure. There was nothing like a ban on women touching the plough.

The second tradition developed in the city with a mix of aristocratic and Chinese-mercantile influences.

The court was totally male-centred and suffused with ideals of masculine militarism. The royal succession was reserved for (warrior) males. By association, all senior posts in the administrative service were awarded to males. Women of the court were excluded from work and office and secluded under harem-like conditions. Kings and senior aristocrats amassed wives and concubines as a mark of status and as a means to generate lots of the sons needed to maintain the family's position. Families exchanged female kinsfolk as a part of political strategy.

The immigrant Chinese brought with them a family tradition focused on the males. In its purest form, the patriarch ruled over the family and over the family business. All property descended to the eldest son in order to keep the family's business capital intact. As in the court, the first role of the women was to generate male successors. Polygamy was justified on these grounds.

But unlike the aristocratic family, the merchant family did not exclude women from work. The upwardly mobile immigrant family business needed all the tied labour resources it could muster. Daughters were usually channelled towards subsidiary, technical tasks — typically accounting, law, marketing. But if the male line failed, daughters could be wheeled in to play a more central management role.

Between them, the aristocratic and merchant traditions in urban society enshrined male dominance. This was reflected into urban Buddhism. Only males qualified to be monks. Only sons could perform some key lifecycle ceremonies which ensured the family's success and the parents' smooth passage to a future life.

In the modern era, these different traditions have fused somewhat, as Thai has married Chinese and aristocrat has married merchant. But the traditions still mould male and female roles in work and business.

First, female participation in the workforce (70 percent) is among the highest in the world. Both rural women and the descendants of the Chinese immigrants expect to work and this ethos now pervades the society. Village girls are pulled into the urban migration stream by a strong sense of their responsibility to contribute to the family income.

Second, women have participated strongly in educational enrolment. In 1990, 42,000 women and 35,000 men graduated from tertiary education. With the rapidly rising premium on professional and technical skills, women have assumed a strong role in many professions and in some specialist niches in business. A few women make it to the very leading ranks of business. The patriarch of the family owning The Mall chain of department stores selected his daughter rather than her elder brothers to take over the key management role.

Third, posts which have any association with political power are strongly biased towards males. The militaristic male tradition of the court was handed down to the modern bureaucracy. From there it has pervaded urban society and helped to reinforce the paternalism of immigrant Chinese business. Few women ascend the heights of politics or administration. Few even occupy roles associated with political power – such as public intellectuals or political journalists.

In 1995, women accounted for 24 of 391 MPs, 8 of 270 senators, and 5 percent of village and district councillors.[27] In the civil service, women contributed almost two-thirds of the lowest grade and none of the top grade. In 1995, Oranuj Osathananda was poised to rise to the top grade and to the top job in the Commerce Department. But the (male) minister gave the job to a less senior man, claiming he would not be able to assign Oranuj night work.[28]

Most women work. A few manage. Almost none govern.

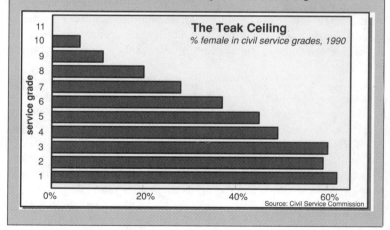

The Teak Ceiling
% female in civil service grades, 1990

Source: Civil Service Commission

7 CITY THAIS

The boom let the city swagger.

Bangkok has long dominated the country as a political and business centre. But this dominance was balanced by the sheer weight of numbers in the villages and by the myth that "Thai culture" was distinctively rural.

The boom changed the balance. The city's businessmen and white-collar workers grew rapidly richer. The city took on a new brashness and self-confidence. This showed first in a new youth culture that broke many old rules. It spread through an aggressive new urban consumerism. It developed much of its style on television.

The city surge affected Buddhism. Middle-class urban society reworked religious practice to suit its own needs and aspirations.

The surge changed the meaning attached to the Chinese origins that so many city people shared. And it brought into question what "being Thai" meant in a nation in which the city had risen to dominance.

City prosperity also sucked in the village poor. They came armed with songs and jokes as defence against the city's strangeness. By the mid-1990s, they had carved a new facet on city culture, hinting at social changes to come.

Through to the early 1980s, Thailand thought of itself as a rural nation. Both radicals and conservatives imagined the villages as the bedrock of the polity. The Communist Party of Thailand promoted a Maoist revolution led by the peasantry. The

National Identity Office called the peasantry the "backbone of the nation". It described "Thai culture" as a mixture of the royal and the rural – a blend of "traditional" court manners and ceremonies on the one hand and "traditional" peasant lifestyles and crafts on the other.[1]

In the early stages of the boom, pundits predicted Thailand's development would still have a strong rural bias. Thailand would become a NAIC, a new *agro*-industrializing country, in distinction to the plain vanilla NICs elsewhere.

Even the leading edge of urban culture was strongly coloured by rural styles and rural attitudes. In the mid-1980s, FM radio and cheap cassettes created a mass national popular music. Its first hit was Carabao's *Made in Thailand*. The band came from the rural northeast. They looked just like the rural migrants flooding into the city. Their music was based on northeastern folk rhythms energized by electrification and borrowings from Western rock.

The song *Made in Thailand* poked fun at the city's sudden enthusiasm for opening up the economy, exporting and importing, looking outwards to the world rather than inwards to Thailand's rural roots. Why did Thailand need all this foreign stuff when everything at home was so good anyway? The song was hugely popular and stunningly prophetic.

Over the next few years, the self-image of Thailand as a rural nation was wiped away with extraordinary speed.

Being Young

The emergence of a new and aggressively urban culture was spearheaded by the development of a distinct youth culture. This was entirely new. It was created by people who thought of themselves as the first generation that had grown up in modern, globalizing Bangkok. They were pioneers. They had little to learn from parents who had grown up in a completely different world. Often they guided the older generations to

Made In Thailand

Made in Thailand, This land of ours.
Kept from way back we have only good things
From before Sukhothai, through Lopburi, Ayutthaya, Thonburi.
Now we're in the age of BMA (Bangkok)
The city where people fall down potholes.
[Oh no! Don't go blaming anyone, huh.]

Made in Thailand. What the Thai do themselves,
Sing a song with meaning, dance a dance with style,
The *farang* love it, but the Thai don't see the value.
Afraid to lose face, worried their taste isn't modern enough
[*Made in Thailand.* So who will do something about this?]
[Well, I think there should be someone responsible]

Made in Thailand. All you fans understand.
The products the Thai make, Thai-made, Thai-used,
We sew the garments, the trousers,
The jeans [you'll lose face]
Well they're sent off by air and come back for sale.
The Thai get the face. The *farang* get the money!

Made in Thailand. But when you display it in the shop
Attach a brand label "Made in Japan".
It'll sell like hot cakes, fetch a good price.
We can tell ourselves it's foreign-made,
Modern style from the fashion magazine.
Nobody has to cheat us. We cheat ourselves!

Carabao, 1984

understand the new world. In the city, the traditional respect for age was balanced by a new reverence for youth.

Music was the main medium of this emerging youth culture. The songs and styles expressed the feelings of the new generation. The singers grew into popular cult figures and role models.

The song that succeeded Carabao's *Made in Thailand* marked the beginning of a shift in style and content. In contrast to Carabao's rustic looks, Thongchai "Bird" Mcintyre was clearly urban – a fresh, clean teen-idol look with affinities to both Hong Kong Canto-pop and Western bubblegum rock.

Thongchai was *luk kru'ng* (mixed race), the product of Scottish and Thai parentage. Amongst the singers, models, and actors/actresses who became the role models of this youth culture, the mixed-race look became massively fashionable. To be successful, such models usually had to have the black hair and eyes that marked them as distinctly Asian. Ideally the Western genes added only secondary features – fair skin, height, Caucasian nose. The look said: I am Asian but I have borrowed from the West.

Thongchai's hit song *Sabai*, however, expressed feelings similar to those of Carabao. The title means ease, comfort. It was seen as a distinctly Thai concept that captured the feeling of satisfaction at living in a country where life was so pleasant. The word itself, and the rhythm of the song, captured the gentle, easy-going pace of the rural lifestyle. The song became so popular, so pervasive, that some dubbed it the "second national anthem".

Within a couple of years, its lazy rhythm and self-satisfied message would seem totally irrelevant.

As the pace of the economy changed in the late 1980s, so did the pace of the music. As change became fast and bewildering, so the songs began to reflect the excitement and the tension.

Just before Bird's *Sabai*, Chantima "Waen" Sudasunthorn had a hit with *Chan phen chan eng*, "I am what I am". The song was among the first to express a theme repeated over and over in the next few years. Although the song's words were directed against a domineering lover, the song was read as a youthful self-assertion against the constraints of family and convention. It said: we are the new city generation. We are a new sort of individual. The old rules do not apply.

Suddenly in the late 1980s, the songs, the films, the TV dramas, the ads, were all about young romance. Until now, the whole subject had been buried by a mixture of taboo and discretion. Now members of the new city generation celebrated teen romance as a mark of their newness, their independence, their role as pioneers. Finding a partner was part of finding oneself.

Many other songs dealt with the difficulties of being pioneers, of growing up in a new city, of coping with the sheer pace and confusion of change. Much of this music borrowed a hard-edged style from Western rock. Asanee and Wasan Chotikul developed a new and surprising style for singing tonal Thai lyrics over Western rock rhythms. Their songs dealt with romance, with being new people, and with urban social concerns – corruption, prostitution, poverty, traffic.

Many of the most powerful and popular singers of urban self-discovery were women. Perhaps this was because the growth of the city brought more change, more opportunity, more bewilderment for female roles than for males. And because the songs helped to spread experience and encouragement. Waen, Masha, Tina, Mai, Beau – a succession of female stars developed a new female role model – sweet but tough, vulnerable but aggressive, approachable but independent. They sang a little about romance and a lot about being themselves, being new women, demanding a better deal from men.

The music was very much a communal experience. It was spread through cassettes, FM radio, TV shows. But the most important events were mass concerts. They were a shared event. They offered the chance for the audience to see the role model in person, in the flesh. The most popular singers like Bird and Mai spent much of these concerts chatting with the audience, sharing thoughts and feelings, explaining the songs, binding the culture.

Through the early 1990s, the music business was rapidly industrialized. The Grammy company specialized in orchestrating the mass concerts that were the focal point of the music culture. It built a cassette and CD business; bought its way into radio; branched out into television; set up chains of music and home entertainment stores; and by 1996 had 1,800 employees and a turnover of 8 billion baht. It began to mass produce new stars on an assembly-line system. Soon other companies like RS followed the Grammy example.

To feed this assembly line, Grammy drew more on Western music. It fashioned stars for rap, grunge, reggae, indie, heavy metal, blues, hip hop. Independent musicians also became more enthusiastic about borrowing from overseas. This was not new. One of Carabao's most successful songs from the mid-1980s had cleverly counterpointed a riff stolen note-for-note from Santana with a typical northeastern folk tune. But in the early 1990s, the borrowings rapidly increased.

Still the music retained a distinctive local character. To some extent this was a function of language. As Asanee had shown, singing a tonal language over a Western beat had a curious result. To an even greater extent it happened because local music – especially northeastern rhythms – persistently crept into the mix. The manufactured rap stars dressed up in floppy shirts and reversed caps but somehow still managed to be distinctively Thai. The Khan-Tee group found *"mor lam* [northeastern folk] music sounds similar to some black American rap music"*, so they mixed the two together.[2] Just as the *luk kru'ng* look said: I am Asian but I have borrowed from the West, so the music still said: this is Thai music but it borrows from the world.

In 1985, the hit band had been Carabao with their rustic looks and their prophetic song about opening up Thailand to the outside world. In 1995, the first group to roll off the music companies' production line was Raptors. These two *luk kru'ng* high-school kids dressed in the regulation floppy shirts and reversed caps of rap, and lovingly reproduced the dance routines copied from MTV. Thoroughly urban and thoroughly globalized.

Being New, World-Class, Fantastic

Bangkok's NASA Spaceadrome opened in 1986. Compared to the existing hotel-style discos, the size was massive. Compared to the usual backdrop of flashing lights, the setting was fantastic. NASA was like an aircraft hangar stacked with millions of lights, computer-controlled video displays, and special effects. At the climax of the evening, a spaceship descended from the roof. The owners claimed it was state-of-the-art, world-class, among the biggest and best in the world.

Many thought that launching such a venture in mid-1980s Bangkok was crazy. The boom had yet to come. The city seemed archaic compared to places like Tokyo, Hong Kong, Singapore. Did Bangkok need NASA?

It was a big success. A decade later, it was still in business and still packed. The owners had tapped something powerful. Bangkok's new youth did not want second best. They wanted the newest, the best, the most fantastic. They might be late arrivals but they certainly did not want the hand-me-downs.

NASA was the first of a string of music venues, each in some way more novel, more fantastic, more state-of-the-art. Some like NASA competed on the basis of size and splendour. By the early 1990s, Bangkok's inner ring road was studded with aircraft-hangar-sized entertainment complexes. Some were simply giant discos. Others crammed in the usual disco along with video, karaoke, snooker, jazz. Other places catered for niche markets that wanted something more exclusive than these disco barns. Smaller "music houses" spread around the more fashionable suburbs. In 1995, a failed retail venture, Royal City Avenue (RCA), sprouted over a hundred pubs and bars.

Big or small, they offered novelty and fantasy. Sharky happened to have a tank with twelve sharks. The Phoebus complex claimed to be one of the biggest ("room for 6,000") and most fantastic in the world. The Party House advertised itself simply as "world class". On RCA, pub-goers had the choice of sitting in a school bus, a replica jail-house, a bar air-conditioned down to zero (patrons were lent overcoats), an old Thai house, a ship's lounge.

By the end of the 1980s, the fascination with the new, the best, the fantastic had spread out beyond the new youth culture into a broader middle class.

Real-estate developers began to remake the city. Even the names chosen for projects reflected the fascination with new, international, and fantastic. Many names were simply looted from the world with no respect for context. An Inn on the Park without a park. Natural Loft for a shophouse in a swamp. House in the Woods amid paddy fields.

A few reached into a fantasy of Thai tradition – Nichada Thani, Chaiyapreuk, Laddawan. Many more played with fantasies of America and Europe – Luna Lanai, California Ville, Le Chateau. Others simply tried hyperbole – Vara Palatial Mansion, Royal Castle, The Icon.

Many projects lived up to their fantastic billing. A white modernist condo surmounted by a classic Roman temple. A rowhouse development disguised as a medieval castle, complete with drawbridge. A shopping mall clad in massive mock-Roman columns. Several tracts packed with Swiss cuckoo-clock houses. And after the advent of prefabricated building techniques, estate after estate that seemed built from jumbo pastel Lego.

Commercial buildings also caught the world-class fever. Some just appropriated names from the globally famous: Wall Street Tower, Centrepoint, World Trade Centre. Others pushed concept to the limit: a bank headquarters modelled on a kid's plastic robot; an M-shaped triple tower tricked up as the Elephant Building; a hotel reminiscent of a beached ocean liner.

Others took this pretension up vertically. In the late 1980s, a developer announced plans to build the world's tallest building. But the project never made it even an inch high. Potential customers knew that Bangkok floats on alluvial goo. By the mid-1990s, tenants had become braver. Baiyoke Tower

II soared up 465 metres, vying with Kuala Lumpur's Petronas Towers to be the world's highest.

Nowhere was the progression towards grandeur and fantasy more evident than in the shopping malls. In 1985, Bangkok had two smallish department store chains – Central and Robinson – plus a smattering of Japanese stores. Over the next decade, Central and Robinson each opened new stores in the city at the rate of one or more a year. Several competing chains appeared. More Japanese retailers came in. By 1995, there were sixty stores in total.

With the increase in the numbers came a growth in pretension. The simple department stores were superseded by elaborate malls patterned after Singapore and Hong Kong, and then by ever larger stores with concept themes and entertainment complexes: Fashion Island, Fortune Town, Future Park, Emporium.

Central City put a funfair on the roof, complete with big dipper. Seacon Square claimed to be the fifth biggest store in the world (new, best, fantastic!). It covered the area of sixteen football pitches and included an amusement park, a multiplex cinema, a roller rink, a mini golf range, a virtual reality parlour. On a weekend day, 150,000 went to Seacon.

In 1985, less than five percent of the city's everyday household purchases came from large modern outlets. By 1995, the proportion had risen to well over half. Shopping was about a lot more than buying. Shopping had become a celebration of rising incomes, of the power of the pocket, of the conquest over envy of more advanced economies. Shopping became the major leisure-time activity of the city's monied classes. The joy at seeing so much merchandise available was half of the fun. The huge stores were the new, world-class, fantastic temples to the boom.

Being Rich: Urban Dramas and Money Games

The confidence and excitement of the new urban society were defined and shared on television.

Already by 1985, virtually every urban home had a TV set. The government reserved the 8 P.M. prime-time slot for locally-made programming. The stations invested in local drama series to replace imported series from Hong Kong. At first many copied the standard Hong Kong genres of action films, family dramas, and ghost stories. But some producers experimented with dramatizing popular Thai novels and stories. The audience reaction was immediate. This stuff was relevant. It tapped into people's lives and concerns.

By the end of the decade, over half of Bangkok sat down every night to watch the Thai dramas. The daily newspapers serialized the stories in parallel. Several papers and magazines ran columns of criticism and comment. The stars of the dramas began to rival the singers as cult heroes and role models. Singers went into acting and actors into singing. Gossip magazines appeared to follow their lives and times.

The Thai TV dramas became one of the peaks of the emerging urban culture, an area of shared experience through the nightly viewing of the tube and the commentary in press, magazine, and daily conversation.

Three variants of drama contributed most of the hit series.

The first were histories – personal dramas in a context of recent history. *Si phaendin* (four reigns) dramatized a famous novel about life in the nineteenth-century royal court. *Nang that* (slave girl) was set in the last years of personal slavery at the end of the nineteenth century. *Chuichai* dealt with the life and times of Phibun Songkram, prime minister from the 1930s to the 1950s. *Khu kam* (fated couple) set a love story against the background of the wartime Japanese occupation. *Lord lai mangkorn* (pattern of the dragon) wove together the biographies of some of the most successful immigrant Chinese entrepreneurs from the 1940s to the present.

Strung together, these historical dramas created a past for the new city that had just sprung into existence. They told of the decline of the old world of the court and slavery, and the rise of a new world made by Protean figures like Phibun and the immigrant entrepreneurs.

The second were family dramas that dealt with becoming rich and often with the difficulties of becoming rich without losing your soul. *Wimanmek* (cloud palace) looked at the internal strains of a family growing rich in the second world war and its aftermath. *La-ong dao* was a modern setting of Cinderella – a sweet ordinary girl marrying a prince. The theme said: it's alright to become rich, even instantly. It was shown in 1990-1, when the successive years of double-digit growth were manufacturing nouveau riche at an unprecedented rate. The story moved slowly as the camera lingered on the setting – grandiose houses, luxury automobiles, fancy Frenchified decor, gorgeous clothes. The audience was huge.

This series was much copied – with the plots getting ever thinner and the trappings ever fancier. The 1993 version (*Nai fun* – in dreams) plunged the Thai cast into a colonial Indian setting and period costume ranging from silk turbans to powdered wigs. The 1994 version (*Silamani* – the gem) conjured up a prosperous nineteenth-century Thai princely state coexisting with the modern world.

By 1995-6, the settings had become globalized. Riffling across channels, a viewer could find Thai dramas set and filmed in Monaco, New Zealand, London, Switzerland, Burma, Nepal, Korea, and San Francisco. In 1997, a Thai cast was stuffed into Arab gowns for a drama set in the middle eastern desert.

The third set dealt with the changing role of women, the largest segment of the dramas' audience. Some looked at women remaking gender roles in situations of crisis and adversity. *Khao nok na* (rice outside the field) dramatized a famous novel about the offspring left behind by the GIs. *Chang mun chan mai khae* (what the hell) contrasted female roles between the new middle class and the urban under-world of crime and prostitution. In *Mongkut dok som* (orange flower crown), the four wives of a Chinese-Thai patriarch wrestled with their personal tragedies.

Others told of women succeeding in multiple roles as lovers, mothers, and tycoons. In *Nuan nang khang khiang* (the pork vendor's daughter), a market-vendor family follows the traditional route of investing all its savings in the education of the son. But the daughter defies tradition both by becoming the family's breadwinner and by choosing her own career and lifestyle. *Rak diao khong jenjira* told the story of a woman's fight against adversity by dove-tailing the plots of Jane Eyre and the Sound of Music.

Apart from dramas (and the news), the most popular programmes were game shows – chances for ordinary people to get rich even quicker than in the real world. By the early 1990s, chat shows also came into vogue. The main guests were the actors, actresses, and singers who had become the role models for the new urban generation. The shows gave the audience the opportunity to get to know them better, to study their clothes, their tastes, their attitudes.

The other popular offering on the TV was the ads.

Borne up by the enthusiasm for consumption, the Thai ad industry soared, in both quantity and quality. For a decade it grew at around 25 percent a year. Thai ads regularly won the TV awards at regional competitions.

The ad industry was not only successful but also glamorous. Ad industry figures joined the fringe of the glitterati celebrated in the gossip columns and the lifestyle magazines. All business newspapers ran columns recording and commenting on the ad industry. University students named advertising as one of the most favoured careers.

The ads both fed on the growing passion for consumption and helped to stoke it. They nudged consumers towards the check-out with a smile of complicity. *You want to spend, don't you. Have fun!* A gentle, smiling humour was used to sell everything from candy to insurance, from household durables to photographic film. For more difficult and boring categories, the ads lured buyers with the testimonials of the role-models. *They use it. So should you!* Stars were used to sell everything from auto tires to feminine hygiene, from fabric detergent to pick-up trucks. As a last resort, the ads simply went for exhibitionism. *You've got the money. Let others know!* Fantasies of luxury sold whisky and credit cards, cars and clothes, mobile phones and condominiums.

In the boom, TV became the most exciting part of the culture. It was locally made – imported shows were a minor part of airtime and even more minor part of viewing. TV reflected the excitement of the urban society that created it. But it was not reserved for the city. In 1985, half of rural homes already had a TV. By 1996, this had grown to 90 percent. Villagers watched the same TV programming as their city cousins. They became eager spectators at this urban-made show about the new urban Thailand, its concerns, its role model stars, its appetite for consumption, its celebration of growing urban prosperity.

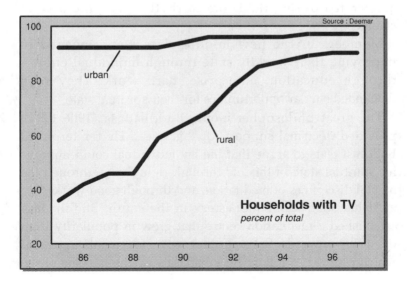

Being Buddhist in the City

The traditional practice of Thai Buddhism allocated the lay person a rather passive role. The monkhood took care of the spiritual well-being of the society and its members. Young men were expected to spend a short, token period as a novice monk. A few would stay on and devote their lives to the monkhood. Lay members of society could gain merit by supporting the monks with alms and donations. Accumulated merit could improve the individual's spiritual status in future lives but not this one. The Sangha, the formal organization of the monkhood, regulated doctrine and practice.

This structure provided few openings for participation, self-improvement, or philosophical debate. It had been developed to serve a rural society. The new urban population found it increasingly less relevant. The numbers of urban youths entering the monkhood for either a short or long stay steadily declined.

Instead, the new urban middle class set out to remodel religious practice more in line with its own aspirations. These moves began earlier in the century. But like much else they accelerated during the boom in rhythm with the pace of change.[3]

Members of the new middle class were engaged in improving their worldly state through individual effort – through education, enterprise, hard work. They soon demanded similar opportunities for their spiritual state.

The great philosopher-monk, Buddhadasa (1906-1994), provided doctrinal support for this quest. He reinterpreted Buddhist texts to argue that the lay individual could improve his spiritual state in this life through right living, through the mental disciplines of meditation, and through good works.[4]

At his Suan Moke monastery in the south, Buddhadasa established a meditation centre that grew in popularity from the 1950s onwards. Several other new movements appeared which claimed to follow Buddhadasa's teachings. One of the most prominent was Santi Asoke, begun in the 1970s by Pothirak, a former television producer. The movement borrowed heavily from the tradition of forest monks who lived remote from civilization and gained high spiritual powers through meditation and ascetic rigours. Santi Asoke offered urban lay members a route to spiritual improvement by similar practices.

The largest of these new movements succeeded by adjusting to the practical needs of the new middle class. Dhammagai was started by two university graduates. It established its meditation centre conveniently on the outskirts of Bangkok. The centre had the clean, modern, hygienic feel of a hospital. It offered short courses that could be managed within an urban lifestyle. It argued that its own special brand of deep meditation not only had spiritual benefits but also cultivated mental disciplines that could bring immediate benefit in everyday life.

Dhammagai became very popular among students, young professionals, and businessmen. Ten thousand attended its main monthly ceremony. Several tens of thousands passed through its courses. Prominent public figures including royalty, politicians, generals, and top businessmen publicly associated themselves with the foundation. The movement marketed itself so ardently and so well that Thammasat University awarded it a marketing prize. Dhammagai announced its plans to build a new stupa by renting advertising lightboxes in the international airport.[5]

Besides the meditation centres, urban society built up new cults surrounding charismatic monks.

The forerunner of this modern wave began in the 1960s. Phra Acharn Mun was a forest monk from the northeast who had lived a life of great ascetic rigour. A few years after his death in 1949, one of his disciples wrote a biography claiming Acharn Mun had attained the spiritual status of an *arahant* or Buddhist saint.

The biography attracted a following of people who sought different ways to tap into Mun's extreme spiritual power. A few took meditation lessons from his disciples. Some sponsored the disciples to build new temples. Many more went on pilgrimage bus-tours to visit Mun's monastery and the sites of his ascetic rigours.

The movement began among high-up members of the bureaucracy. It extended to include the royal family, which visited Mun's shrine and patronized his disciples. It expanded to a large middle-class following during the 1970s.[6]

City Buddhists were not limited to their local wat. Just as the urban supermarket had more and better selections than the village shop, so the range of choice for the modern urban Buddhist had widened. Disciples flocked to the Mun cult because they believed Mun was the most powerful spiritual figure of the century. From the 1980s, the ranks of charismatic monks multiplied. These monks became popular for many reasons – for their powerful sermons, their good looks, their modern and relevant interpretations of Buddhism, their good works – but always for their sheer *presence*. Their charisma signified spiritual power. Followers honoured them and patronized them to benefit from this power.

Some popular monks derived their power from the forest tradition. Luang Phor Koon wandered in the forests for several years before settling in Korat where he became famous for his rustic advice – blunt and simple pronouncements delivered in an outrageously broad local dialect. He developed several engaging habits including tapping votaries on the head with his knuckles or a roll of paper, and blessing mass meetings with a water hose. He gained a reputation for predictive insight which made him especially popular among politicians.

In his homeland of the northeast, any politician who sought popularity was obliged to sit at Phor Koon's feet, be rapped on the head, and hear his prediction (usually comfortingly favourable). This political following in turn added to Luang Phor Koon's fame.

Others became popular through adapting Buddhist traditions to the urban setting. Most notably, Phra Payom Kallayano. He extended the methods for alms-giving by using bank debit systems and credit cards. He spent monastic funds on urban development and social welfare schemes including drug rehabilitation, employment creation, and cooperatives. He spread his message through modern urban technology – through radio, television, and sermons distributed on audio and video tape. He specialized in aphorisms which translated Buddhist teachings into sound-bites with modern relevance.

In parallel with these charismatic movements, the market in religious amulets boomed. There was nothing new about wearing amulets bearing the image of the Buddha or a famous monk. But the expansion of scale was also a change in kind. Wearing an amulet was one way to translate spiritual power into personal fortune. For the modern urban dweller, this concept had enormous appeal.

In the 1970s, disciples distributed amulets with Mun's image to the urban followers of the Mun cult. When they found how popular the amulets were, they mass-produced them for sale to fund the maintenance of their temples. During the war in Indochina, Thai officers sometimes distributed these amulets to their men as a protection from danger.

By the 1980s, the trade in amulets had become big business. Collectors paid hundreds of thousands of baht for rare amulets with a reputation for special power. Amulet markets sprung up in various parts of the city. On evenings and weekends, they were packed. At peak periods the amulet market at Tha Prajan was reckoned to have a turnover of ten million baht a day.

Several magazines appeared devoted exclusively to the amulet trade. Major dealers took expensive full-page ads in the leading newspapers. Popular charismatic figures like Luang Phor Koon manufactured amulets to meet the demand. Politicians openly espoused the cult of amulets and often distributed them to followers, constituents, and associates. By one estimate, a third of all MPs wore amulets and three MPs were among the most enthusiastic and lavish collectors.[7]

The city also generated new cults and practices to help predict and control the future. Businessmen and politicians regularly patronized fortune-tellers. Many prominent public figures confessed to having their personal seers. Some leading economists who specialized in building models of the economy's future practised fortune-telling as a sideline. Spirit mediums, who had long been popular in the villages, grew in popularity in the city. So did spirit shrines which offered people the facility to beg help in controlling the future in return for a boon, often paid only on condition of success. The wife of Chavalit Yongchaiyudh combated her husband's political decline by propitiating Rahu, a minor Hindu monster-god.

Many of these elements came together in the Kuan Yin cult which spread among the Bangkok business and professional classes in the 1990s. The popularity of Kuan Yin owed something to her Chinese origins but rather more to her role as an all-embracing mother goddess who protected her adherents from all kinds of uncertainty. The Kuan Yin cult offered meditation for personal involvement, spirit mediums to foresee the future, and the chance to ask for boons to control it. Business people built up Kuan Yin as a new "goddess of trade". Women especially liked the cult's difference from Buddhism's enshrined male dominance. Kuan Yin helped followers to overcome many difficulties of city life: "Our business has taken a turn for the better," reported one devotee, "our health has improved . . . and my husband stopped being unfaithful after he started meditating and going to the temple with me."[8]

Another new cult arose around Rama V, King Chulalongkorn. Amulets with his picture became the most popular of all. Many households set up small shrines around his portrait. People gathered around his equestrian statue in the centre of old Bangkok to make offerings of flowers, candles, sweets, and the Scotch whisky he reputedly appreciated. Around 1990, the gatherings happened one evening a week. By mid-decade, there were mass attendances on two evenings and a steady stream of devotees at any other day or time.

At first the people who gathered below the statue came mostly from the Bangkok middle class – officials, small businessmen, professionals. But the catchment rapidly broadened to include the whole urban spectrum. And the statue became part of the itinerary of upcountry visitors.

Everyone had learned at school that Chulalongkorn was the great King whose reforms at the end of the nineteenth century had created Thailand as a modern nation. The devotees honoured a great figure in history and asked for his help. They hoped he could reduce the insecurity in their lives and increase their chances of prosperity and success. When the police chief, Sawat Amornwiwat, was threatened with dismissal for misconduct, he called on the old King for help. He had a ladder placed against the statue's plinth so he could climb up and make obeisance as close to the image as possible.[9]

Several themes ran through many of these new religious movements – the meditation centres, the charismatic monks, the amulet craze, augury, and the new cults.

First, they answered a demand for more direct and personal involvement in religious practice in ways compatible with a modern urban lifestyle. The adherents wanted some means to participate which was less drastic than entering the monkhood but more involving than just giving alms to a monk, listening to an abbot's sermon, and hoping for some pay-off in a future incarnation.

Second, the new practices offered remedies for the insecurities and uncertainties of urban life. The most successful meditation cults combined short-term retreats and mental exercises that reduced stress, with a promise of self-improvement in both this life and the future. The charismatic monks, amulets, spirit mediums, and new cults all in different ways offered protection against insecurity and some hope of good fortune.

Third, like so much in booming Bangkok they were about money. They offered opportunities for the adherents to invest some of their increasing wealth in the search for religious benefit. The leading charismatics attracted funding for wealthy religious foundations. In 1994 Luang Phor Koon collected and donated over sixty-three million baht. Phra Yantra, a leading charismatic undone by sexual scandals in early 1995, had commanded donations of fourteen million baht a day at the peak of his popularity.

The big meditation centres became spectacularly wealthy. Dhammagai's suburban headquarters covered thirty hectares. Its founders travelled in a fleet of cars including a Rolls Royce.[10] Two of the biggest contributors to Dhammagai's new stupa were two of the leading figures on the stock exchange – Anant Asvabhokin who had used the exchange to build the Land & House property empire, and Sia Song who was said to be the exchange's most famous stock manipulator.

Religion had been adapted to the new urban world of rising prosperity, growing individualism, and increasing insecurity.

Being Chinese

The vast majority of the commercial families of the city could count some Chinese blood. Very many were pure Chinese.

Through the first half of the twentieth century, the Chinese in Thailand had to suffer occasional outbursts of criticism and repression. The large flow of migrants meant the city always had a floating population of *jek*, new arrivals who could not speak the language or fit into the local scene. They easily became the butt of jokes and the target of resentment.

More important, the government constantly worried that the migrants would bring with them the turbulent politics of China. These fears were not unfounded. In the 1910s, Chinese nationalist groups raised money and support for Sun Yat Sen. In the 1930s and 1940s, they agitated against the Japanese. In the 1940s and 1950s, the Chinese Communist Party had a branch in Bangkok.[11]

The government stomped on these political movements. This antagonism occasionally spilled over into broader movements of racial antipathy – restrictions on Chinese employment, business, education. But these were usually minor and short-lived. The government welcomed the immigrants' enterprise and manpower as long as they left their politics behind (see chapter 2).

Yet in the 1950s, American scholars could still write as if Bangkok was divided between a bureaucracy of Thai ethnic origin and a commercial class of Chinese migrant origin. They suggested the bureaucrats lived off the merchants by deft use of cultural repression and mandarin squeeze.[12]

By the time of the boom, the situation had changed. A fifteen-year old who had arrived in the last wave of migration around 1950 would be entering retirement by the 1990s. By this date, most of the working population of Chinese origin had grown up speaking Thai. They had passed through the Thai schooling system. They had taken to Thai ways in enthusiasm for the new country that granted such prosperity. The *jek* were fading away.

The TV dramas show the new Chinese-origin family with its gradation of generations. The current generation speaks Bangkok Thai, dresses in the styles of Bangkok yuppiedom, and affects attitudes of the globalized age. The mother-in-law lives in a house full of severe wooden furniture of Chinese design. She speaks Thai with the trace of an accent and plays the role of the Chinese matriarch. Tucked away in some corner of the house is grandma. Her silence suggest something about her language skills. Her whole appearance looks as if it had not changed much since she got on the boat in Swatow.

While the Chinese have changed over the past generation so too have the officials. The bureaucracy still has a core of Thai aristocratic origin who affect traditional attitudes. But they are gradually being moved aside by the new technocrats, many of whom come from the same background of Chinese origin/Thai education as the businessmen.

Just as the Chinese are becoming absorbed, the pressures on them also are relaxing. With no new migration for over a generation, there are few *jek* left to excite crude racial attitudes. More important, China has suddenly ceased to be a political threat and has become a political ally.

From the 1970s onwards, it became gradually easier to be proud of a Chinese heritage. Kukrit Pramoj, prime minister in 1975-6, was one of the first to make a public point of claiming Chinese blood. Kukrit was a titled member of the royal family but could also claim a Chinese grandmother.[13]

By the mid-1980s, government lifted a ban on electoral candidates making appeals based on Chinese origins. Several city candidates now touted their original Chinese lineage, their *sae* name, and their place of origin. Gradually it became not just acceptable but chic to claim Chinese roots.

The boom accelerated these trends. More than ever before, the nation was growing rich, powerful, and internationally recognized from the commercial enterprise of its sons of China. On top of that, China itself had become a magnet for investment and was poised to become the economic engine for the whole region.

The TV drama series *Lord lai mangkorn* (pattern of the dragon) crystallized this growing sense of pride and confidence. A generation earlier, Botan's novel *Jotmai jak muang thai (Letters from Thailand)*[14] had gone over some of the same thematic ground about the experience of the Chinese migrants. But *Jotmai* had a downbeat feel. The hero's moderate commercial success in Thailand was balanced against a host of petty discriminations. By contrast *Lord lai mangkorn* was a celebration of immigrant tenacity, an upbeat story of spectacular success. The central character progressed from Chinatown street smart to the king of a great business dynasty.

Not only was the series wildly popular but its popularity stimulated the fashion for outing one's own "Chineseness". Several journalists and intellectuals used *Lord lai mangkorn* to reflect on their own Chinese origins.[15]

The series title song became an "unofficial anthem" for the Bangkok Chinese: "From the Chinese land overseas, On a small boat drifting afar, Penniless like a beggar. . . . Through the days and nights of struggling . . . Dragon begins to spread its wings, Pays back things it owes to this land".[15] In the later series *Mongkut dok som* (the orange flower crown), the older characters conversed in Chinese with Thai subtitles.

In the early 1980s, the government had frowned on the imported Hong Kong serials and had pushed them out of TV prime time. The popularity of the Thai dramas had made these regulations redundant. But in the early 1990s, after the success of *Lord lai mangkorn*, the Chinese series returned to great audience acclaim. In 1994 the television began screening *Sam kok* (*The Romance of The Three Kingdoms*).

This tale of Chinese origin has been popular in Thailand since the nineteenth century. Its popularity grew further with the expansion of the city from the 1960s onwards. The book was published several times. The story appeared also in abbreviated and cartoon versions. The theme of dynastic conflict also provided the basis for a whole range of "how to" books that used the characters of *Sam kok* as examples. These included both manuals of the art of war but, more specially, of the art of business.[17]

The TV series of *Sam kok* ran three nights a week for seven months. Newspapers ran intricate analyses of the plot. Political figures publicly identified themselves with leading characters. For the true fan, the complete series was available on a set of forty-two video cassettes.

But *Sam kok* was dwarfed by *Paobunjin* (Justice Pao) which started running around the same time. Several versions of this story had appeared in TV and cinema in the past. But its appearance in 1994 was quite different. Two different TV companies imported versions of the story and showed them in competition. The press followed the drama with constant criticism and comment. The audiences soared. One TV channel ran the Taiwan-made version five days a week for over a year. When the series ended, the station immediately began screening a Hong Kong version.[18]

By mid-decade, the trend had gathered momentum. At the 1995 and 1996 elections, city candidates and party leaders vied to show off their Chinese origins. Prime minister Banharn was nicknamed "Deng" in reference to his stature and his origin. Department stores celebrated Chinese New Year with ads stuffed with dragons, Chinese characters, swirling red silk, and painted cranes. A Bangkok MP invited to preside at a charity function dedicated to the "prolongation of Thai culture" got up on the stage and sang an old Chinese song.

In 1996, this trend spilled into the youth music culture. Pornphan Chunhachai performed under the name Jennifer Kim, dressed up in Suzy Wong style cheongsam, sang about *Rabum ngiew* (the Chinese opera dance), and talked about preserving Chinese culture. Much more powerful was Apisit O-pasaimlikit, a third-generation Thai-Chinese who had grown up speaking no Chinese and ignoring his parents' attempt to keep up the old customs. Under the name Joey Boy, he sang and danced in rap style. But he also wore pyjamas and pigtail to emphasize his Chinese looks, and led with a song, *Ka Ki Nang* (no stranger), which used some of the pugnacity of rap to assert pride in his Chineseness. He recorded in Toronto and joyfully mixed Thai, Chinese, and English words into one line. Here was being Chinese for the era of globalization.

Being Thai in the City

The "traditional Thai culture" to which everyone was introduced at school was a mix of the royal and rural, the arts of the court and the folklore of the villages, the lineaments of a peasant society ruled by a monarchy.

This definition of Thai culture was formalized in the publications of the National Identity Office in the late 1970s and early 1980s. The Office's book on *Thailand in the 1980s* defined Thai culture as a blend of "classical court culture, which includes Buddhist art" and "popular culture . . . concerned with age-old village realities associated with birth, death and the cultivation of crops".[19]

Members of the new urban society had more and more difficulty finding this version of Thai culture relevant to their lives and their lifestyles. The rural portion was exactly what they were fleeing from.

From the 1960s, the social activist, Sulak Sivaraksa, had railed that urbanization on an American model would undermine Thailand's cultural specialness.[20] Sulak himself conducted a personal rearguard campaign by affecting traditional courtly and rustic forms of dress. But few others saw this as a practical form of defence.

Similarly, the 1980s prime minister, General Prem, wore the royal-inspired *chut prarachathan* for many formal occasions. During his premiership, many other public figures adopted this alternative to Western styles. But for the rising business-men, the garment smacked too much of the bureaucratic culture they were in the process of overthrowing.

The replacement of Prem by Chatichai in 1988 occasioned a sartorial revolution as well as a political one. The *chut prarachathan* virtually disappeared from high-level political occasions. Business ruled and with it the business suit.

Some sections of business openly took up the task of defending "Thainess" in the modern world. Siam Cement was the most aristocratic of all Thai companies. It was among the oldest, had the Crown Property as a major shareholder, and saw itself as a pioneer of Thai business. Siam Cement established a tradition of running corporate public relations campaigns around the defence of Thai culture. It sponsored the restoration of historical buildings and other aspects of the Thai heritage.

Siam Cement also set out to define "what is Thai" for the modern urban world in terms not of dress and customs but of feelings and ideas. Its corporate campaigns highlighted what Siam Cement considered typical, defining characteristics of what it was to be Thai. Siam Cement focused on concepts like *vinai* (discipline) and filial piety.

As many newer companies became rich in the boom, several followed Siam Cement's example in presenting themselves as defenders of ideas and sentiments at the heart of Thai culture. But where Siam Cement had championed sentiments to do with authority and obedience, these newer companies highlighted sentiments like *nam jai* about mutual assistance and cooperation.

In 1994, government officials organized a Year for the Promotion of Thai Culture. They set out to support customs, ideas, sentiments presumed to be distinctively Thai. Grants were offered to each province to organize some promotion of Thai culture. A national campaign of advertising and public relations was launched.

Addressing the topic on this grand scale immediately raised the issue: what exactly is this "Thai culture" which we are going to spend money to defend? On this issue, the campaign seemed to fall apart. The central event of the national mass campaign was a television ad and poster campaign about the *wai*, the gesture of joined hands used for greeting, worship, respect, thanks. Was that it? In the end, was Thai culture a gesture?

On an academic plane, the origins and meaning of "Thai culture" had become a matter for elusive but important debate.

In the establishment history written into the schoolbooks, the Thai had come down from the north in the thirteenth century and established a series of kingdoms in the Chaophraya plain. From the start, the monarchy and a martial aristocracy had been the core of these kingdoms. Their traditions had formed the centrepiece of Thai culture down to the present day.

Since the early 1980s, new urban intellectuals had been trying to blow this mythology up. In two ways.

First, they challenged the history of Sukhothai. The root-stock of the Thais, they argued, consisted not of migrants from the north but people who lived in the area already, mostly on the Lao plateau. Thais were Laos mixed in with other peoples from around Southeast Asia. Sukhothai had been founded not by northern warriors but by Lao traders.

Second, they pointed out the importance of the Chinese in Thai history. Charnvit Kasetsiri suggested that the Ayutthaya kingdom had probably been founded by a Chinese trader. Nidhi Eoseewong wrote about early Bangkok, showing the importance of the Chinese and trade.[21]

Nidhi also turned the pejorative term *jek* into a positive. He used it to describe the Chinese-in-Thailand as against the Chinese-in-China. "A society which is powerful", he wrote in 1986, "allows variety in ways of life and values. The *jek* add to the cultural richness of Thai society."[22]

In 1987, the writer and editor Sujit Wongthes brought these two strands together. Thai culture is *jek bon lao*, a mixture of Lao and Chinese, just like Sujit himself.[23]

The Year for the Promotion of Thai Culture restated the old idea of a traditional Thainess. This provoked the urban intellectuals to stronger stuff. An anthropologist-historian wrote that Sukhothai was an offshoot of an earlier kingdom centred on the Lao capital of Vientiane. Charnvit pointed out that students were bored by the conventional Thai history but the *jek* history about the role of the Chinese sold like hot cakes in books and magazines.

Sujit said that the bureaucrats promoting Thai culture were just "turning this country's heritage into a mere commodity for consumption". Nidhi compared Thainess to "a product that doesn't sell". The political scientist, Kasian Tejapira, said he felt "raped" by a version of Thainess which simply left out the contribution of the Chinese.

Kasian also pointed out how difficult it was to be Thai in the age of globalization. The bureaucrats defined Thainess as something very classic and traditional. But urban people now lived an international urban lifestyle. They worked in an office, wore a tie, ate fast food, watched TV, bought international brands. How could they relate traditional Thainess to their everyday life? "Cultural schizophrenia" Kasian concluded, "is reaching epidemic proportions".[24]

Being Country

Villagers have been migrating to Bangkok for over half a century. But with the boom, more came and more stayed. By the mid-1990s, this group reached some sort of critical mass. Figures are hard to come by. But at the 1997 Songkran (Thai new year), an estimated 1.8 million migrants travelled back from city to village for the holiday. The village migrants began to change the culture of the city. With over half of all migrants coming from the northeast, this change had a strong *isan* tinge.

Northeastern food was the first element to follow the migrants to the capital. In the 1970s, an *isan* restaurant added a string of girls who could be hired for dancing. The format was quickly copied in many bars. In the mid-1980s, another restaurant in Bangkapi became famous for offering a new and exciting adaptation of northeastern music. Again the copies soon appeared.

In the 1980s, many suburban areas began to sprout new *cafes*. The English word adapted into Thai meant a bar with entertainment catering for a middle and lower class clientele. *Cafes* came in two main varieties – comedy or music. The first featured solo comedians and small comic troupes. The acts were improvised, loose, topical, sometimes rough and knockabout, always irreverent, usually risqué, often downright vulgar.

The music *cafes* featured strings of singers, mostly young and female but with a sprinkling of male crooners and occasionally older men and women famous for singing in traditional styles.

The decor was simple, the lights less dim than a night-club or lounge, and the atmosphere noisy and boisterous. To show their appreciation of the comic or singer, and also to show off their own success, patrons gave money directly to the performers. For the male comics, the gifts were usually folded notes. But female singers received flower garlands garnished with banknotes.

The migrants to the city brought along their local music. Once in the city, the lives of the migrants changed. New jobs. New wealth. New problems. The music changed too. New technology. New influences. New concerns to reflect.

Phleng luk thung (country music) developed this way in the 1960s when central-region migrants first came to Bangkok in large numbers. They brought their folk music, added the new electric keyboards, and dressed it up with Latino rhythms and stagecraft popular in the international films and TV shows of the era.

The songs were often specifically about the life experience of the migrant – missing the village life back home, struggling with the strangeness and unfriendliness of the city, grasping at new opportunities. With new technology of cassette tapes, radio, and roadshows touring the country's new highway network, *phleng luk thung* developed a national audience.

The flow of migrants from the central region was soon overtaken by a flood from the northeast. They brought their own style of *moh lam* music. Originally *moh lam* was a form of local poetry set with music and dance for religious ceremonies and festivals. Performers improvised a lot, adding in humour and political messages. Transported to the city, *moh lam* got caught up in the *luk thung* craze, producing a style which mixed *moh lam* lyrics with *luk thung* tunes.

Phleng peu chivit (music for life) developed in the 1970s by a similar route but among a different social group. For the first time, students from the provinces were sucked into Bangkok's colleges and universities in large numbers. Some student musicians from the northeast mixed their local riffs and rhythms with borrowings from country'n'western and rock music. The songs were shaped by the social conscience and political awakening of the decade. The resulting *phleng peu chivit* became the soundtrack for political protest.

Despite their vitality and popularity, none of these styles penetrated the urban mainstream. *Phleng luk thung* and *moh lam* were too rural, *phleng peu chivit* too political. In the 1980s, they were pushed aside by the surge of slick, modern, international, optimistic grammypop. By 1990, many of the big *luk thung* troupes had stopped touring. Most of the famous singers had retired. Both the big *peu chivit* bands, Caravan and Carabao, had stopped recording, squabbled among themselves, and disbanded.

But in the 1990s, this decline was suddenly and spectacularly reversed. The music found a new audience and moved towards the urban mainstream.

In 1989, the self-appointed archivist and enthusiast of *luk thung*, Jenphop, staged a sell-out concert in the Thailand Cultural Centre. In 1992, the tragic death of the queen of *luk thung*, Poompuang Duangjan, allowed many prominent people, including the prime minister Anand Panyarachun, to confess a secret love for this music. Over the next couple of years, this nostalgia was converted into full-blown revival.

Several new singers appeared. Some mixed up *phleng luk thung* with bits of rock, pop, techno, and rap. Some threw in humour. Others offered a self-consciously traditional and pure version of the sound and style. A handful of songs, particularly Yingyong's *Somsri 1992*, became national hits. FM radio stations started to feature *phleng luk thung* shows in the graveyard slots. Then television too. Then as the audiences grew, the shows gravitated towards peak time.

Several new music-publishing companies put out classic reissues and new albums. Cassette sales mounted. Performers began to make music videos for the new TV shows. The *cafe* nightspots increased in number and popularity. Finally Grammy took Got, a young urban pop star whose career just would not spark, and remodelled him as a new-age *luk thung* artist. With huge success.

In 1995, a TV channel remade a 25-year old movie musical as a series, *Monrak luk thung* (the wonder of country music). The series caught on, driven largely by the sound-track of the original songs. Two million tapes were sold. The urban actors who played the main roles were converted into country singers, earning more from appearing in touring provincial roadshows than from doing yet another TV family drama.

In 1996, a *luk thung* singer who shunned publicity because he looked too downright rural produced the biggest national hit since Thongchai's *Sabai*. Monsit Khamsoi's *Sang nang* (while I'm away) was played everywhere from country concerts to discos. All other singers had to learn it because it always came up in the request section. Businessmen crooned it at karaoke. The Bangkok Symphony Orchestra made a cover version. Monsit appeared at NASA, on TV talk shows, and in glossy magazines. *Luk thung* had arrived in the heart of urban culture.

The northeastern folk style of *moh lam* was not far behind. Young performers added bass guitar, synthesizer, and drumkit. The resulting *moh lam sing* had the stagecraft of *luk thung*, the improvised and often bawdy comedy of *moh lam*, and the energy of rock. Touring troupes of young performers attracted big audiences. An experienced performer set up a *moh lam sing* school, complete with distance learning by mail and cassette. Traditionalists were so troubled that conferences were held to lament the perversion of an old craft.

By the mid-1990s, the revival had spread to more esoteric styles. *Kantruem* was originally a Khmer-language folk style popular in the Thai-Cambodian border area. It was modernized by borrowing from everywhere – the rock energy of *moh lam sing*, the lyricism of *luk thung*, some of the social concerns of *phleng peu chivit*, and even songs from Grammy stars.

Phleng peu chivit revived in parallel. In the early 1990s, a few new singers took up the style. Weekend out-of-town festivals attracted small but devoted audiences. Then in 1995-6, the music suddenly became fashionable. Several of the old stars were winkled out of retirement and launched on tours looking a little battered and beer-bellied. The Carabao group got together again after a seven-year break and made albums which outsold Grammy's carefully crafted teen idols.

The *peu chivit* revival was transformed into a movement. Rustic bars were rechristened as "for life pubs". Several new ones were built with size to match booming demand. The biggest blended the size of a German beer-hall with decor emphasising simplicity and nature.

Phleng peu chivit now reached a much wider audience than it had in the 1970s. Still the students. Also many of the new upcountry migrants. Plus some who deserted the discos and the yuppie bars, moving out of a glossy world of neon and chrome into a deliberately understated environment.

Cafe-style comedy also enjoyed a surge of popularity and made the leap into television. Before the early 1990s, it was hard to find much laughter on the box. A few review style programmes had some short-term success. A handful of comics had support roles in game-shows and talk-shows. In the early 1990s some channels tentatively experimented with bringing the *cafe*-style format onto the small screen. The audience went for it. All the stations quickly competed to offer comic shows. The popular troupes were hired for corporate and society events. A few figures became household names.

Often the keepers of the urban culture had difficulty adjusting to these new rustic imports. In the TV series *Monrak luk thung*, the village setting was curiously sanitized, as if an urban audience would not accept the real thing. The village characters were played as comic bumpkins, confirming an urban view of rural backwardness. Rural audiences tuned in for the songs and the main love story. But found the rest hard to take.

Urban producers could not resist trying to "improve" the *luk thung* concerts which suddenly became fashionable. Songs of other styles were added to the repertoire. Television-style emcees swarmed all over the performance. In one glittering hi-so concert, the *luk thung* singers were stuffed into evening gowns and backed by a symphony orchestra – successfully draining away the music's vitality.

The gameshow, the glossy ad, the bourgeois family drama, and the clean-cut Grammy star still dominated the new urban-based public culture. But the resurgence of bawdy comedy and modernized folk music had given this culture another side – often more rugged, less pretentious, more direct, and simply enjoyable.

City Thais

The boom stopped Thailand thinking of itself as a rural nation. The city had seized the initiative – not just in the economy and politics but in the realm of culture and national identity.

The growing wealth of business and salariat overflowed into an ebullient new urban culture which valued modernity, prosperity, individualism, globalism. Youth pioneered the trend. Television quickly became the main medium on which the culture was formed, expressed, broadcast.

The urban middle class began to rework the practice of Buddhism to meet their new aspirations and to cope with their new insecurities. Popular culture began to change the meaning of a Chinese origin. Intellectuals and artists began to recast history to give better roots to the new urban society.

When the National Identity Office revised its Thailand volume for the 1990s, it no longer attempted to define Thai culture in largely rural terms. The description of village society that had taken up so much of the 1980s volume had disappeared completely. *Thailand in the 90s* focused on the growing urban economy and on Thailand's qualifications to be considered a *world-class* modern society.

But beyond these modernist, middle-class pretensions, something both stronger and simpler was beginning to take shape. The villagers were arriving by the bus-load, with songs and laughter.

8 THE ABANDONED VILLAGE

In the boom, the countryside was discarded.

In the 1930s, a Bangkok newspaper described the peasant farmer as the person "on whom we all live".[1] Up to the 1970s, this was still largely true. The urban economy floated on crop exports.

By 1990, agriculture was reduced to a minor role. Industry contributed twice as much to GDP. Industry was growing at 15 percent a year while agriculture stagnated. Among major exports, rice had slid from first to tenth. The economy was powered by exports of manufactures.

Industry now seemed to be the future and agriculture the past. The transition had been very sudden.

Urban business now looked on the countryside as a source of cheap labour for urban work, land for housing and factories, water for generating hydroelectricity, raw materials for industry. With business very much driving the boom, these attitudes mattered.

But agriculture retained a major role in the society. The majority still lived in the villages and worked on the land.

Many people in the countryside were not ready for a new role. They would rather fight to retain their way of life and to defend rural resources against urban predators.

For over a century, agriculture had been the mainstay of the economy and society. Though agriculture was now eclipsed, this "peasant century" left behind a powerful legacy, which served as a foundation for resistance to the city rampant.

The Legacy of the Land Frontier

The success of Thailand's agriculture had been based on one simple factor – large reserves of unused land. In the early nineteenth century, over 95 percent of the land area of modern Thailand was covered by swamp and forest. The small population of a million or so was limited to narrow strips along the coasts and the major rivers. The rest was the province of the elephant and the crocodile.

Clearing these tracts began in the 1820s and accelerated from the 1870s. Through to the 1950s, the swamps of the river valleys and deltas were drained and planted with rice to feed Asia's growing population. From the 1950s onwards, the forests were felled to plant maize, jute, sugar, cassava to meet strong world demand. Over 150 years, peasants cleared twenty million hectares.[2]

The expansion of this land frontier shaped the rural society and economy in many important ways.

The frontier drew in a large rural population. By 1990, there were some forty-three million people living in the villages.

Agricultural productivity was low. Thailand expanded its crop exports by clearing more and more land rather than by investing in better techniques. Most of the settlers had no access to sophisticated and expensive technology. Government saw no need to invest in upgrading productivity as long as the frontier expanded so successfully. Only from the 1950s onwards did it promote better seeds and other productivity improvements, and even then with limited enthusiasm. Thailand's yields per hectare were among the lowest in Asia.

Largely because of this low productivity, most peasants were poor. The first attempt to survey incomes in 1962-3 found just under half of all families in the countryside were living below the poverty line.[3]

Peasants were poor but proud. The frontier moulded a distinctive peasant culture, marked by a strong sense of freedom and independence. The settlers were a mixture of

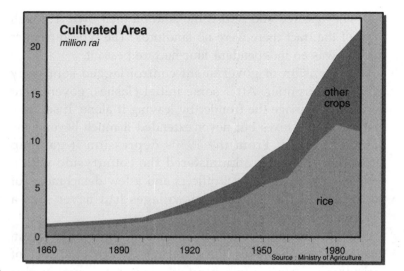

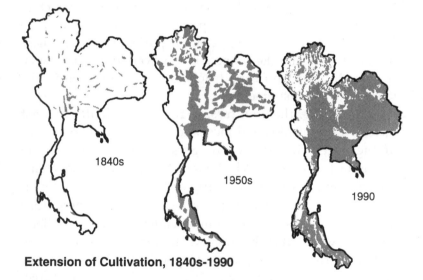

Extension of Cultivation, 1840s-1990

bondsmen escaped from old feudal ties, migrants fleeing poverty or oppression in adjacent regions, and a sprinkling of Chinese migrants from famine-ridden Swatow. For many the frontier was an opportunity to escape hardship and domination. They cleared and settled the land on their own. Through most of the tract there were no landlords. The typical frontier colonist was an independent four-hectare peasant.

The extension of government control lagged some way behind the frontier. After some initial clashes, government decided to manage the frontier by leaving it alone. It set up a system of land taxes but never extended it much beyond the Bangkok region. From the 1930s depression it gave up altogether. Bangkok administered the countryside with a skeletal network of district officers and a few detachments of police. Up to the 1960s, many villages had never seen a government official.

In the last twenty years of its expansion, the frontier was in turmoil. From the 1950s, the government drove the pace of agricultural expansion to generate the export revenues needed to finance urban growth. It promoted agribusinesses which in turn invested in agricultural expansion. It built roads into the countryside to bring the crops out. It pushed the government machinery out into the countryside to oversee the expansion. It posted district officers, teachers, and policemen in the villages for the first time.

In the 1970s, the countryside reacted violently against increased exploitation and increased control. In the provinces of the outer rim, many villagers were drawn into the communist insurgency which spread across from Indochina. The communists recruited support by fanning resentment against the intrusions of tricky merchants and predatory officials. They played on the independent-minded frontiers-men's conviction that the countryside was theirs because they had converted it from jungle to paddy field: "It was our ancestors, the peasants, who grew the first coconut tree, planted the first rice field and cultivated the first fruit farm," ran a communist tract, "but the oppressive system has trampled all over us and our ancestors."[4]

The army's clumsy attempts to suppress the insurgency often confirmed the peasants' conviction that officials were unsympathetic meddlers. The army resettled whole villages, terrorized suspects, used its firepower carelessly. By the mid-1970s, the insurgency had spread to half the nation's provinces. Government reckoned some six thousand villages housing four million people were affected.[5]

The insurgency did not penetrate some of the longest and most densely settled areas in the central region and the north. But these areas were in turmoil nonetheless. Peasants agitated against increased exploitation by merchants and landlords. They demanded lower rents, higher crop prices, measures to limit loss of land through debt. They formed a Peasants Federation, took petitions to government, and marched in demonstration through the centre of Bangkok.[6]

Eventually, the authorities suppressed these protests by violence. In the space of four months in 1975, eighteen leaders of the Peasants Federation were assassinated, probably by vigilante groups.[7] In the late 1970s and early 1980s, the army defeated the insurgency. First it felled and burned the forests around the communist bases. Then it launched massive armed attacks while simultaneously offering amnesty to defectors.[8]

With peace restored, the authorities set out to quieten the countryside for the longer term through kindness. They set up programmes to support crop prices; to improve local infrastructure; to spread local irrigation works in the poor northeast; to provide funding for local councils; to upgrade agricultural research and extension activities; to accelerate development in the poorest areas which had been so susceptible to the insurgency.

But this enthusiasm was very short-lived. As long as urban business depended ultimately on agricultural growth, and as long as the insurgency threatened to wreck the whole political structure, the city cheered the authorities' attempts to pacify the peasantry. But by 1983, the insurgency had been defeated. From 1986 onwards, the urban economy spurted ahead. More and more, the city could not care less about the countryside.

Many of the rural programmes just withered away. "Bangkok is Thailand and Thailand is Bangkok" was the cry. Government should allocate all the resources to the urban economy which had the highest potential for growth. Every low-productivity peasant converted into a more productive urban worker would boost the economy. It would also get rid of troublesome peasant protests. And make available the resources of the countryside for urban capital to develop. In the 1980s, government closed off the land frontier by banning logging, policing entry into the forest areas more strictly, and moving some settlers off marginal land.[9]

For decades, young villagers had migrated to work in the city. The closing of the land frontier and the spurt of industrialization sharply increased the flow. Over the boom decade, 6-7 million moved into non-agricultural jobs. In some villages, the generation of younger adults was virtually stripped out, leaving just the children and the old.[10] The loss of village labour was dramatic. In some areas, marginal land fell out of cultivation. Elsewhere, farmers replaced lost family members with machines. In a few years, rice harvesters spread widely in the central plain and parts of the northeast.

But most people did not quit the village completely, either physically or mentally. Planting rice was more difficult to mechanize than harvesting. Some farmers gave up trans-planting seedlings and sowed broadcast. More commonly, sons and daughters still went back home for at least this one annual task. At other times, as Phongsit Kamphi's 1997 song "Home" claimed, they carried the village with them in their heads. The song's music video showed young people paused in front of TVs in an urban shopping mall. As they listen to Phongsit's song and watch scenes of old women dancing in the village, their limbs are pulled into the poses of the local dance.

Over one generation, the countryside had changed from important to peripheral, from neglected to controlled, from expansive to stagnant, from coddled to threatened. But there were still over forty million people left in the villages. And they were still very much the product of the freewheeling history of the land frontier.

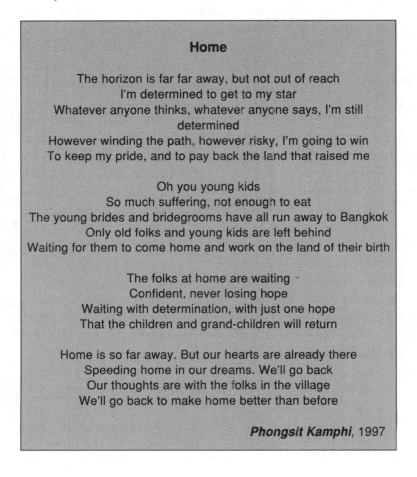

Home

The horizon is far far away, but not out of reach
I'm determined to get to my star
Whatever anyone thinks, whatever anyone says, I'm still determined
However winding the path, however risky, I'm going to win
To keep my pride, and to pay back the land that raised me

Oh you young kids
So much suffering, not enough to eat
The young brides and bridegrooms have all run away to Bangkok
Only old folks and young kids are left behind
Waiting for them to come home and work on the land of their birth

The folks at home are waiting
Confident, never losing hope
Waiting with determination, with just one hope
That the children and grand-children will return

Home is so far away. But our hearts are already there
Speeding home in our dreams. We'll go back
Our thoughts are with the folks in the village
We'll go back to make home better than before

Phongsit Kamphi, 1997

Whose Resources?

As the city grows richer and more powerful, it gobbles up resources which once belonged to the countryside. Industrial estates, housing projects, resorts, golf courses take over land which had been under crops. Dams to provide the city with hydroelectricity flood areas of forest, displace villages, and disrupt fish stocks. Factories pollute the air, the rivers, and the soil.

For villagers, these resources of land, water, and forests are the basis of their livelihood. They fight to defend them.

Most of these fights have been very localized. Villagers around Mae Moh in Lampang complained that a lignite-burning electricity generating plant spewed out so much air pollution that the locality became unlivable ("a mini-Chernobyl"). In Loei, villagers complained that quarries and rock-grinding plants overwhelmed the village with noise and dust. Along the Phong river in the northeast, villagers protested when the Phoenix pulp factory released waste which killed all the fish stocks. They protested again when the factory introduced a water-recycling plant which poisoned the area's water table. They protested yet again when the factory owners attributed this poisoning to rain water. In the lower northeast, villagers complained that rocksalt mining operations disturbed the water table and made the surrounding fields dry and saline. In Saraburi, villagers protested against a cement factory which planned to blast a limestone hill where the villagers grazed animals, collected firewood, and gathered foods and herbs.[11]

Some protests took on a broader meaning. They became public issues. They helped to dramatize the city-countryside battle over resources.

The first of these major public protests concerned the Nam Choan dam.[12] The electricity authority planned the project in the late 1970s. The dam would supply the growing urban demand for electricity and reduce the dependence on imported oil as an energy source. Since 1960, the authority had built several similar dam projects in different regions. Each had flooded large areas of forest and displaced large numbers of people. There had been local protests but they had been stifled. During the communist insurgency, the government authorities found it quite easy to cast protesting

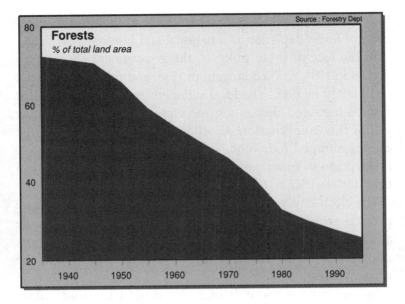

Source : Forestry Dept

villagers – and anyone who tried to help them – as evil communists.

In the case of Nam Choan, the time and the place were different from these earlier dam projects. The insurgency was collapsing and could no longer be summoned up as a credible threat. The dam project would flood a large area of the forest along the Thai-Burmese border. This "western forest" was the largest remaining forest in mainland Southeast Asia. Some parts of it had been designated as wildlife reserves. The opponents of the dam were not "communist troublemakers" but environmentalists.

The protest against Nam Choan began in the locality. Villagers did not want to be moved, did not want the local forests flooded. Local townspeople added their voice. They resented a project which benefited the capital at the expense of the locality. But what gave the protest its extra force was the environmental dimension.

Thailand's forested area had been reduced by half over the past generation. Nam Choan would destroy another chunk of a particularly large and important forest. Environmentalists took a stand on Nam Choan as a way to dramatize the whole issue of forest depletion as a national and international issue.

In the face of these protests, the government shelved the project in 1981, revived it again in 1984, and then abandoned it completely in 1988. The local villagers and environmentalist groups heralded this as a great victory. Over the next five years, this combination of villagers and environmentalist groups stopped four other dam projects which would have flooded forest areas and displaced villagers to feed the urban need for electricity.

The electricity authority changed its strategy. It focused on projects which would create less local disruption to people and trees, which would bring some local benefits in irrigation, and which would not intrude on emotive areas like the western forests.

In the early 1990s, it launched a project to build a dam across the Mun river close to the point where it flowed into the Mekong. The authorities claimed it was a "run-of-the-river" dam which would not flood forest, disrupt the river flow, or force many people to relocate.

Still there was a long and bitter battle. The environmental lobby argued a 17-metre-high cross-channel structure was not "run-of-the-river"; the whole northeast river system would be affected; and fish would never negotiate the dam's fish ladder because "Thai fish cannot jump". But the authorities rode out the protests and completed the dam in 1994.

With this victory, the electricity authority regained the upper hand. It now launched several new projects to build similar dams on the Mun-Chi river network in the northeast and on upper tributaries of the Chaophraya river in the north. It revived one of the projects halted by earlier protests – the Kaeng Sua Ten (dancing tiger rapids) dam on the Yom river in Phrae province.

Non-governmental organizations (NGOs) pointed out the plans for the Kaeng Sua Ten dam were unclear and the benefits questionable. The site was dangerously near a geological fault line. Several thousand villagers would be disrupted. Thailand's last remaining natural forest of golden teak would be drowned.

But officials and politicians seemed keen to build the dam *for almost any reason.* The dam had been first proposed in 1980 to generate electricity. It was promoted again after 1985 as an irrigation project. After bad flooding in 1995 and again in 1996, it was claimed as a flood control scheme.

Irrigation officials perhaps wanted to confirm the victory won at Paak Mun. Politicians wanted the kudos of bringing big projects to their constituencies, and perhaps also the side-benefits from logging and contracting. The golden teak alone was valued at two billion baht.

Government seemed desperate to launch the project. Banharn's agriculture minister claimed the golden teak simply did not exist (newspapers published photographs to disprove this). The science minister convened a meeting of flooded-out downstream villagers, told them the dam would prevent flooding, then announced the project had been supported by a "public hearing". Army TV aired a documentary presenting

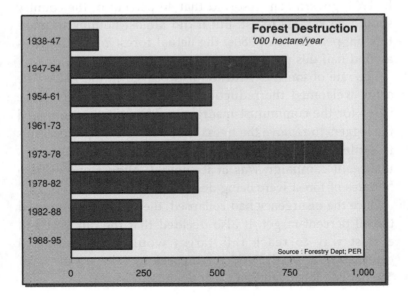

Forest Destruction
'000 hectare/year

Source : Forestry Dept; PER

the case for the dam, then cancelled the second part which aired the case against.

The World Bank stalled its funding because the environmental impact study was inadequate. The science minister commissioned the "experts" responsible for the rejected study to try again. A Chulalongkorn University team ruled that the environmental destruction outweighed the dam's benefits. The minister asked the team to change the data. The government's own environmental watchdog ruled that a geological report was "crude" and "inadequate". But the cabinet accepted the report.[13]

Kaeng Sua Ten grew from a small dam project to a big issue because it lay right across three major fault-lines in society, politics, and economy – locality against city, cost-benefit against sustainable development, top-down authoritarianism against participation.

Tree wars

In 1964, government resolved that 40 percent of the country should be kept as forest. But it did almost nothing to make this happen. By the 1980s, the actual forest remaining was around half this proportion.[14]

The rate of forest destruction had peaked in the 1970s. The army welcomed the reduction of forest zones which were bases for the communist insurgents. They often encouraged the loggers to remove the trees. They helped move in peasants to settle the cleared areas. In the mid-1970s when the anti-insurgent campaign was at its height, almost one million hectares of forest were being destroyed each year.

Once the insurgency had collapsed, the government revived the 40 percent target. It also decided that the quickest and easiest way to reach this target would be commercial reforestation. It allowed businesses to take up areas of "degraded" forest land on cheap long-term leases.

The idea of "reforestation" conjures up images of hardwood plantations or the natural regeneration of tropical forest. The reality was very different. Businesses seized the opportunity to take up cheap land for plantations of fast-growing trees for input to the pulp-and-paper industry. The favoured tree was the eucalyptus. Taiwanese, Japanese, and European firms entered the business along with many large local companies.

The idea of "reforestation" also suggests planting new trees on *empty* land. But most of the areas in question were occupied. Over the past generation, government had *encouraged* farmers to clear new land to expand crop exports. It had not put up any signposts to show what land was officially "forest". Government had refused to give land deeds to settlers on official forest land. But in other respects it had taxed and administered them like everyone else. Now it suddenly decreed that they were "squatters" and wanted to throw them off. These "squatters" numbered up to twelve million people, over a quarter of the whole rural population.[15]

The forestry department, which already had a reputation for some internal corruption, exercised very loose control over the reforestation project. Some areas granted out as concessions were still covered with original forest. Some were actively "degraded" to qualify for reallocation. Some were the homes of peasant settlers who had been working the land for many decades.

In the valleys of the north, the forestry department was specially aggressive in classifying land as "forest" to reach the 40 percent target. Many of the settlers inside these "forests" were hill peoples. Some had no Thai nationality or had acquired it only recently. Few had the confidence and contacts necessary to get land deeds. Some cultivated opium. It was easy for forestry officials to blame these settlers for destroying the forest through slash-and-burn.

In the early 1990s, this official aggression provoked a groundswell of resistance led by local headmen and activist

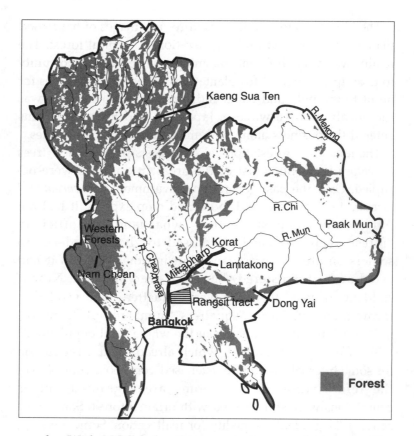

monks. With NGO help, these protests were drawn together into the Northern Farmers Network.

NGOs and academics argued that hill peoples were responsible for only a small fraction of deforestation. Much more was due to logging, colonization by lowland farmers, and tourism. Hill-dwellers like the Karen were better than the government at protecting the forests because they relied on them for livelihood. "We drink from streams, we must protect streams," ran a Karen saying, "we eat from the forest, we must protect the forest."[16]

To resist eviction, villages set out to prove they were better at forest conservation than the forestry department. They "ordained" fifty million trees, protested against loggers, demanded removal of sawmills. In imitation of the government, villages made maps and models showing their zoning of forest and land use, and put up signs defining forest and village boundaries.

In 1995, the Northern Farmers Network organized a march of twenty thousand farmers through Chiang Mai and Lamphun. They forced the minister of agriculture to negotiate. But the agreement came to nothing when the government fell a few weeks later.[17]

In the northeast, the struggle over the forests took a different form. Here the eucalyptus tree became the symbol of the battle between peasant and urban business. In some cases, villages petitioned to take up degraded areas to use as community forest but were rejected in favour of eucalyptus plantations. In others, villages were turfed off the land to make way for the plantations.

Villagers complained that the eucalyptus tree was an ecological menace. It siphoned water out of the soil with disastrous impact on the water table of neighbouring cultivation. It offered no shade, no grazing, no firewood, no edible herbs, roots and mushrooms – none of the amenities of a community forest. "They have taken away our super-market," complained one village leader whose neighbourhood forest had been planted with eucalyptus.[18]

Through the mid-1980s, protests against the eucalyptus increased in number, force, and violence. Villagers blocked tractor ploughing, tore up eucalyptus saplings, assaulted forestry officials, and burned down forestry department buildings. Environmental campaigners raised public protests against the government's enthusiasm for the eucalyptus tree. They blocked a government plan to increase promotional support for eucalyptus plantations. The press exposed the corruption involved in the granting of reforestation con-cessions. One firm which was closely associated with the agriculture minister had managed to acquire vast areas, some of which were still under forest cover.[19]

Protests came to a head in the late 1980s in the Dongyai forest in the lower northeast. The clash here summarized the conflicting forces involved. The villagers in Dongyai had been moved in by the army during the counter-insurgency campaign. They claimed the army had promised to grant them land rights. They were now called illegal squatters and instructed to move out to make way for reforestation. They stayed put and resisted the loggers who came in to cut down the remaining forest ready for eucalyptus planting.

A conservationist monk built his monastery in the disputed forest and "ordained" trees to protect them from the axe. The forestry department and army tried to move the villagers and the monk by force. The clashes aligned monk and settler against logger, eucalyptus planter, forestry official, and soldier.

The guns carried the day. The monk was harassed with bombs, threats, and lawsuits until he fled the forest, disrobed, and went into hiding. Twelve other leaders were arrested for firing tracts of eucalyptus. The villagers were marched out of the forest at gunpoint. The loggers and the planters moved in, guarded by groups of gunmen.[20] But Dongyai was one battle in what was rapidly becoming a much broader war.

In 1990, the army decided to take control of the issue of forest land. It prepared a plan, known by the Thai acronym *Khor Jor Kor*, to move six million settlers out of 1,250 different forest areas to make way for reforestation. In 1991, it began to implement the plan, again in the lower northeast.

The plan was flawed from the start. What moral authority did the army have for deciding the allocation of land between peasant and planter? Where was the land for resettling so many people? The army's first experimental moves created a howl of protest. Some settlers resisted the attempts to be moved. Some protested strongly after they were taken to hopelessly barren areas. Other villages complained when the army dumped settlers on them and expected them to share out their existing lands.

In mid-1992, scattered local protests against *Khor Jor Kor* gelled into a single movement. NGO workers helped to bring the protesting villagers together in a meeting which prepared a petition to the government and resolved to march to Bangkok.

The march dramatized the contest between peasant and city over rural resources. The marchers set out along the Mitrapharp, the US-funded highway which had first opened the northeast up for economic development in the 1960s. The government did not want this column to reach Bangkok. A junior minister rushed up to meet the marchers before they reached the escarpment which formed the symbolic boundary between the northeast and the Bangkok-dominated central plain. The government agreed to kill the *Khor Jor Kor* scheme and the march dispersed.[21]

Government now approached reforestation with more subtlety. It continued to give out plantation concessions but was more careful to avoid displacing settler communities. It limited its resettlement attempts to key watershed areas and major forests (such as the western forests) and it planned them better. It began a programme to give land deeds (*SPK 4-01*) to people who had been long settled on land officially designated as forest. In honour of the King, several companies undertook to sponsor a scheme to plant a million hectares with real forest trees.

These efforts were still sabotaged by the underlying conflict over resources. The attempt to distribute land deeds to settler communities was corrupted to enable urban businessmen to seize land. In Phuket, businessmen with strong links to the local and central administration secured deeds to land which was still forested and to seafront land ideal for tourist developments. The reforestation project was undermined by the obscure workings of the forestry department. Real estate dealers, golf courses, and resort developers continued to exploit the chaos of land administration to seize tracts which were either public property or settler homes.

The protests against the eucalyptus tree diminished. But the success of the Mitrapharp march had shown a new way to bring rural issues to the attention of a government which preferred to ignore them.

In 1992, farmers and NGO leaders formed the Federation of Small-scale Farmers of the Northeast. The prime mover was Bamrung Kayotha, a farmer who had received a political education in the city. From 1965 to 1976 he worked for the Siam Cement Company, took part in union activities, and was caught up in the protests of 1973-6. After returning to his native Kalasin and starting a pig farm, he began working with the NGOs.

The Federation publicized a string of local protests – over crop prices, over compensation for displacement by dam projects, over land rights for forest settlers, and over compensation for those involved in failed development schemes.

These schemes had been launched in the late 1980s, in the tail-end of the rush to placate the countryside with kindness. Most aimed to increase farmers' productivity by transferring land to higher-value crops. Largely because of the department's relative inexperience, several of these schemes were disasters. Red millet grew well but nobody bought it ("even my chickens did not want to eat it"). Plantations of cashew trees bore no fruit. Cows imported as expensive high-quality breeding stock turned out to be infertile ("plastic cows"). Farmers who had participated in these schemes were left carrying large debts to the government's agricultural bank.[22]

In 1994 the Federation brought together peasants aggrieved at dams, land rights, rice prices, urban pollution of the countryside, and the failed development schemes. The protesters rallied at the Lamtakong reservoir beside the Mitrapharp highway around 160 kilometres from Bangkok. They drew up a list of complaints. They started to march along the highway towards Bangkok. Again government sent up officials to negotiate a compromise.

A year later, ten thousand northeasterners again assembled at Lamtakong to protest. Government had not fulfilled its previous year's promises to resolve their problems. Conflicts over resources had increased. This time the protesters would not be fobbed off by a minor official. Bamrung negotiated directly with the minister of agriculture. The protest dispersed only after the minister had undertaken to set up a complex machinery to solve the protesters' complaints.

The Mitrapharp highway had first conveyed Bangkok merchants and administrators into the northeast in the 1960s. Now it served as a richly symbolic highway to convey back to Bangkok protests at what these merchants and administrators had done.

The Assembly of the Poor

Behind these marches, protest was becoming better organized. New leaders had emerged who could knot local groups into wider alliances. Issues were discussed in meetings at fairs, funerals, and festivals. The tracks of battered NGO pick-ups criss-crossing the provinces mapped out a new network of rural politics.

Nothing came of the minister's promises at Lamtakong. Three months later, one of the leaders was shot dead – an echo of the fate of rural leaders in the 1970s. The gun belonged to a police officer. No culprit was found.

In February 1996, the northeastern leaders met in Korat to plan a new march. Ministers rushed up by helicopter and asked them to delay until after the prestigious Asia-Europe summit in Bangkok. The leaders agreed but also decided on tougher tactics. Two months later, they dispensed with the march altogether and brought over ten thousand villagers into the heart of Bangkok. They were fed up with talking to officials who did nothing. They wanted to deal directly with ministers.

This move brought new groups into the protest alliance. Slum groups, worker groups, and environmental protesters joined in. The Assembly of the Poor was formed to act as an umbrella organization. The list of demands grew to forty-seven items. For three weeks, the leaders negotiated with ministers and senior officials, ending with an eighteen-page cabinet resolution. Then the summer rains began. Camping on the Bangkok pavement became a lot less comfortable. Work in the fields beckoned. The protest dispersed.

Again almost nothing happened. Out of twenty-eight local land disputes listed in the cabinet resolution, only two were resolved. Out of twelve issues over dams, one was settled. Others were buried in committees or smothered by bureaucratic resistance. Yet another leader was shot dead.

Three months after the protest dispersed, the leaders met the prime minister to register impatience. Another three months later in October, groups invaded the science and agriculture ministries to publicize their growing anger. Still nothing happened.

In December 1996, immediately after a new (Chavalit) government was formed, the leaders started drawing up a new list of demands. In January, they met in Buriram to map out strategy. On 25 January, they arrived and set up camp alongside Government House. Within days, ten to fifteen thousand had joined the protest.

The camp was well organized with its own commissary system, brigade of guards, sanitation department, fundraising committee, entertainment council, and internal system of political organization. The Bangkok municipality laid on water and sanitation. The police watched from a safe distance.

The protest started with a precise agenda of 121 demands. Most were the old issues – land, forest, dams, and failed development schemes. The northeastern protests were still the core. But now the northern group had also merged. A group of fishermen from the south had joined. And some slum and worker groups.

The leaders insisted on getting firm cabinet decisions, not just promises and sub-committees. This time they would not leave until they had real results. The next three months proceeded like the negotiation of a peace treaty. Twice a week, Assembly members met with ministers and bureaucrats. Decisions were referred to the weekly cabinet meetings for approval. Many of the simpler issues were decided quickly – stopping some eucalyptus projects, changing some forest demarcations, settling compensation for new dam projects, amending the Eighth Plan, changing rules on worker compensation.

Then the negotiations stuck. Solving disputes over land, forests, and dams would mean changing or overriding laws. Junior ministers did not have the authority. Bureaucrats were obstructive. Cabinet was distracted by the economic crisis.

In mid-March, twenty thousand marched through the centre of the city. A few weeks later, there was a scuffle at the gates of Government House. Academics and NGO organizations urged the prime minister to intervene personally to break the deadlock. On 11 April, he met the Assembly leaders. A week later, cabinet approved "in principle" the major remaining demands. Optimists hoped the villagers would now go home, celebrate Songkran (Thai new year), plant their fields.

But the Assembly members knew about agreements "in principle". Only a few went home. Most stayed on, through the rising heat and the early rainstorms. The leaders beat out the details of the remaining three big issues: payment of six billion baht in compensation to almost 7,000 families who had lost their land to dam schemes; cancellation of one dam project and review of five others; and an end to eviction from "forest" lands.

On 2 May, the camp dispersed after ninety-seven days on the Bangkok pavement. Some twenty thousand had taken part. Ten had died and two had committed suicide when their hope failed. "We will return," said one of the leaders, "if we don't receive what the Government has promised."[23]

The Assembly had galvanized other rural protests. In Chiang Mai, five thousand farmers demonstrated in support. The Federation of Small-scale Farmers of the Northeast, which had split away from the Assembly, rallied fifty thousand farmers in Khon Kaen to protest against debt, and collected a hundred thousand signatures on a petition. In Kanchanaburi, farmers demonstrated over land rights. In the east and northeast, thousands of farmers blocked roads to protest at low cassava prices. Rubber planters did the same in the south, and garlic growers in the north.

Just before the Assembly dispersed, the cabinet held a meeting in a remote and poor area of the northeast. The prime minister announced: "We must ensure people can live in forests and protect them. No more arrests, no more harassment . . . The people can now live where they are without worries."[24] Evictions would stop. Forest boundaries would be redrawn, zones reclassified, land deeds issued. A Community Forestry Bill, shelved a year earlier, was placed back on the parliamentary agenda.

Fears and splits emerged. Would another scheme to issue land deeds just be exploited by politicians and influential figures? Would local communities really manage the forest? Some environmental groups doubted it. "If the policy goes ahead", claimed one dark green, "Thailand's forests will be gone in five to ten years."[25] But the forestry department cannot defend the forests, countered the light greens. And how else to solve the human problem of millions of "squatters": "There is no unoccupied land, or if there is, it's not good for growing anything."[26]

Over a decade, rural protests had slowly worked their way from village and forest to the heart of the capital.

In 1992-5, the northeasterners had been the spearhead. In 1996, they linked up with slum and worker groups in the city. In 1997, northern and southern movements merged in.

In 1992-5, the protests had been kept in the provinces. In 1996, they jumped into the city. In 1997, thousands had camped in the heart of the city and captured the media spotlight.

Behind this rising wave lay a larger issue. Farmers still formed over half of the population. Yet not a single MP could be called their representative. Parliamentary politics were part of modern, urban Thailand. Rural issues went unheard. Some of the grievances raised by the Assembly had lain around for thirty years. "We don't believe" said an Assembly leader, "that political parties are the real representatives of the people."[27]

The parliament of the rural poor met on the pavements of Bangkok.

Defending the Peasant Community

The protests in defence of resources drew on powerful traditions in the peasant community. Over the century of the expanding land frontier, Thailand had developed a peasant society which was possibly unique. Most settlers had access to as much land as they could manage. They developed customs of cooperation to battle the harsh conditions of life on the frontier. They were not under the control of landlords, merchants, or government officials. The countryside developed a relatively egalitarian society of small-scale independent cultivators with little urban influence and strong traditions of independence and community.

In the 1980s, urban allies brought a new dimension to this rural resistance. NGOs and student organizations helped to bring the scattered protests together. The press provided a platform for publicizing the issues and conflicts.

Some of these urban allies were graduates from 1970s radicalism. Many NGO workers had been student activists in 1973-6. Others were motivated by a simple sense of equity and humanism. Many were affected by a historically ingrained belief that the peasantry was the true Thailand and that the peasants deserved sympathy and help.

Through the mid 1980s and early 1990s, peasant leaders, NGO workers, and intellectuals pieced together an ideology of peasant defence. They began from the belief that government's top-down strategy of development aided urban exploitation. They looked to build an alternative model from the bottom-up – founded on peasant needs and built upwards from local knowledge and local technology.

Such efforts would have to be based on the peasant community. The first task would be to strengthen this foundation – by reviving traditions of cooperation, rebuilding institutions for local autonomy, and reducing the local interference by government officials. In the late 1980s, NGOs and rural leaders helped to launch self-help schemes and campaigned for more autonomous local management of community forests and water resources.

By the late 1980s, these ideas were identified as the *wattanatham chumchon* or "community culture" movement.[28] By the early 1990s, some of its proponents had begun to explore some more radical implications of this way of thinking.

They saw the culture of the peasantry as totally different from the urban culture of government and business. It was also more truly "Thai". The original village settlements had existed before government was imposed. Much of the urban culture was imported and was shaped by the strong Chinese presence in urban Thailand. The peasant culture revolved around ideas of community, mutual welfare, and harmony with the natural environment. These ideas were strongly opposed to the urban conceptions of capitalism, individualism, exploitation of the environment, and government domination.[29]

Behind these propositions lay the idea that the peasantry ought to be preserved. It enshrined better social values than urban capitalism. It would have to struggle for survival on the basis of its own culture and resources. Urban society should help it or leave it alone.

Many officials, businessmen, and intellectuals held opposing views. They expected that the peasantry would be swept away by the rise of the city. Many wanted it to happen quickly. Every peasant converted into an urban worker would increase the national wealth and reduce the danger of rural protest. In 1994 the prime minister, Chuan Leekpai, said that ideally the peasantry should be reduced to just 5-10 percent of the total population.

Chuan was probably thinking of Japan, Korea, and Taiwan. In these countries, the rural population had been reduced to a very small proportion. Government had helped the few remaining behind in the villages with technology to raise their productivity and subsidies to keep them happy. In 1992, some Thai technocrats suggested that Thailand should embark on a similar route.[30]

But with over 60 percent of the population left in the villages, the process was likely to be long and wrenching. Most urbanites preferred not to think about the future of the countryside at all. The technocrats' suggestions were greeted with a resounding silence.

From Isan to Beijing

Yupin (not her real name) was born to a smallholder family in one of the poorest provinces of the northeast *(isan)*. She went to school long enough to read but not to write. When she was sixteen, her mother fell ill. To pay the medical bills, the family first sold their livestock and then sent Yupin, the eldest, off to work as a construction labourer in Bangkok.

In her first few weeks on the job, Yupin learnt some major lessons. First, power easily leads to abuse. The gang foreman liked to use his position to have his way with the new female recruits. Yupin escaped rape by climbing up onto the roof of their shed. Second, organization works. When the whole gang threatened to quit, the contractor raised their pay from 600 to 700 baht a month.

By the time Yupin went home six years later to get married, she had learnt a third lesson. Living in the village was much better than in the city.

For the next fifteen years, life went relatively smoothly. The marriage worked well. Four kids appeared. The small farm enabled them to get by. Then in 1990, Yupin saw on the TV news soldiers throwing villages off their land as part of the *Khor Jor Kor* resettlement programme.

Yupin organized her fellow villagers to travel to Korat to see what was happening. When the soldiers later came to Yupin's village, the villagers were ready to resist. But the soldiers came with guns, ploughed over the crops, and set fire to the field shelters. When Yupin led the resistance, some soldiers raped her twelve-year old niece in retaliation.

After the collapse of the *Khor Jor Kor* programme, the villagers cultivated the land again. But soon after, forestry officials turned up and announced they wanted to "reforest" the unoccupied land which the village used for grazing animals and collecting edible shoots, herbs, and fungi. The villagers were sceptical. But the officials said they would plant only local trees.

Some months later, the officials ploughed over fifty hectares and planted eucalyptus. The village felt cheated but could still survive using other areas for grazing. Then the forestry department announced it planned to multiply the eucalyptus area by six times. The villagers protested, petitioned, marched in demonstration, took their case to the local officials. To no avail. So one night they went into the eucalyptus plantation and cut it down.

Now the officials had to take notice. Yupin played a leading part in putting together a plan to manage the area as a community forest. She negotiated with officials from the local forestry unit right up to the provincial governor. The government finally agreed. Yupin went on to work with NGOs to set up a women's conservation group covering twenty-one villages.

Yupin had now become an important force in the locality. People asked her to help them with grievances against government. Yupin took their cases to the district officials and, if necessary, the governor.

In September 1995, Yupin was invited to the NGO International Women's Forum outside Beijing. She spoke on the role of women in the conservation of natural resources. She met the Korean and Chinese "comfort women" who had been forced into prostitution by the Japanese military during the war. She spoke with women's activists from all over the world. She was interviewed by Japanese TV. When she was introduced to a female minister from Finland, she immediately complained that Finnish aid and Finnish consultants were responsible for the forestry master plan behind the eucalyptus planting.

Yupin never had the chance to become fully literate. But politically she has become highly educated. She learnt that military power is easily abused to commit rape, to seize land, to force women into prostitution. She came to know through experience how ordinary people can resist exploitation through organized defiance. She learnt to value rural life and to fight in defence of the natural resources on which it depends.

A combination of peasant directness and unaffected eloquence has made Yupin into a natural leader. The back-currents of globalization have carried her political career from construction gang strike, through resource conflicts, to the international NGO movement and the media glare of the Beijing conference.

Village and City

By the mid 1990s, it was reckoned that on any one day Thailand had two rural protests.

From the 1940s onwards, Thailand's development strategy had leant on the village to build the city. For a generation, the village was asked to hand over most of the profits from crop exports. More recently it has been pressed for labour, real estate, and hydro-electricity.

The city has learnt to be very complacent and to expect the countryside to absorb this kind of treatment. For a century, the masses of vacant land acted as a social shock-absorber. Under pressure, most peasants would take off to the frontier rather than stand and fight. The few who did fight could be managed with the Gatling Gun and later the M-16. The closure of the frontier has jammed the shock-absorber. The rising murmur of local protest is the result.

The Thai countryside has become very diverse. At one end of the spectrum are long-settled, commercialized villages producing multiple crops of rice. At the other are new settlements scratching a precarious, semi-subsistence living in the forest fringe. Both variants have reason for complaint.

The commercialized villages are vulnerable to the market. Often they are submerged by debt. Typically they protest when crop failures or price-falls undermine their delicate accounting.

The frontier villages suffer from insecurity over land rights. Often they are vulnerable to ecological decline. Sometimes they are disrupted by government schemes of dam-building and land settlement.

Movements of rural reaction are common in countries undergoing rapid industrialization. But in Thailand several factors ensure that this movement has acquired special force. The rural economy was buoyant for so long and was brought to such a sudden stop. The frontier expansion bred an independence of mind which easily changes to truculence. The peasantry has long played a central role in the nation's image of itself. Most of all, the peasantry is simply so large it cannot easily be ignored.

The villagers did not rush off to the city at the first opportunity (see chapter 6). Most still have some land. Few have enough education to succeed. Until the late 1980s, only a marginal surplus of people went off to the city. Even then, most of them went only temporarily. In the 1990s, the flow to the city increased. Urban wages were rising, while in the villages the problems of debt, income, and insecurity were getting worse.

But even this movement turned out to be temporary. The bust of 1997 emptied the building sites, reduced the demand for taxis, cut back the returns to prostitution, and brought lay-offs in the factories. Not all could go home. Many had become more committed to the city. It was not clear that the weakened village economy could stand the strain of so many returning.

Rural protests had at first been fragmentary. But since 1990 they had gelled into a movement with growing organization, focus, and vision. Rural issues were still effectively excluded from the world of modern politics. But other routes had been developed to express rural issues.

The defence of the abandoned village is both economic and political. At the start of each year when the rains stop and the harvest is gathered in, some farmers go to earn some extra cash in the city and some go to camp on the pavements of Bangkok.[31]

9 OPENING UP POLITICS

During the boom decade, Thailand's long-standing military rulers were pushed aside by new political forces emerging from dynamic urban society.

In 1985, the prime minister was General Prem Tinsulanonda. He had risen to the post by "promotion" from the headship of the army. For all but eight of the past forty-seven years, Thailand had been ruled by prime ministers who came up this way. The three other key ministries (interior, finance, foreign) were held by soldiers and officials. The two major political events of the year were attempts by other military figures to unseat General Prem – one by coup, the other by intrigue. Politics was very much a military affair.

At the start of 1995, the prime minister was Chuan Leekpai, the son of a Chinese language teacher and a market vendor from a southern provincial town. In July 1995, he was replaced by Banharn Silpa-archa, son of a Chinese immigrant who traded in the provincial town of Suphanburi. Neither had ever been in the civilian bureaucracy or the army.

Their key ministers were businessmen and an ex-soldier who had been flung out of the army. The major political issues of the year were all about the development of Thailand's democracy – constitutional reform, administrative decentralization, and land reform.

The contrast in the personnel and issues over the span of a decade is striking. The transition was eventful: one failed coup, one successful, six prime ministers, eleven major changes of the cabinet, three political crises over the

constitution, six general elections, and mass demon-
strations of over half-a-million people leading to a bloody
confrontation with the army.

Thai politics can seem chaotic, arcane, esoteric, and beyond comprehension. The drama has such an unlikely cast of characters: one of Asia's few surviving monarchs; starring roles for generals, retired generals, and provincial boss politicians rumoured to be involved in smuggling, drug-running, gambling, and arms trading; walk-on parts for small-time lawyers, lay ascetics, and retired policemen; and a chorus of strutting gangsters, professional opinion-makers, vociferous monks, new media moguls, and cashiered colonels. The big scenes are full of coups, demonstrations, crumbling coalitions. The plot is hard to follow because the characters change sides so regularly. The whole script is overloaded with rumour, scandal, anonymous pamphlets, corruption charges, and backstairs intrigue.

The day-to-day sequence of political events can seem arcane and confusing. The underlying forces make more sense.

The boom decade saw a major political change: the collapse of the military influence which had dominated Thai politics for over half a century. The generals were moved aside by three new forces from urban society – Bangkok big business, provincial business, and an urban middle class.

The Bureaucratic Polity

When American academics arrived in the 1960s along with the GIs and the aid officials, they described Thailand as a "bureaucratic polity".[1] In many ways this was just a fudge for "military dictatorship". But the term did convey how much politics was the preserve of bureaucrats, both civil and military. To understand how this came about, we have to look briefly at the transition from the traditional kingdom.

Until the turn of this century, the kingdom had a simple three-tiered structure: the King; a mandarinate-aristocracy; the peasantry. At the end of the nineteenth century, the King converted this mandarinate into a centralized bureaucracy modelled on colonial systems.[2]

This new bureaucracy was much more than an administrative frame. It had a core of royal and aristocratic figures who ensured it retained the prestige of the old ruling class. It still functioned like a mandarinate with the degree of the new Chulalongkorn University controlling entry just like the examination systems of the Chinese bureaucracy. It now had the authority copied from colonial systems of policing and governance.

This combination of aristocratic hauteur, mandarin elitism, and bureaucratic rigour made it a peculiarly powerful and self-regarding ruling class.

In the early twentieth century, the growth of the city brought new men and new ideas. In neighbouring colonial territories, such new men turned against the European rulers. In Siam, they revolted against the absolute monarchy. In 1932, dissident soldiers and bureaucrats demanded a constitution, parliament, and cabinet government.

Urban businessmen, intellectuals, and labour backed this change. But at this stage these new urban forces were relatively weak. Unlike in many other Asian countries, they did not have the added fire of anti-colonial nationalism. In the fifteen years after the 1932 revolt, the bureaucracy regained the upper hand – with the army as its spearhead.

The army head took over the prime ministership for the first time in 1938. When the parliament refused to bend to military dominance, it was crushed out of existence. At the end of the Second World War, some veterans of the 1932 revolt staged a comeback. But within a couple of years, they were again blasted aside by a coup that began a generation of military rule.

In the post-war era, urban society grew rapidly and with it urban opposition to military dictatorship. But Cold War politics sustained military-bureaucratic domination.

From the early 1950s, the Thai generals and the US government negotiated an alliance. The US could use Thailand as a base for defending Southeast Asia against communism. The price was US political and material support for the military regime.

Over two decades, the US poured US$2 billion into Thailand, mostly in military aid and spending. The generals got more troops, sophisticated hardware, fat bank balances, and American political backing.

The US also helped to strengthen the bureaucracy as a whole by providing cash and technology. The total size of the bureaucracy grew from 75,000 in 1944 to 250,000 in 1965. As the communist insurgency spread across from Indochina into Thailand, the US gave both money and advice to enable the police, the army, and the Interior Ministry to gain a firmer grip over the country.[3]

With all this help, the army institutionalized its control over the country. In 1957-8, General Sarit seized power by coup and installed his subordinates from the First Army below him in the political structure. Senior military officers took over key posts in ministries and in state enterprises. They fanned out into corporate boardrooms and all kinds of private organizations. When Sarit died, his subordinates moved up in orderly succession, army-style. To be military was to be powerful. To be powerful was to be military.

The generals fortified their rule with ideologies of military dominance. The generals had the right to rule because only the army could defend Thailand from communism: "the country is your house, the army is its fence". Generals and bureaucrats had special "merit" as political leaders because they were disinterested. Civilian politicians, by contrast, represented personal and sectional interests. They were by nature selfish and corrupt. They were unfit to rule.[4]

Of course this contrast between good soldiers and bad businessmen had nothing to do with reality. When Sarit died, his fortune was 2.8 billion baht, equivalent to eighty billion in 1990s' money. Most of this had been accumulated during his six years as premier. Some 600 million was ruled to have been acquired corruptly. Sarit's two successors were later accused of looting around a billion baht.[5]

But such details had minor importance. The army and bureaucracy kept a tight grip on radio and television and used these media to drum in their message of dominance for over thirty years.[6]

Thailand's military dictators were the defenders of bureaucratic absolutism – a form of rule by a mandarin-aristocracy, created under absolute kingship, embellished by colonial systems, and strengthened with modern American technology. It would prove hard to dislodge.

"Ethnically homogenous"

Some attribute Thailand's underlying stability to "ethnic homogeneity". But a couple of generations back, most of the population would probably not have answered "Thai" when asked to give their "race" or "people". Most would not have grown up speaking Thai as a first language.[7]

Many urban people would have replied "Chinese". Most in the northeast would have said "Lao". Many others would have replied Malay, Khmer, Mon, Shan, or more local identities like Lao Phuan, So, Song Dam, Thai Yai, Phu Tai.

Thainess is quite a new idea. Around the turn of this century, the court borrowed from the Europeans the idea of a nation. It also took up the myth that a nation is somehow fuzzily based on a race. The kings applied this concept to the country that had only just been defined by geographic boundaries and that contained a lively mix of peoples.[8]

The rulers used four main strategies. First, they decided that many of the peoples (Lao, Shan, Khmer etc) which they had

---

recently described as conquered and inferior races, were actually variants of a larger "Thai" or "Tai" racial family.

Second, for those who could not possibly be included in this fiction (like the Chinese) they provided a route to become "Thai". The 1911 Act gave Thai nationality to anyone born within the borders.

Third, they fortified the race myth at the heart of Thainess with a race history. The Thai originated in south China. They migrated south and conquered the Chaophraya plain. They established a succession of kingdoms at Sukhothai, Ayutthaya, and Bangkok.

Fourth, they set up a project to put all children through compulsory education in the Thai language and in the rudiments of Thai culture.

This last and crucially important part of the scheme was planned at the turn of the century but not properly implemented until the 1960s. Then the US provided the subsidies and the Indochinese threat concentrated the mind. Only then did the mass of the children grow up learning about the Thai alphabet, the Thai king, the Thai flag, and the Thai nation.[9]

The project met some resistance, particularly from some parts of the Lao northeast and from the small pocket of Malay Muslims in the far south.[10] During the dictatorship period, the military tried to beat these areas into submission. With little success. After the decline of authoritarianism, officials took a more relaxed attitude, and local leaders found their place in the representative politics of locality and nation. Resistance diminished.

One fact indicates how successfully "Thai" has become a cultural rather than an ethnic definition. Some of the strongest supporters of the nation myth have come from the ranks of the immigrant Chinese. From the 1930s to the 1950s, Luang Wichit Wathakan wrote a stream of histories, songs, dramas, tracts, and speeches elaborating the race myth of the Thai people. In the late 1930s, he incited the "Thai" against the Chinese. He was the son of Chinese immigrants.[11] So too was Anuman Rajadhon, the foremost chronicler of Thai folk culture.[12] So too is Sulak Sivaraksa who has defended traditional Thai culture against the onslaught of modernism.

It is true that Thailand has no Chinese problem like Malaysia or Indonesia, no Mindanao-style succession movement, no

> equivalent of Burma's mass of liberation armies in the hills. But this is not some magical result of a "homogenous" ethnic heritage.
>
> The Thai rulers have been quite successful in persuading most of the people thrown together inside a fairly arbitrary boundary to imagine that they share something more than the same government. But the roots of Thailand's long-run political stability lie elsewhere – in its relative success at resolving the political conflicts generated by rapid social change.

City Business

The first challenge to the general's power began in the 1970s. It came from the ranks of Bangkok businessmen who had until recently been the generals' dutiful allies.

Many businessmen had supported the liberal surges of 1932 and 1945-7. But through the 1950s, they fell into step with the dominant military. On American advice, Sarit created a benign environment for private enterprise. Leading companies received profitable political favours from the generals in return for letting the generals share in their profits and rule without challenge.

But in the 1970s, businessmen and generals drifted apart. Bangkok's business leaders grew rapidly richer and more confident. They became less sure that they needed to share their profits with the generals. An explosion of social protests made them ponder whether military repression was the best technique for managing Thailand's increasingly complex society. The failure of the Americans in Indochina made them consider ways to deal with their neighbours other than as Cold War enemies.

In 1973 the military regime was brought down by student protests. Bangkok business welcomed the fall and participated eagerly in the replacement of military dictatorship by parliamentary rule. Businessmen joined a constitutional convention. They supplied over a third of the successful candidates at the 1975 elections. They occupied over half of the seats in the cabinet. They helped form three major parties – the Democrats, Social Action, and Chat Thai (Thai Nation).[13]

The Democrat Party was founded in 1946 as a pro-royalist grouping. It declined in the 1950s but then reformed when military rule faltered in the 1970s. Its new incarnation retained some of its royalist heritage. But the party now included a much larger group of businessmen and professionals from the city and from the old, established port towns of the south. One of these was the lawyer, Chuan Leekpai, from the province of Trang.[14]

The core of Chat Thai was an old military faction that had been prominent in the 1950s but had been drummed out by the rise of Sarit. They now had extensive business interests particularly in textiles. The party also attracted other big business interests especially from the buoyant agribusiness sector.

Social Action was led by Kukrit Pramoj, a minor royal family member and leading journalist who projected himself as an enlightened traditionalist. He was supported by businessmen like Boonchu Rojanastien of the Bangkok Bank and Pong Sarasin who combined a bureaucratic family heritage with a modern business interest including the Coca Cola franchise.

All three of these parties were a mixture of the traditional authority of royalists, bureaucrats, and generals along with the new wealth and assertiveness of business.

After Kukrit became prime minister in 1975, his policies reflected the wish to move away from Cold War strategies of the military era. To pacify urban labour, he introduced a minimum wage and labour law. To quieten the countryside, he brought in a rent-control act, rice price support, and rural development fund. To break out of the Cold War stricture, he travelled to China and held talks with Chairman Mao.

But the traditions of the bureaucratic polity and military rule were not so easily overridden. This first civilian parliamentary government in a generation faced huge difficulties. Some bureaucrats resented being ruled by civilian politicians. Some were too imbued with the policies and methods of military dictatorship to accept the changes of policy direction. Many of Kukrit's reforms were savaged in implementation.[15]

Within a couple of years, the military regrouped. Ironically the defeat of the Americans in Indochina gave a new lease of life to military rule. It enabled the Thai army to present itself as the sole bulwark against communism both inside and outside the country.

As the Indochinese capitals fell to the communists in mid-1975, the army organized political support for a return to military rule. It formed para-military and propaganda organizations that set out to persuade businessmen that only the military could save Thailand. It orchestrated a campaign to portray any opponent to military rule as a communist, including Kukrit and two future prime ministers (Anand and Chuan).[16]

Through 1976, the para-military forces used threats, bombs, and assassinations to disperse the student, worker, and peasant protests. The campaign culminated in October with a massacre of student demonstrators.

The generals again took control by coup. To root out the threat of communism, they claimed the right to control not just the cabinet but every type of social and political organization. In the villages, the army established vigilante groups and propaganda organizations. In the city, it set up a powerful intelligence organization.[17]

General Prem, who had been the most successful counter-insurgency general, rose to the top of the army and then to the prime ministership. He stayed there for eight years, sustained by the backing of palace, military, and bureaucracy.

But the army recognized that 1973-6 represented a break from total military dictatorship. In 1979, the military rulers restored parliament, though under a constitution that ensured considerable military control.

For the next eight years, the polity had a dual structure. Prem held the premiership and his official allies filled the key Ministries of Defence, Interior, Finance, and Foreign Affairs. The three business-dominated parties won the majority of seats at the elections in 1979, 1983, and 1986, and shared out the remaining ministries. Chat Thai established a hold on the Industry Ministry, Social Action on Commerce, and the Democrats on Agriculture.

The "bureaucratic polity" still controlled the political core. But the businessmen politicians now had some influence over policy and some access to the privileges and favours they had once secured by befriending generals. This share-out was dubbed semi-democracy or sometimes "premocracy".[18]

By 1985, the rise of Bangkok business, the first shock to military dictatorship, had been resolved with this compromise. The second shock was about to happen.

Provincial Business

Both business profits and political power had been heavily concentrated in the capital. In 1960, Bangkok was thirty-five times the size of the next largest town. But from the 1960s, the boom in agribusiness sparked growth in the provinces. Towns expanded. A new generation of rich provincial magnates appeared.[19]

Much of the new money was made dealing in the boom crops. Some was made by investing in real estate, retailing, and services that expanded on growing local demand. But *big and quick money* was made in two other ways.

First, by tapping into the large sums spent by government on the development of local infrastructure and services. Banharn Silpa-archa, for instance, started off supplying chlorine to the Public Works Department. During the Vietnam War–era expansion of provincial infrastructure, he became one of the department's biggest construction contractors, building roads and water mains. The proceeds were generous. Between 1968 and 1974 alone, he reaped some 200 million baht at a 40 percent margin. He invested part of these funds in his native Suphanburi – a rice mill, finance company, service stations, school, land, and distributorships for cars, trucks, and motorcycles. By the early 1970s he had become the province's richest and most prominent figure.[20]

Second, quick money was made from investing in illegal businesses with large profit margins: running opium from the Golden Triangle to the international drugs trade; planting marijuana along the Mekong to supply the US troops and exports; smuggling oil, consumer goods, dollars through the many seaports of the long coastline; running logs, gems, guns across the long and remote borders with Burma and Indochina; operating underground casinos and lotteries to meet the age-old Asian love of gambling.[21]

Many successful provincial businessmen operated completely within the law. But some of the richest and most prominent rose on the fast money available in illegal operations. Somchai Rerkvararat (Sia Yae) of Ang Thong made his first fortune running a gambling den. He invested the proceeds in construction and timber businesses and went on to become a powerful figure in local and national politics.[22] Charoen Pattanadamrongjit (Sia Leng) started from crop trading around the northeast, added an illegal lottery business to his itinerant dealings, and graduated from there to Bangkok casinos and party politics.[23] Somchai Kunpluem (Kamnan Po) made his first fortune smuggling dollars into Cambodia on fishing boats before spreading out into property and tourism and becoming the business and political boss of the Chonburi region.[24]

With these illegal businesses went a gangland lifestyle of gunmen, spectacular assassinations, and wars of revenge. The provincial bosses were dubbed the *jao phor*. The term meant a local spirit with powers that transcended natural and human laws. It had been used to translate the title of the film *The Godfather*.

By the mid-1970s, these provincial magnates had begun to attract the attention of Bangkok. The generals building their anti-communist networks sought their support. The civilian politicians looking around for a provincial seat tapped their local influence to organize elections. For the local magnates, these celestial connections added to their local status.[25]

At first, many local magnates were happy to organize the electoral bases for Bangkok leaders. Kamnan Po of Chonburi, for instance, orchestrated the election of Boonchu of the Social Action Party. But in each successive election, more of the local magnates decided to stand themselves or support their local friends.[26] Kamnan Po dropped Boonchu and lent support first to cousins and business colleagues and later to his own two sons.

The provincial magnates controlled elections on a patronage system. They lavished their own wealth on schools, clinics, bus shelters, and other local amenities. They promised the electorate that as MPs they would bring more government funds into the locality. They dished out banknotes on polling day. For both short and long term gain, the villagers voted them in.[27]

The provincial MPs attached themselves to the Bangkok parties. Then in the mid-1980s, through a combination of cash and numbers, they took them over. They dominated the party councils. They contributed the finance for electioneering. They controlled key posts in the party organization. And finally they demanded the party leader posts. Montri Pongpanich of Ayutthaya took over Social Action. Banharn Silpa-archa of Suphanburi climbed more slowly to the top of Chat Thai.

For many old Bangkok politicians, these new arrivals were hard to take. Some of the old guard of Bangkok businessmen quit politics completely. Some like Boonchu were shunted off into a netherworld of minor parties. Chat Thai made the best job of compromising with the new arrivals. When Prem decided to retire after the 1988 elections, Chat Thai's large contingent of provincial MPs made it the single largest party.

Chatichai Choonhavan, the Chat Thai leader who became prime minister after the 1988 elections, straddled the old world and the new, the city and the provinces. He belonged to a prominent military family and still in retirement carried the title of general. He had extensive interests in Bangkok business, especially in textiles, hotels, and finance. He had built an electoral base in the major northeast provincial town of Korat by making close friends with the local magnates. They cheered his appointment to the premiership. He put five of them in the cabinet and another in the senate.[28]

The transition from Prem to Chatichai signalled a major crack in the bureaucratic polity. In all thirty-three of the forty-five in the Chatichai cabinet were businessmen, with a heavy weighting from the provinces. The Interior Ministry was held by Chatichai's brother-in-law, like him a soldier turned businessman. Finance went to a leading provincial magnate who had bankrolled the party at the elections.

The new ministers were quickly engaged in skirmishes with the senior ranks of the bureaucracy. In many ministries, they pushed aside the more obstructive officials. In some, they shifted authority between the minister and the permanent staff.

The new government began undermining some pillars of military dominance. In the past, the military budget had been inviolable. Now ministers and MPs argued that the military was over-inflated and that the money could be better spent on development. The press and the rumour-mill took the argument further: the generous budget for arms-spending generated large commissions that paid for the generals' lavish life-styles and financed their continued political strength. During the budget process, parliament for the first time made cuts in the military allocation.[29]

The army tried to isolate the arms budget from such open political debate. It drew up a plan for arms purchases up to the year 2000 and asked the cabinet to give a long-term commitment on funding. The cabinet refused.

The clash between the interests of military and of provincial business extended to foreign policy. Chatichai announced a new direction in foreign policy towards Indochina. His government would "turn battlefields into marketplaces" – would make friends with the Indochina states so that Thai business could profit from their opening markets.

The policy was especially attractive to the businessmen of the provincial northeast who were a large factor in Chatichai's coalition. The army did not like it at all. The army still justified its need for arms and for a domestic political role on grounds of combating the "threat" of aggression from the east. Chatichai's new direction would remove this justification.

Again as in 1975-6, the generals fought back. They seized on the issue of corruption to restate their old adage that businessmen were unfit to rule.

In the bubble economy of 1988-90 with exports soaring, land prices multiplying, the stock market taking off, there were many opportunities for quick fortunes. Many businessmen were ready to pay to get the necessary licences, contracts, concessions – especially for big public projects in transport, communications, power generation, and port facilities. Ministers kept close control over these allocations. The rumour-mill told tales of huge sums of money changing hands. After the fall of Chatichai, investigators found many gift cheques presented to ministers in return for the small favours that opened up big opportunities in the boom.[30]

Corruption of this sort was not new. But the boom economy made the sums larger. And the shift of power from bureaucracy to business changed the beneficiaries. For many Bangkokians, both businessman and bureaucrat, the provincial politicians seemed greedy upstarts. They had been pulled into politics as an extension of their business interests. They were now promoting those interests from their seats in the cabinet with the business ethics of the provincial frontier. They were grabbing the corruption revenue which once had disappeared into more established pockets.

The press dubbed it the "buffet cabinet", a deft play on the term "eating the province" used to describe old-style political corruption.

In February 1991, the army staged a coup and threw out Chatichai's government. To drum up support among business, bureaucrat, and middle class in Bangkok, the generals cited the rising tide of corruption as a main justification.

But again there was a gap between rhetoric and reality. Members of the coup junta had already become rich, partly from lucrative government construction contracts.[31] One later bought a restaurant in France. Just two weeks before the coup, the cabinet had again rejected the army's huge long-term arms package. It was the shift of power and corruption revenue that was at stake rather than the issue of corruption itself. The coup was a last-ditch attempt to defend army and bureaucracy against the growing power of parliament.

The coup-makers knew they had to compromise with the powerful new forces of Bangkok and provincial business. They set up a prominent Bangkok mandarin-turned-businessman, Anand Panyarachun, as prime minister. They allowed him the freedom to introduce many economic reforms on the agenda of Bangkok business.

With the provincial magnates, they used a mixture of cajolery and intimidation. They set up a commission to hear charges of corruption against members of the Chatichai government. They quickly dropped the charges against those who promised support for the junta. In the provinces they launched a campaign against "dark influences", targeted at the *jao phor* who had played a large role at elections. They then set up a new political party (Samakkitham) and invited the provincial magnates to join. Many provincial politicians, including ministers and MPs of Chatichai's coalition, flocked to this haven.

With the Bangkok and provincial business lobbies apparently under control, the junta set about writing a new constitution that would restore firm military control over cabinet and parliament. They planned to restore the framework of the early 1980s, which had allowed the military to dominate politics by remote control. They were surprised when this strategy ran into fierce opposition from a new quarter: the urban middle class.

The Wild East

In the 1960s, the rural market town and fishing port of Chonburi began its own boom. Many types of business contributed to Chonburi's surge. First, the forests in the town's hinterland were slashed down to plant sugar and cassava for export. Logging and land speculation created big profits. Next, the neighbouring area of Pattaya mushroomed as a resort for the US troops on R&R and nearby Bang Saen developed as Bangkok's Coney Island. Fortunes were made in hotels and entertainment businesses. Finally, government located one of the main sites of the Eastern Seaboard project just outside the town. More fortunes were made in land speculation and service businesses of all kinds.

Chonburi grew not just rich but violent. The huge profits in land speculation tempted people to extreme strategies, including gunplay. The fishing port was ideally placed as a centre for smuggling goods into Bangkok. The booming local Chinese community provided a market for all kinds of illegal gambling. The resorts ran a lucrative sex trade. As everywhere, these activities created a gangsterish milieu.

Chonburi soon ranked top among provinces for the number of murders. The town became known as the place to go if you wanted to hire an experienced hit man. The region was nicknamed the "Wild East".

For those with the right kind of talents, the route from rags to riches in Chonburi could be fast and exciting. Long Ju Kiang, the local boss of the 1960s, started as an accountant, went into mining, then grew rich during the crop boom by trading, logging, land speculation, and crop processing. Sia Jiew began as a bus conductor, ventured into pork slaughtering, took over Kiang's empire in the 1970s, and added service businesses and government contracting.[32] Somchai Kunpluem (Kamnan Po) who became Jiew's lieutenant and then took over the empire, was a fisherman who reputedly made his first fortune smuggling between Thailand and Cambodia.[33] He invested in land speculation and entertainment businesses during the tourism boom.

Many such bosses were rumoured to have iceberg-shaped businesses with the profits from smuggling, gambling, and other illicit activities concealed below the surface.

The route up could also be rough. After Kiang died, his two sons were gunned down in separate gangland-style hits. Sia Jiew was possibly responsible and certainly took over Kiang's empire.[34] Some years later, Jiew and his Mercedes were blown off the Bangkok-Pattaya highway by a rocket launcher. His son was assassinated a few months later. During Kamnan Po's rise, his chief rival was killed after a chase and gun battle along the main road. Po denied any involvement but did comment "in Chonburi, bad guys must die".[35]

Four years later, in what looked like revenge, three of Po's henchmen were shot dead and left beside the road.[36] In 1994, Po's right-hand man was gunned down by an Uzi while he was drinking coffee at his regular morning coffee-shop. Opinion was divided. Some thought the hit was a blow against Po. Others suspected it was an inside job against an over-mighty lieutenant. In 1995, another friend of Po was gunned down by M-16s. Again identifying the culprit was difficult because there were so many potential causes – a simmering dispute between local sugar barons, a conflict over mining rights, backwash from the recent election campaigns, a dispute over construction, or just plain old revenge for other killings.[37] In 1997, another aide was shot dead at a construction site.

To be secure as a boss in Chonburi, it was not enough just to dodge the bullets. You also needed friends in Bangkok. Kiang and Sia Jiew both cultivated close relations with the old military strongmen. From 1975, Sia Jiew started "arranging" parliamentary elections. Kamnan Po continued the practice. The old gangland rivalries were now reproduced as competition between the political parties. Po was so good at arranging elections that he became a regional party head. The large turnout figures in Chonburi, he admitted, may have occurred because his men were over-zealous in stuffing the ballot-boxes.[38]

In 1992 and again in 1995, Po's sons were elected into parliament. In 1995, the elder joined the cabinet. With their US education and the status of MP, they strenuously disassociated themselves from the mythology of the "Wild East". They wore suits, talked nicely, preached democracy.

But Chonburi seemed secretly to like its notoriety. Why else would it have a provincial festival of buffalo racing so like the American rodeo?

The Mobile Phone Mob

Thailand's economic growth created a rapidly rising demand for technicians, managers, executives, professionals. Between the 1960s and the late 1980s, the numbers in white-collar jobs grew from around half-a-million to around four-and-a-half million. In the space of a couple of decades, Thailand acquired a new urban middle class.

These new salarymen and salarywomen were different. They passed through the university system but not into the bureaucracy. They moved out of the family homes in the old city centre and colonized the suburbs. They grew prosperous on the rising salaries paid for skill and talent. They shopped in modern department stores that offered them the pick of the world's brandnames.

The political impact of this new social class was mixed. Their interests for the most part were tied up with their economic well-being. They were inclined to support any regime that maintained stability and kept the urban economy growing. But this passivity coexisted with other impulses.

They were children of the new, globalizing world. They had grown up in the period of American influence. They matured in the age of global information – CNN, MTV, satellite news, Internet. They wanted to see Thailand as a modern nation – not just prosperous but also sophisticated and politically mature.

They wanted to be ruled by people as enlightened and sophisticated as themselves, not strutting generals or corrupt, gangsterish businessmen.

They developed strongly individualist attitudes. Their own lives showed the possibilities open to individual effort and self-improvement. They resented restrictive traditional structures. Some joined new Buddhist movements that allowed more individual involvement and more individual control over spiritual destiny. A few formed organizations demanding human rights.

More than anything, their political attitudes were shaped by the events of 1973-6. The students of these years, the first to benefit from the expansion of higher education, were the vanguard of this new urban middle class.

In 1971-3, they were mobilized by the student activism that swept around the world during the Vietnam War. In 1973, their street demonstrations brought down the military junta. In the liberalization that followed, they studied Marxism and helped organize movements of protest by peasants and workers. They demonstrated against American militarism and Japanese economic exploitation. They argued fiercely about the nature and future of Thai society. In 1976, the student movement was brutally crushed by the army. Some 2-3,000 fled to join the communist insurgents in the jungles of Thailand and Laos.[39]

In 1979-83, the insurgency collapsed in a mess of quarrels between China and Russia, Vietnam and Cambodia, the 1976 students and the communist party old guard. Under an army amnesty, the students returned from the jungle. Many were disillusioned by the bickering within the rebel movement, by the futility of the attempt to mount a revolution from the jungle, and by the extreme polarization of views between Thailand's radicals and conservatives.[40]

In the 1980s, many of the "jungle graduates" were swept along the upward curve of the urban economy. Several became successful businessmen. Some made their fortune and returned later to contest parliamentary elections. Many more were absorbed into the ranks of the salariat. A few continued as journalists, artists, broadcasters, teachers – positions from which they could pass on some of the radical spirit to future generations.

The "jungle graduates" were only a small core. Many others lived through the same period at a lower intensity but still gained a political education from the tumultuous sequence of events.

In the early 1980s, parliament became better established and more important than it had been in the past. Some middle-class intellectuals were enthusiastic about entering. Yet it quickly became clear that this new middle class was not large, rich, or coherent enough to form a base for parliamentary politics. The capital included less than ten percent of all constituencies. Provincial elections were dominated by the money of the local magnates. Parties formed in the hope of capturing a middle-class vote were spectacularly unsuccessful.

But if they did not have the money or the numbers to make an impact *inside* parliament, they had the talents to make a noise *outside*. The new middle class played politics *nok rabop*, "outside the system", through organizations, agitations, and especially through the press.

Since the 1920s, Thailand had a small but active political press. In the 1980s, the rising numbers and incomes of the new middle class boosted numbers and circulations of newspapers and magazines. As the repression of 1975-9 retreated into the past, the press became steadily more ambitious. During the Chatichai government, it campaigned to cancel old dictatorial press controls and fought off politicians' attempts to apply the muzzle.

The press provided a platform for very open debate on political and social subjects. Papers mounted campaigns on specific issues and provided a forum for monitoring the work of officials and politicians. Many dealings that the ruling elite could once keep discreet were now exposed in this new public court – petty corruption, suspect business dealings, backstairs intrigue, abuse of power.

The *Manager* and *The Nation* press groups went beyond this to carry a torch for middle-class issues such as the environment, corruption, globalization, human rights. Suthichai Yoon of *The Nation* extended these campaigns into TV and radio. Sondhi Limthongkul of the *Manager* set up a foundation that carried out research and activist projects intended to influence the future course of politics.

The press provided a major outlet for public intellectuals who the middle class built into mouthpieces for their evolving attitudes. These public intellectuals wrote regular columns, appeared often in public meetings, were asked by reporters to comment on day-to-day events. Several were veterans of the 1973-6 period. Thirayuth Boonmee had been a prominent student leader. Both he and Kasian Tejapira had graduated through the jungle. Chai-Anan Samudavanija had been a more moderate force during the debates of 1973-6 and had gone on to become a leading political scientist.

Others had different credentials. Prawase Wasi was a doctor who had won the Magsaysay award for his work in rural medical care. He wrote passionately about rural development, Buddhism, and individual responsibility. Sukhumbhand Paribatra, who sported a royal lineage and an Oxford degree, commented especially on foreign affairs, and campaigned for the reorientation of policy towards Indochina.

Prawase was also a key figure in another political expression of the post-1976 era – non-governmental organizations (NGOs). For many veterans of 1973-6, NGOs provided an avenue to work for social and political ideals without inviting confrontation and polarization. Many NGOs were founded to promote a bottom-up approach to rural development as an alternative to the government's authoritarian ways. Others became involved in medical care, slum work, rural education, media liberalization, human rights.

Through the decade of the 1980s, the politics "outside the system" grew more prominent and more assured. The newspapers became more assertive. The public intellectuals more strident. The NGO movement more active.

Within the city, this middle-class assertiveness fed into electoral politics. In 1985 Chamlong Srimuang stood for election as Bangkok mayor. He campaigned on the single issue of cleaning up the city's corrupt and inefficient administration. To emphasize his difference from the old municipal regime, he sported a simple peasant shirt and used scarecrows as election posters. Bangkok voted him in decisively and then voted him in again by a landslide in 1990.

Chamlong had been a dissident soldier in the 1970s and had joined one of the new urban reformist Buddhist sects (Santi Asoke) in the early 1980s. He named his political party Palang Dharma (moral force) to signal a crusade for change. The core of the party consisted of other ex-soldiers, members of the sect, and several city businessmen. At the two parliamentary elections in 1992, Palang Dharma won most of the seats in Bangkok.

Chamlong was far from ideal as a candidate for political canonization by the Bangkok middle class. He had been a soldier. Some alleged he had participated in the bloody suppression of students in October 1976. The asceticism of his adopted Santi Asoke sect conflicted with middle-class consumerism. But he promised to bring in the clean, responsive, and principled administration that the middle class favoured. And he represented the *change* that the new middle class hankered for. In the short term, that was enough to make him a political flag-carrier for the middle-class upsurge.[41]

After the 1991 coup, the immediate reaction was muted. Middle-class opinion felt little affinity for the Chatichai ministers and little regret at their fall. But many felt uneasy about the return of the military. It fitted badly with their image of Thailand as a modern state. It aligned Thailand with the select group of countries – Burma, Panama, Nigeria – still run by a coup regime.

More importantly, the coup had a rapid impact on Thailand's globally oriented economy. Tourists thought twice about coming. Investors delayed projects. Risk analysts marked Thailand down a point or two. The economy was already past the peak of the boom. As it decelerated through 1991-2, it was difficult not to believe the coup had something to do with it.

Opposition emerged when it became clear that the junta intended to restore military control for the long term. The generals planned to fix the constitution, herd the provincial MPs into a tame political party, and put the army head, General Suchinda, into the prime ministership. The opposition to this plan emerged through the networks developed over the past ten years to express middle-class opinion.

The press and public intellectuals criticized the military's new draft constitution. NGO groups formed a Campaign for Popular Democracy to oppose the military's attempts to control the polity. Chamlong came forward to lead the popular movement. When Suchinda was appointed prime minister, the protesters took to the streets.

On 17 May 1992, up to half a million joined demonstrations in Bangkok. The Social Science Association conducted a spot survey. Most were married, aged 25-45, white-collar, and reasonably well off. This was not the mob. Nor was this the student demo of the 1973-6 period. This was the middle class. Festooned with Rolexes and mobile phones.

After three nights of violence, the King intervened. The soldiers went back to barracks. The demonstrators went back to work. Suchinda resigned. Anand was brought back to the premiership. The most objectionable parts of the constitution were rescinded. New elections were called.

The mobilization of the middle class was the most dramatic element in the crisis. The pressed coined the term *mob mu' thu'*, the mobile phone mob. But there was more to the story. Many of Bangkok's poorer groups had joined the demonstrations and had borne the brunt of the army violence. After the King's intervention, the associations representing Bangkok big business had come out to oppose any return to military rule.

On the backwash of the May crisis, the new middle class was enthusiastic about taking a more prominent role in politics. Associations of 1973-6 veterans were reactivated to organize support for candidates. The PollWatch NGO mobilized sixty thousand volunteers to combat vote-buying at the October elections. More educated professionals ran at the polls than at any election since 1974. Around forty of the elected MPs had been student activists in the 1973-6 era.[42]

The press and NGOs shaped the contest over a single issue – the military role in politics. Videotapes of CNN and BBC footage showing soldiers firing into the May demonstrations were sold on the streets of Bangkok and distributed upcountry through NGO organizations. The press dubbed the contesting parties as "angels" or "devils" depending on whether they had opposed Suchinda or supported him.

Despite all this noise, the devils almost won. The angel Democrat party won the largest number of seats and by convention was given the first chance to put together a coalition. But it won by only two seats from the devil Chat Thai party. If Chatichai had not formed the breakaway Chat Phatthana party during the electoral campaign, Chat Thai might have won easily. The Democrats had to bring in one devil party to make up the coalition.

Middle-class politics "outside the system" spearheaded the move to thwart a military restoration. But once it had to play "inside the system" again, the weakness of the middle class was obvious. Parliament belonged to the provincial politicians.

A King and his people

In March 1995, King Bhumibol Adulyadej appeared on prime-time television to tell the nation about his recent heart operation. Surrounded by family and medical staff, he used a flip chart to show what the surgeons had done.

The moment captured something of the unique relationship between Thailand's King and his people: the audience transfixed by respect and concern; the monarch dispensing reassurance and medical education; the moment made possible by mass television.

King Bhumibol once remarked that the role he played was not the one usually expected of a king. Certainly not a traditional king. But then the twentieth century has turned most monarchies into museum pieces or tabloid curiosities. In a reign lasting half a century, King Bhumibol has redefined Thai kingship for an age of mass development, mass politics, and mass communications.

In theory, the king is the "personification of the Thai nationhood" – "the King and the People become one".[43] King Bhumibol has given humanity and meaning to this theoretical construct in two major ways.

First, he remade the relationship between king and people by a personal commitment to better the nation's well-being.

Until 1932, the Thai monarch was still an absolute ruler, rendered remote by power and ritual. In 1932, nationalists revolted against this absolutism and demanded a constitution. In 1935, the King abdicated. For over a decade, the country had no resident, ruling monarch. This gap might have signalled a trend of decline. Instead it provided the opportunity to rebuild kingship for a new era.

From the late 1950s, contact between king and people dramatically increased. The King and Queen travelled around the country. They appeared at hundreds of functions. They presided over marriages, handed out degrees, accepted military salutes, graced charity events.[44]

Then from the 1960s, they focused their contact on one group – the rural peasantry which was the largest element in the nation and the least well-equipped to handle the surge to modernity. In the palace grounds, the King started projects of agrarian research. For most of the year, the King and Queen toured the provinces, starting and supervising scores of projects in rural development. The King concentrated on irrigation, new crops, reforestation; the queen on handicrafts and off-farm work.

Millions of people far from the capital had the chance to see their monarch and his commitment to their own well-being. As television spread, the recurring image on the daily news showed the King in a rural setting, map or blueprint in hand, directing officials in a project of rural uplift.

In the 1990s, in line with the economic shift from country to town, the King increased his attention to urban problems. He donated funds to relieve traffic congestion. He directed the construction of new roads and bridges. In the great flood of 1995, he galvanized officials into action and laid out plans against a future recurrence.

Second, the King helped to guide the nation through the difficult process of political development.

Officially the king is "above politics", free of any attachment to a political group or cause. Yet the king is also head of state and plays a subtle but critical role in the unfolding of a new polity.

Since the late 1960s, in birthday speeches and other public occasions, the King has offered guidance on political development. The main themes running through these addresses are the responsibilities of leadership, the demon of corruption, the dangers of extremism, and the importance of unity and harmony.

From time to time he has acted against the wayward swings of political change. These interventions have been short and decisive – a tap on the tiller to nudge the ship of state back towards a middle course.

In the late 1960s, when the military junta threw away the constitution and censored the press, the King told the student audience: "So I say to the generals . . . they must learn to listen to the people."[45] When four years later students rose in revolt, the King ordered the junta into exile. In 1976, against a backdrop of polarization and violence, the King endorsed the reimposition of firm rule. In 1992, the King used his influence to stop the clash between populist and military and to allow the reinstatement of parliamentary democracy.

In 1995 this democracy delivered up a cabinet studded with faces suspected of past corruption. The King delivered them an inaugural address on the social responsibilities of political power: "you must have honest minds, or the intention to do only good things and avoid bad things".[46]

A memoir compiled on the King's sixtieth birthday recalled the concept of kingship from thirteenth-century Sukhothai: "The King . . . having been entrusted with the task not out of any divine right, but by the consent of his fellow peers, felt an inherent obligation to rule the country 'with righteousness', not for the glory of himself or his family, but 'for the benefits and happiness' of the people in his trust."[47] As the King explained his own role: "I do things that will be useful and that is all".[48]

By taking on responsibility for the economic needs and political aspirations of the mass of people, King Bhumibol had redefined Thai kingship for an age of democracy and development. Through his long reign of good deeds, the institution of monarchy has grown steadily stronger. Little more than a century before, the people could not look at the royal person. Now they could see him on television, as with pointer and flip chart the King reassured his people that he was going to be all right.

The Politics of Boom

Thailand's expansive urban society generated powerful new social forces that demanded political expression. From the 1970s, these forces battered against an authoritarian bureaucratic regime with strong historical roots. They invented institutions and tools to modify the old bureaucratic regime – not just constitution, parliament, and parties but also a strident press, a movement of NGOs, a cadre of public intellectuals, a realm of open public debate.

The military's difficulties in managing these new forces bubbling up through Thailand's dynamic urban society began in 1972-3. They increased after the army lost its US patron and its role as the bulwark against communism. They increased again with the urban upsurge of the boom.

Thailand's politics often seem chaotic because so much is changing, so much is at stake, and so much is out in the open.

Bangkok big business, provincial business, and the urban middle class have been the driving forces of the new politics. Each has its own agenda, and occupies a different kind of political space. Provincial business dominates the parliament through its grip over the rural electorate. The middle class dominates public debate over politics. Big business exerts the power of its wealth, its economic role, and its celestial connections in the dim background. These three realms whirl and clash to create the lively day-to-day drama of politics.

The results often seem frighteningly disorderly – "institutionalized anarchy" in the words of one leading political scientist.[49] Parliament houses a revolving carousel of scrapping factions. The press indulges in scandal and revelation. The rumour mill traffics in stories of intrigue, double-dealing, and plunder.

But the openness of political debate and conflict is one of the country's major strengths. The society is remaking itself, and resolving the resulting stresses and strains from day to day. In many neighbouring countries, politics are bottled up out of sight, with uncertain consequences.

But once the military had been pushed aside, who would rule? "The positive side of the event," noted a financier in the aftermath of the May 1992 crisis, "is that business people now pay attention to politics. From now on, business will determine the pattern of Thailand's future."[50]

10 WRESTLING WITH DEMOCRACY

Making democracy work was tough in a time of jolting social change and tantalizing economic opportunities.

Fifty years of military domination had come to an end. Parliament could now rule. After May 1992, many businessmen and intellectuals talked about entering politics. Many hoped Thai politics would now progress and modernize, rather as the economy had already done.

But political stability proved elusive. The new prime minister hoped to last the full four-year term to show democracy was maturing. He didn't make it. Over the next five years, there were three prime ministers from three different parties. Counting major reshuffles, each cabinet lasted around nine months.

The 1995 elections brought in a government which seemed a direct descendant of the "buffet cabinet" of 1988-91 – dominated by provincial bosses and riven with scandals. Had rule by generals simply been replaced with rule by godfathers and gravel-pit owners? Had "semi-democracy" succeeded to "money politics"?

By mid-decade, politics were seen as a drag on Thailand's progress. "Political reform" sprang to the top of the national agenda.

The ending of the 1991-2 crisis was a moment of hope. The military had been retired from the political stage. Thailand's democracy could now flourish. Many veterans of 1973-6 radicalism decided it was now safe to enter politics. Business associations organized campaigns to restore international confidence in Thailand's economy. The press became bolder. New chat shows surfaced on TV and phone-ins on radio. Thailand could now start to clear away the debris of the military-dominated era – the over-centralized government, the domineering and often corrupt bureaucracy, the tight controls on the media, the pervasive role of "influence".

It would not prove so easy.

Wealth and Numbers

Thailand's parliamentary democracy was young and tender. Parliaments had existed on-and-off since the 1930s. But only with the 1974 constitution was the system truly established. And only after the 1979 elections did it acquire some continuity. Thailand's parliament was really a little over a decade old.

It was also under intense pressure. The boom had created new social forces, new demands, and new conflicts. The boom had changed the whole pattern of business opportunities. Politicians often had the agony and ecstasy of deciding who would profit from these opportunities. The boom had also created a swathe of urgent issues – how to build the infrastructure, expand education, improve the legal framework, overhaul the bureaucracy, manage the economy, and spread the benefits of the boom to more people.

Moreover, the parliamentary system now had to cope with Thailand's huge social paradox: *most of the people are in the countryside, most of the wealth in the city.*

This division created two separate political cultures and two competing agendas.

Two-thirds of the electorate lived in the villages and over 80 percent of all constituencies were dominated by the rural vote. But villagers had not been tied into democratic politics. Rural organizations had been suppressed in the Cold War period. Farmers had not been able to get together to form pressure groups or political parties. Parliament had always been concerned with urban issues.

Rural voters viewed national elections from a local perspective: a chance to get something for themselves and for their locality. They voted for the candidate who could get their wells dug and their roads paved; who would be strong enough leaders to get something out of the central budget; and who were generous enough to give them some money.

This electorate formed a base for local bosses – businessmen who had the cash to invest in patronage, the contacts to distribute it to the voters, and the hope that electoral success would allow them to recoup their investment. As provincial MPs, they fought for the budget to build more highways, schools, and colleges in their hometowns. They trickled more funds down to the villages for paving roads, digging wells, hooking up electricity. They were much more successful at bringing public goods and services to the localities than the centralized bureaucracy had ever been.

But these achievements came at a cost. Many of the provincial boss-politicians were in politics *as a way to do business*. Some were construction contractors and gravel-pit owners, for whom electoral politics was self-liquidating. They could promise to build the villagers roads and then make a profit when they delivered.[1] Others found that parliament was a great marketplace – for licences, deals, kickbacks, commissions, contracts, even just market knowledge, and especially for that little extra leverage so important in business success. In 1996, three-fifths of all MPs described their *profession* as "politician".

Party affiliation was governed not by conviction but prediction – which party would be part of the next ruling coalition and thus worth joining. The Political Parties Law tried to encourage party development by forcing MPs to be a party member and by placing restrictions on switching. But provincial politicians still moved with the log-rolls and faction shifts. "I am a man who can go anywhere," announced Snoh

Thienthong when he abandoned the Chat Thai party in 1996. "We welcome any who have the same ideology," said Chavalit Yongchaiyudh before accommodating Snoh and sixty-nine other sitting MPs into his party.[2] Many provincial politicians were in Chat Thai in 1988. Switched to Samakkhitham in 1992. Turned up again in Chat Thai in 1995. And flooded into New Aspiration in 1996. Parties which could turn deftly with the political current were known as "eel parties". Chat Phatthana, which could turn faster and sharper than any, was dubbed "eels on skates". Smaller parties appeared and disappeared like glow-worms.

ELECTION RESULT	75	76	79	83	86	88	92a	92b	95	96
Democrat	72	114	32	56	100	48	44	79	86	123
Chat Thai	28	56	38	73	63	87	74	77	92	39
Social Action	18	45	83	92	51	54	31	22	22	20
Palang Dharma	-	-	-	-	-	14	41	47	23	1
New Aspiration	-	-	-	-	-	-	72	51	57	125
Chat Phatthana	-	-	-	-	-	-	-	60	53	52
Samakkhitham	-	-	-	-	-	-	79	-	-	-
Prachakorn Thai	-	-	32	36	24	31	7	3	18	18
Other	151	64	116	67	109	123	12	21	40	15
Total	269	279	301	324	347	357	360	360	391	393

A very different political culture emerged in Bangkok. The city's business and middle class of professionals, executives, and small businessmen had done well out of the boom. They hoped the good times would continue. They wanted to concentrate resources in the more productive modern urban economy. They believed Thailand must reform to become a modern, prosperous, and efficient nation. Some had a broader view of Thailand as a better society with less corruption and influence, more equity and justice.[3]

But city politics faced a problem. The city's wealth certainly translated into political power. Businessmen made their deals in the lobby room and on the backstairs. The middle class shaped the agenda of political debate through the press, public intellectuals, and NGOs. But in terms of numbers, votes, and electoral constituencies, the city was a minority. And in parliamentary politics, numbers matter.

City politics fell into a cycle of hope and disappointment. Urban voters would invest a party with high expectations. But the party would fail to gain enough power in parliament and cabinet to deliver. The press and electorate would then trash it in frustration.

The Democrat party, which had reflected urban aspirations since the late 1940s, had been spun through this cycle several times. It rose on the liberal surge of the mid-1970s, then dwindled in the subsequent reaction. It revived in the mid-1980s but then failed to reflect the optimism spurred by the boom.

The Palang Dharma party was spun through the cycle from 1985 to 1996. With his ascetic air, Chamlong Srimuang promised a cleaner politics. The party swept two Bangkok municipality elections and most of the Bangkok seats in the two general elections of 1992.[4] But as a minor partner in the Chuan and Banharn coalitions, Palang Dharma could not deliver the changes it promised. Chamlong quit. The party dissolved into warring factions. At the 1996 elections, Bangkok rejected the party, reducing it to a single seat.

Because of the provincial bosses' roving habits and the urban electorate's fickleness, parties had grown fitfully. Only the Democrats had developed much of a party organization and funding. The provincial parties were held together by the stickiness of money. They depended on big financiers who bank-rolled election campaigns and paid retainers to MPs.[5]

More importantly, not even the Democrats had machinery for evolving policies or drafting legislation. On the eve of elections, party leaders typically hired academics to throw together a party platform. Most were predictable boilerplate. New ministers gathered together teams of "advisers" including academics, friends, business associates, and assorted experts. Few of these had much experience in policy-making. Democratically elected government passed sadly little legislation.

Since 1975, parliament had developed a few conventions to structure this fluid system. The party which won the largest number of seats had the first chance to form a cabinet. In the run-up to an election, an ambitious leader would try to log-roll factions into his party to become first-past-the-post. Many of these new additions were only loosely attached to the party and its leader.

With the parties so fragmented, the largest usually had around a quarter of the total seats. To achieve a majority, it had to negotiate with a raft of smaller parties. Ministerships were shared out by quota according to the number of MPs in each coalition party. With some forty cabinet posts and something over two hundred MPs needed for a majority, around 1-in-6 of coalition MPs got ministerships. Ambitious politicians financed the election campaigns of relatives and friends in order to build a six-plus faction which could bargain for a cabinet position. Each election was followed by fierce horse-trading to secure the plum ministerships.

Every 6-9 months, the opposition would assault the government with a no-confidence motion. The lack of party infrastructure meant the opposition was poorly equipped to monitor the cabinet performance from day to day. It relied on press reports, leaks, and rumours to identify ministers' misdeeds. Then it presented these in a no-confidence debate rather like impeachment charges.

These new democratic politics were conducted under the media spotlight. The press had played a big part in the urban revolt against the military and especially in the crisis of 1991-2. It had won a measure of freedom which politicians found difficult to revoke. Television and radio were still under official control. Yet even here, there was an expansion of talk-shows, phone-ins, and magazine programmes on political issues. The television news functioned as an everyday court of popular scrutiny. Ministers struggled down the steps of government house through a barrage of microphones, cassette recorders, and video crews.

The press carried a torch for urban interests, campaigned for reforms, monitored the politicians' performance, and exposed corruption and malpractice. But a section of the press was itself susceptible to money. The line between legitimate revelation and interested rumour-mongering was so fine as to be invisible. The press surrounded parliament with a swirl of rumour, allegation, and scandal.

How to win an election

Thai elections in the 1990s are major economic events. The Thai Farmers Bank Research Centre reckoned 20-30 billion baht was spent of the 1996 campaign[6] – more than on the US presidential campaign. Much of it went for simple handouts to voters.

Winning such an election could look easy. Just hand out a lot of money. But it's more complex. Here's a guide on how to succeed.

First you have to answer a question. How many of the following businesses do you, your relatives or your patron own: hotel, pawn shop, whisky agency, gravel quarry, automobile dealership, petrol pump, trucking firm, construction business?

If you counted fewer than four, you should give up now. If you scored over six, you are in with a chance.

Next, who will be your running mates? Most constituencies have three slots. Unless you choose your partners carefully, they can get you into trouble. So what about your family? Any promising sons, nephews, even wives or daughters? Many experienced politicians stand in family groups. Costs are shared. Voters have to remember only one surname. And all the benefits stay in the family.

There are no real party organizations. Instead there is the underground lottery which in many ways is a lot better. Just about everybody bets on the underground lottery. And the network of lottery agents is probably the largest and most efficient organization in Thailand. Underground lottery agents make far the best election canvassers.

If you have to find your canvassers on the open market, it's a lot trickier. The freelancers charge high fees. They also have a habit of "working" for both you and your rivals.

You can also use the lottery network for another campaign tactic. Arrange for the lottery agents to take bets on who will win the election and rig the odds so most will bet on you. Who will vote against you if that means they lose the bet? If you want to be even more sure, run another book for betting on your opponent losing. This trick needs a lot of nerve and a good numbers man. But it has a track record of working very well.

Now 100-200 baht a head is not so much to pay for votes. But every village is going to ask you for something much bigger – a well, street lights, bus shelter, community hall. Paving the road is the most popular. Don't panic. At this stage, all you have to do is promise. If you get elected, there's the fund of thirty million baht per MP to pay for these promises. You can deliver on all of them and increase your chances of getting elected next time too.

Now you see why it is so important to own a gravel quarry, trucking firm, or construction business. Who do you think makes a profit out of paving all those village roads?

Handing out money is getting more difficult every time. People from PollWatch sneak around all over the place. But there are still lots of ways to give out money which are very nearly legal.

Invite lots of people to rallies and give each of them a little payment as an attendance fee. Put up your posters on every house and pay the owners a fee for the advertising space. Appoint just about everybody in the village as your paid election agent. Host a boat race or dancing contest and hand out prizes to all and sundry.

If you have a hotel or restaurant, arrange some free buffets. If you have a car or motorcycle shop, offer free repairs. If you run the whisky dealership, let a few cases run out the back door. If you have a pawn shop, be a bit generous. (Now you see what the quiz above was all about.)

The important thing is to make people feel so indebted to you they could not possibly vote for anyone else. In the last few days before the poll, there is really no alternative. Just give out cash.

But don't do it yourself. That's what canvassers are for. Even if things go wrong, they will arrest the canvassers rather than you. Unless they catch them pressing the money into the voter's hand in the presence of the entire national press corps and the provincial governor, then your canvassers should still get away with it.

Lastly, you need to know how people really vote, village by village. If you win, you don't want to go paving the road of a village that took your money but voted for your opponent. If you lose, you want to find out which of your election agents were really working for your opponents. And fix them.[7]

Luckily they still count the votes in the locality. You are not supposed to get a peek at the results village by village but there are ways around this. Presumably you are in the habit of drinking with the right kind of people and are very generous about buying the bottles.

So now you see that vote-buying is not just about money. All the candidates will hand out cash. It's part of qualifying as a candidate. No-one will take you seriously unless you do it. But equally, no-one will vote for you just because you give them a few red ones. For that, you need to show them you're a "big guy". That's why you need the gravel quarry, the hotel, the lottery network, and the right drinking circle. That's what will get you elected.

Chuan Leekpai, 1992-95: Fallen Angels

The September 1992 election brought in a coalition of "angel" parties headed by the Democrats. Chuan Leekpai was the first prime minister who came from a common background and who had no experience in the military or bureaucracy. Just by occupying the post, he signalled a break from the lingering traditions of the bureaucratic polity.

Chuan's agenda had two main points. First, he had to deliver on the expectations of the urban business and middle class which had put him into power. Most of all that meant fixing the economy and meeting middle-class expectations for further liberalization and improvements in the quality of life.

Second, he had to build firmer foundations for Thailand's democracy and for the Democrat party. That would mean forestalling a military resurgence, controlling the ambitions of the provincial bosses, and bringing more benefits to the mass of the population still in the countryside, to wean them away from support of the bosses and the generals.

Chuan needed to show the business community that a democratically-elected government could produce top technocrats to manage the economy. He drafted in the non-MP banker, Tarrin Nimmanhaeminda, to serve as finance minister. Tarrin helped to restore local and international business confidence after the crisis of 1991-2. He continued the process of reforming taxation, the capital market, and the tariff regime in the interests of the export economy.

Tarrin also reached beyond the usual scope of the finance minister to tackle longer-term problems for the economy. He worked up plans to improve the education level by providing grants and loans to keep children in school longer.

Chuan also appointed another ex-banker, Supachai Panitchapakdi, to drive negotiations for an Asean Free Trade Area, an idea started by Anand and widely supported by Bangkok business.

In 1993, international confidence flowed back. The growth rate rose out of its post-coup dip.

On political liberalization, Chuan's government moved more cautiously. It launched a reform of the constitution. The preamble for the first time contained a declaration of civic rights. The senate was made smaller. The voting age was lowered to eighteen. New institutions and procedures were set up to control corruption and abuse of power.

But several more radical proposals for constitutional reform were blocked, often because of opposition from the bureaucracy. The liberalization of the electronic media moved very slowly. Plans to allow several new private TV stations were whittled back to a single new UHF channel. The politically active element of the middle class expected more after the drama of 1992.

Chuan's government gave more power to *tambon* (sub-district) councils. But more ambitious plans for decentralizing government were battered back by the powerful Interior Ministry. Plans to remove the government-appointed village officials from ex-officio posts in local government were defeated in parliament. Proposals to choose provincial governors by election were totally suppressed. Judicial reforms ran into opposition from the judges and were quietly dropped.

On the political side, the record was similar – some initial success but then increasing frustration.

Chuan gently urged the military to stay in the barracks. He continued Anand's efforts to weed generals out of powerful sinecures in the administration, the national airline, and other state enterprises. The cabinet turned down several further requests for special arms budgets. The press exposed abuses of power that the generals had once managed with impunity: big military construction projects allotted to companies in which the generals had holdings; arms sold to the Khmer Rouge in defiance of international agreements; a state-owned vintage train parked on a general's rural retreat.

The new army chief foreswore any future army intervention in politics. Generals talked about a new professionalism in the armed forces.

But after laying low for a year or so, the military began to reassert its presence. The army produced a White Paper justifying big arms budgets for defending Thailand's growing economic interests in the region. By mid-1994, generals were again prepared to mutter in public about the importance of the military, its claim to a political role, and the possibility it would be "forced" to defend military honour. The defence minister (a military man) voted against his own government over constitutional reforms which the military opposed. In mid-

1995, the army began to rehabilitate the careers of some prominent figures sidelined for their role in May 1992.

For the longer term, the Democrats needed to break the hold of the big provincial bosses who had undermined Chatichai by their own greed and who had then lined up behind Suchinda.

This was a delicate business. Things happened in mysterious ways. Somehow, several more obviously gangsterish MPs were embroiled in scandals. One was formally charged in the US with smuggling fifty tons of marijuana. Two others were reported to have been denied US visas on suspicion of involvement in the drug trade. An unusual casino raid netted one MP and reportedly narrowly missed a couple of others.[8] An MP was forced to explain why an illegal casino was operating in a house he owned. Rumours circulated that certain MPs were smuggling oil on fishing boats.

At the same time, Chuan looked for ways to break the provincial bosses' grip on the rural vote. The constitutional reforms included new rules designed to limit the vote-buying and other electoral malpractice on which the provincial bosses relied. But these measures were not enough. The Democrats also launched policies designed to appeal directly to the rural electorate. They devoted more funds to rural development. They placed more of these funds under the control of local bodies (the *tambon* councils). They intervened in markets to bolster agricultural prices. Most of all, they tackled land reform and made it the showpiece of the government.

Several million villagers occupied land which government defined as "forest" but which had long been cleared and cultivated (see chapter 8). The Democrats planned to give non-transferable land deeds (known as *SPK 4-01*) to villagers who could prove they had occupied the land before 1954 and were truly poor and in need of land. The policy set out to solve a long-standing problem. It also took the responsibility away from the army, which had tackled the same issue with the disastrous *Khor Jor Kor* scheme in 1991.

But these efforts to win rural support were shaky. When northeastern farmers organized to demand government help over debts, land issues, and failed development schemes, Chuan refused to take any personal interest in the issue. The farmers' leaders felt fobbed off with empty promises and bureaucratic inertia. When one of them was shot, it recalled the bad old days when rural leaders were systematically assassinated.

Increasingly the press and NGOs which had focused the urban movement of 1991-2 came round to the view that Chuan had squandered a great historical moment. He was too cautious, too indecisive. At heart, the Democrats were still too conservative.

The business lobby also became more critical. The Chuan government had not been good at building the infrastructure which the economy desperately needed. The Bangkok traffic was grinding to a halt. Two leading business figures peeled away and headed parties designed to appeal to the business lobby at the next election.[9]

The Democrats' Achilles heel was their showpiece, the *SPK 4-01* land reform. In late 1994, the leading mass-circulation newspaper, *Thai Rath*, published that businessmen in Phuket had secured land under the scheme. They clearly did not qualify as poor farmers. Some of the land had big potential for tourist development. One of the beneficiaries was husband of the Democrat MP who served as secretary to the minister overseeing the scheme.

At first the story did not catch fire. But *Thai Rath*, which in the past had been known for its military links, published the same allegations day after day for several months. The story gradually eroded the last traces of the Democrats' angelic virtue.

The rest of the press took up the issue. Prominent NGO leaders held public meetings to castigate the government for its failures. No rural voice emerged in support of the land-reform scheme and the Democrats. In May 1995, the opposition staged a dramatic no-confidence debate, displaying blow-up maps and photographs of the Phuket land for the benefit of the TV audience. Chuan resigned and called an election rather than face the final vote.

The *SPK 4-01* land scandal showed the difficulties of an urban-based government in a rural-based democracy. For the villagers, land was livelihood. For many urban businessmen, land was an opportunity to generate great wealth. The Democrats' ambitious scheme was sabotaged by the greed of a few of its own supporters. The *SPK 4-01* issue was not just another scandal. It highlighted the urban-rural division at the core of Thai society and politics.

For the first time, the election was a relatively clear contest between two major parties and their respective leaders – Chuan of the Democrat Party, and Banharn of Chat Thai. For the first time too, the media played a large role. Press, radio, and TV carried a barrage of party advertising, debates, personal appearances, and commentary.

The campaign highlighted the political divide between city and provinces. Three major parties – Palang Dharma, Prachakorn Thai, and Nam Thai – were anchored in the city. A fourth, the Democrats, was intent on retaining its city support. These parties campaigned heavily through the modern media and emphasized policies and slogans with city appeal. They promised to improve the city's infrastructure and to make Thailand a yet more successful player in the globalizing world. Their candidate lists were packed with technocrats, professionals, and city businessmen. The leaders of Palang Dharma and Nam Thai both sported a foreign Ph.D, a background in the bureaucracy, and a base in modern business.

By contrast, the main provincial parties of Chat Thai, Chat Phatthana, Social Action, and New Aspiration ignored the city and between them won only a single city seat. They promised to spread growth into the provinces by building roads, developing the cross-border economies, improving agriculture.

They used the modern media but not very seriously. Many of their candidates placed much more emphasis on old-style machine politics of local vote-banks and envelopes of money.

By simple electoral arithmetic, the provinces won. Banharn of Chat Thai rose to the premiership. Bangkok held its breath in fear and anticipation.

Banharn Silpa-archa, 1995-6: The 7-Eleven Government

Banharn was the very model of the provincial politician. He made his fortune as a contractor and supplier to government departments. He rose by befriending powerful officials. He built a political base in Suphanburi by securing extraordinary amounts from the national budget for the town's roads, schools, hospitals, and other public facilities.[10]

He became general secretary of the Chat Thai party through generosity which earned him the title of the "walking ATM". He held the two powerful Ministries of Interior and then Finance during Chatichai's "buffet cabinet" of 1988-91. A newspaper quoted his offhand remark that "for a politician, being in opposition is like starving yourself to death".

After 1992, he clambered to the Chat Thai party leadership. Before the 1995 election, he gathered back into Chat Thai many of the provincial boss politicians who had dispersed since the 1991 coup. He promised them a lot. Three were expecting to be awarded the Interior Ministry.

Banharn also promised his cabinet line-up would "not disappoint the people". But three members (including Banharn) were among those investigated as "unusually rich" in the Chatichai era. Two others were sons of Thailand's most famous godfathers. Another three came from Group 16, a faction of young provincial MPs known for their aggressive approach to both business and politics.

The King delivered this new cabinet a stern lecture on the responsibilities of power.[11] Over the next three months, he twice criticized the government for failing to deal with problems of infrastructure. In the inaugural house debate, Chuan warned the ministers to take "not one satang" in corruption.

But the scandals soon emerged. The Chidchob family ran the poor northeastern province of Buriram with an iron hand. Banharn gave Newin Chidchob a deputy ministership in finance. Just before the election, Newin was challenged for intimidating rival bidders on a construction project. During the election campaign, his canvassers were caught stapling eleven million baht in small denomination notes together with Newin's campaign card. Newin's father (also an MP) complained his son was being victimized. Vote-buying, he said, happened in every constituency. As for the bid-rigging, that was "normal business practice".[12]

Suchart Tancharoen, a deputy interior minister, was found to have acquired thirty thousand rai of land in Nong Khai province, while his father had got title to tracts on Samet Island. In both cases, the documents were suspicious and some villagers complained they had been tricked or intimidated.[13]

Newin, Suchart, and two other MPs were found to have taken large loans from the Bangkok Bank of Commerce (BBC). In Suchart's case, the suspicious Nong Khai landholdings had been used as collateral at vastly inflated prices. The loans had been used for leveraged takeovers and share speculation. Suchart insisted he had done "nothing illegal".[14]

Agriculture minister Montri Pongpanich came under suspicion for promoting a suspicious fertilizer scheme and a dam project which would generate big logging profits. A foreign journalist alleged large backhanders in the purchase of submarines.[15] The local press raised similar suspicions about armoured cars. A foreign NGO linked Banharn and other ministers to the illegal flow of timber from Cambodia into Thailand.[16] Some ministers were rumoured to be selling promotions to their subordinates. Cases to recover back-taxes from the "unusually rich" of the Chatichai era were conveniently dropped.[17]

The house speaker and deputy leader of Banharn's party announced that half of all budget project money was lost to corruption: "the budget is like a popsicle that's passed around. Everyone gets a lick at it."[18]

In his inaugural speech, Banharn presented himself as a leader of the poor and of the provinces against the over-privileged city. He also promised to make all Thailand as smart as his home province of Suphanburi. But Banharn had beautified Suphanburi by getting more than the town's fair share from the government budget.[19] This strategy did not work if all provinces tried to do it. But that was what Banharn stood for and what his supporters emulated. Newin openly boasted to his Buriram constituents that he used his deputy ministership to favour the province.[20]

The press dubbed this the "7-Eleven government" – composed of seven parties and eleven factions and, like a convenience store, open for business twenty-four hours.

From the start Banharn was aware that he would face opposition from the city. He pulled two small city-based parties into the coalition and entrusted them with the traffic and economic problems which the city people cared about. But the traffic proved too difficult. And the economy was rapidly sliding into trouble.

In the past, the Ministry of Finance and Bank of Thailand managed the economy relatively free of political meddling. But political pressure had been on the increase. And Banharn increased it further. He chose finance ministers who were weak and dependent on him (see chapter 5). They complied with plans to boost government spending, especially on the construction projects which MPs loved. The budget surplus, which had countered the economy's overheating for the past five years, was converted into gravel.[21] Banharn also drew the Bank of Thailand governor into his schemes to remove uncooperative technocrats and to cover up the looming crisis in the economy.

Under Banharn, the political pressure on economic policy reached a critical stage – partly because the economy was becoming fragile, partly because Banharn's cabinet did not want to be obstructed by strict bureaucrats, partly because Banharn simply did not understand economics or its importance. At an early cabinet meeting, Banharn let slip that he did not know the Thai term for inflation. Later he produced his own solution to inflation – reintroducing small-denomination notes and coins on grounds these would reduce the scale of price rises.

The city's swelling opposition to the Banharn government was focused through the press. Banharn reacted with suppression.

In February 1996, government closed down a TV talk-show and six radio programmes, all run by a Thammasat academic. The TV show, *Mong Dtang Mum* (different perspectives) had pioneered free TV debate on political issues. Banharn had appeared on the show on the eve of election and been asked to name the key figures in his prospective cabinet. He closed the programme down on grounds it was "uncontrollable".[22]

Some TV reporters were ordered off the political beat for asking tough questions. Several radio talk-shows were taken off the air. The Thai-language daily *Siam Post*, which publicized several ministerial scandals, was battered by libel suits and forced to close. The Carabao band had a song banned for sarcastic political references. A leading public poll announced it would stop polling political matters for reasons of prudence.[23]

Banharn was chaining up the guard dogs after letting loose the wolves.

The Mass Communications Organization of Thailand oversaw the government's two TV stations and several hundred radio stations. With the boom in advertising and broadcasting, this had become a highly profitable fief. The Democrats had appointed a talented and honest official, Saengchai Sunthornwat, to sort out the gangs of percentage-men who drained away much of the profit. In April 1996, Saengchai was shot dead gangland-style as he drove home. It was not difficult to work out why he was killed. It was more difficult to identify which of the many candidates had done it. Four gunmen were jailed but no mastermind.[24] The murder seemed to symbolize the age of Banharn. Pirates ruled. Honest men challenged them at their peril.

The political scientist, Chai-Anan Samudavanija, had described a "vicious cycle" in Thailand's politics from the 1940s to the 1980s. At the start of the cycle, popular protest removes dictators and installs a democratic government; after a time, corruption and disorder increases; eventually the military carries out a coup to restore dictatorship; and the cycle returns to the beginning.[25] Did this cycle still revolve? Was this the rise of corruption and social disorder which preceded a coup? By mid-1996, some liberals were voicing fears of a coup.[26] Some conservatives took up the theme of corruption. Anand Panyarachun, who had been premier under the 1991-2 coup regime, labelled the Banharn government as "shameless".

But the coup of 1991 had turned out to be a strategic disaster for the military. Some other method had to be found. Many people began to discuss the need for "political reform" to stem the rise of "money politics". General Chavalit Yongchaiyudh took up the issue. Since he left the army and entered politics in the late 1980s, he had made no secret of his ambition to be premier. Now, borne up by imperceptible forces, he began to rise towards his goal.

In May 1996, the Democrat opposition mounted a no-confidence debate. The Democrat MPs started out with charges on the BBC affair and Suchart's land deals. Before they had time to turn to the prime minister himself, Banharn closed the debate.

Banharn had commanded some residual admiration for his sheer guts and effrontery. When he ducked this debate, admiration dissolved.[27] He reshuffled the cabinet and spilled out promises. But now he was on the run. The opposition demanded another no-confidence debate. It turned the event into a three-day impeachment of the prime minister, broadcast on national television.

The opposition alleged Banharn had plagiarized his MA thesis; fiddled records to avoid charges of being "unusually rich"; profiteered from selling land to the central bank; taken money from those involved in the BBC scandal; perverted the budget process to beautify Suphanburi; awarded infrastructure contracts under suspicious circumstances; and suppressed evidence about his nationality status which would disqualify him as an MP.[28]

At the close of the debate, Chavalit and other ministers threatened to withdraw support and let Banharn face defeat. In a tableau reminiscent of the murder scene from Julius Caesar, Banharn appeared on TV surrounded by his recent supporters. He announced he would resign and call elections instead.

Chuan had stumbled over the emotive rural issue of land. Banharn ran into the problem of a provincial party managing the city-based modern economy. For the city's businessmen and middle class, the modern economy was livelihood. It needed careful tending. But for many of the provincial politicians, the modern economy and the government coffers were lucky dips – for contracts, pay-offs, and paved roads. As the economy deteriorated, the city lobby grew rapidly less tolerant.

The elections focused on the crises created by Banharn's government. The economy was deteriorating fast. The leading election contenders were the Democrats, who had staged the no-confidence debates, and Chavalit, who had served in Banharn's government but then delivered the *coup de grâce*.

The Democrats focused on the economic crisis. They led with the old economic team of Tarrin and Supachai. Their campaign promised to bring economic recovery. They swept the polls in the city where people could feel that the boom was dissolving.

Chavalit concentrated on the political crisis. He promised political reforms which would mean the Banharn era could not be repeated. "What Thailand needs most is a strong political system," he claimed, "with good economy as a back-up . . . My feeling is that if the political system is strong, the economy will be strengthened too."[29]

He took his campaign into the city with a media campaign but failed to win a single seat. In the provinces, he played electoral politics with some skill. The result was a cliff-hanger, decided only when a recount turned a dead-heat into a two-seat margin for Chavalit.

The two no-confidence debates and the heated election campaign had been a remarkable political education. Scandals had long been the stuff of rumour. In the no-confidence debates, they were aired on national television. While previously such crises had brought back the men in green, this transition was managed within the rules of parliament.

But was the result really the same? A general again occupied the premiership.

Chavalit Yongchaiyudh, 1996-7 : A Coup by Other Means?

Chavalit Yongchaiyudh had been a career soldier. In the late 1980s, he was ascending the old ladder of success through the army command to the premiership. But just at *his* moment, the ladder was kicked away. He resigned from the army, entered politics, and in 1992 formed his own party under the crusading title of "New Aspiration".

In the early 1980s, he had helped to formulate politico-military strategy against the communist insurgency. He believed that business profiteering had caused the nation's social and political divisions. He once referred to Thailand's business-dominated political parties as "trading companies".

He believed in strong leadership. He openly admired the military-backed Golkar party in Indonesia. He noted that Deng Hsiao-Ping was effective because he held the Chinese leadership for a long time. He once let slip the idea that Thailand might be better run by a "presidium".

After entering politics, he submerged these views. But he carved out a role as the defender of military-bureaucratic interests against the rising power of parliament. As interior minister under Chuan, he championed the interests of village officers; scrunched decentralization proposals, particularly attempts to make provincial governors elective; and supported better pay and conditions for teachers. As defence minister under Banharn, he manipulated military reshuffles to place his own men in key posts; supported increases in the military budget; defended military chiefs against scrutiny by parliament; and tried to develop new businesses in banking and mobile phones under the Veterans Organization.

Throughout this rise, Chavalit presented himself as an agent of reform. In naming his party, he rejected words like national, development, people, progress which most parties used. "New Aspiration" promised change with overtones of almost religious fervour. Early recruits to the party contained many other ex-soldiers and ex-bureaucrats who felt Thailand needed a new direction.

Over the next few years, Chavalit broadened this base. He contacted businessmen, intellectuals, academics, NGO workers, and pressure groups. He sought support from those who felt Chuan had been a failure and Banharn a disaster. He recruited from across the political spectrum. Several businessmen joined. So did some veterans of 1973-6. By 1996, the party stretched from ex-generals to ex-communists.

In contrast to the polarizing effects of Chuan and Banharn, Chavalit promised to represent the whole of society. Previous premiers, he claimed, had helped only the rich but "I will also be responsible to the poor and the middle class".[30] Later he would say "I view myself as a central link that brings about harmony in society".[31]

But to win power, he had to play the same political game as everyone else. He rose by acting just like another provincial boss. He built an electoral base in a poor and neglected northeastern province by traditional patronage.[32] He log-rolled a majority before the election by welcoming refugees from Banharn's collapsed coalition. One third of his parliamentary party were defectors from other parties, mostly from Banharn's Chat Thai.

His cabinet looked little different from Banharn's. Six ministers were among those investigated in 1991 for being "unusually rich" from the buffet days. Three party financiers were given potentially lucrative ministerial posts. For the first time, cabinet posts seemed distributed across ministries according not to workload but to potential income. The four ministries which spent 60 percent of all budget projects had nineteen ministers and deputies.

Ascending to the premiership, Chavalit was an enigma. Was he just another political soldier who had completed the "vicious cycle" through a coup by other means?[33] Or had he become so compromised by his friends and allies that he was just another provincial boss enmeshed in money politics? Or was he the avenging angel who played the system only in order to gain the power to change it?

In style, Chavalit's government clearly marked a return to a military-dominated pattern. In the first few days, he took personal control over the intelligence services. He put his military men in key posts in the state-run media. He worked with a kitchen cabinet and controlled the agenda of formal cabinet meetings with a firm hand.

The military heads became more outspoken on political topics than at any time since 1992. The military again pressed hard to increase its share of the national budget. Chavalit took all the service chiefs on an official trip to China to inspect hardware. Speaking at the military academy, Chavalit simply assumed future prime ministers would come from the ranks. The annual military reshuffle recovered a lot of its old importance. The old military power blocs resurfaced after a five-year eclipse.

In his first few weeks, Chavalit set out a spectacular agenda of reforms. He welcomed the movement to draft a new constitution and promised to resign when the new system was in place. His secretary announced plans to overhaul the bureaucracy on a scale not seen since the reforms of the 1890s, to shake up the judiciary, and to revise the budgeting system established since the 1950s.[34]

But Chavalit's wish to harmonize the conflicting interests in Thailand's changing society ran into difficulty. He was soon caught in the tension between right and left, city and provinces, the demand for reform and the interests of the old political bosses.

The backing of the military and the local bosses tilted the government to the right. A series of incidents revealed this bias and provoked liberal opposition.

A notorious police officer shot six suspected drug traders within the hearing of several journalists. Despite a press outcry against "judicial killings", government blocked any official investigation.

Chavalit secretly moved to rehabilitate one of the generals disgraced for shooting protesters in 1973. Challenged by the press, Chavalit said the general had shown "efforts to promote democracy".[35] This time the protest forced the government to back down.

Bothered by accusations of election malpractice by his party and in his own constituency, Chavalit lashed out at the retired general who headed PollWatch: "he is so old that death is close, but he likes to act childishly."[36]

Snoh Thienthong, the provincial boss who had led the defection from Banharn, became one of the most high-profile figures in the cabinet. As interior minister, he advocated legalization of cock-fighting, supported a plan to build casinos in Phuket, tried to raise the weight-limit for trucks (his business), revived an old right-wing vigilante organization, and scoffed at every form of protest. On the summary killings of alleged drug-traders, he said: "Frankly, I don't care how many of them die. They must be wiped out."[37] In reaction to media criticism he announced: "The economy is falling apart and it's all because of the word 'freedom' . . . I will resort to any measure to help ensure national stability."[38]

Corruption scandals emerged around several ministers with track records. Projects to buy computer equipment and fertilizer carried suspiciously high price tags. So did contracts for building local roads. Press and opposition laid out details. Chavalit used two cabinet reshuffles to move the suspects out of the firing line.

The ex-radicals enticed into the party by Chavalit's image as a reformer became steadily more uneasy. Some student recruits publicly burnt their party cards.

Chavalit's attempt to span city and countryside ran into similar difficulties.

At the outset, he cultivated rural support with some skill. In the election campaign he presented himself as *luk isan*, a son of the rural northeast. He handled the protest by the Assembly of the Poor more sensitively than his two predecessors (see chapter 8). His cabinet approved a land reform scheme which would provide titles to the millions settled in areas reserved as "forest", and announced an ambitious scheme to develop the poor northeast through infrastructure, industry, and new agricultural technology.

But as the economic crisis consumed more of the government's attention, these rural issues languished. The Assembly leaders were again tangled up in negotiations with un-sympathetic bureaucrats. Cabinet ministers again espoused rapacious plans to build dams in national parks.

At the other end of the spectrum, city support was eroded by the government's failure to combat the deepening economic crisis. In the election campaign, Chavalit promised to form a "dream team" to manage the economy. But many technocrats looked at Chavalit's base of support and recalled what had happened to technocrats under Banharn. Some refused. Some turned off their mobile phones. Some hid. Some left the country. In the usual haggling over cabinet posts, the size of the "dream team" was cut back from five to three, and the members were not so dreamy.

Amnuay Virawan served as finance minister for six months. He resigned when premier and cabinet refused to back a tax scheme to balance the budget. The governor of the central bank quit a few weeks later. Again many senior figures refused to be drafted for the vacant posts. The head of the Thai Military Bank took on the finance post. He resigned after four months when again a tax package was revoked.

As the economy lurched through the finance crisis, the unpegging of the baht, and the IMF bailout, businessmen called on the premier to quit. Chavalit argued that the problems had been inherited from previous governments and that he had been let down by the technocrats. But these excuses did not appeal to businessmen who saw the economy as the government's priority.

As with Banharn, the press focused the growing urban discontent with the premier. And as with Banharn, the government reacted by imposing controls. At first Chavalit attempted an old strategy of holding cosy and slightly intimidating chats with editors. Then some papers were sued. Radio stations were warned about critical chat shows. Subjects were declared off-limits for the news on the four TV stations owned by government and army. A radio programme was closed down.

Government set up a media monitoring centre which combed the electronic and printed media, and fired off intimidatory warnings. When this attempt at censorship only stimulated the appetite for rumours, government mounted a campaign to hunt down rumour-mongers. Reporters who asked searching questions were accused of "creating chaos in this country". The wording echoed the old claim that it was the military's duty to impose order (*khwam riaproy*) over the chaos and confusion (*khwam wunwai*) of uncontrolled political demands.[39]

Ten months after Chavalit had become premier, the issue of constitutional reform brought these growing divisions to a head. The draft charter was ambitious (see next section). It challenged many of the centres of power and influence left over from military dictatorship. It aimed to roll back the "money politics" of the past decade.

The draft deepened the divide in Chavalit's own party between the ex-radicals and the provincial old guard. In the country at large it drove a rift between an establishment of office and privilege, and all those who hoped for change. Chavalit had built his support in the establishment – among military men, officials, village heads, and the local bosses. These interests opposed the new draft. But the deepening economic problems persuaded many people, especially businessmen, to support constitutional reform as one solution to the growing crisis.

In line with his mission of harmony, Chavalit wanted to find a compromise. But over such a polarized issue, the attempt only made him appear two-faced. He prevaricated. He called the drafters of the new charter "dreamers". Then he told *Time* magazine he would support it. Then he led an eleventh-hour attempt to make alterations.

The city press demanded Chavalit resign for mismanagement of the economic crisis, duplicity over the constitution issue, and dependence on the corrupt and conservative old guard. In desperation, Chavalit and Snoh trucked in villagers to provide displays of public support. Snoh argued that the draft constitution was supported by "communists". Chavalit pictured himself as the leader of rural Thais fighting the self-interest of the city:

> "Thai people own this country and allow others to share the land. But when this second group of people loses benefits and doesn't get what it wants, they make noise. . . They want to destroy this land. I want to see my people rise up to protect our country."[40]

Chavalit's vision of harmony had dissolved into the rhetorical divisions of the Cold War, complete with fear of communists and hints of disloyalty among the city people of Chinese origin.

In the face of growing popular support for the constitution, the conservative opposition to the draft backed down. Parliament passed the draft grudgingly. The popular wave now turned against Chavalit. Major business figures and business organizations called on him to quit as his government had lost all chance of restoring investor confidence. Small businessmen and salarymen at the sharp end of the economic crisis joined street demonstrations. Foreign investors and analysts pointed out that politics was getting in the way of any chance of economic recovery. The government's own top technocrat commented: "The only problem we have here is politics."[41] Colleagues in the coalition government moved in for the kill. To buy time, Chavalit prettified the cabinet with ten technocrats. They held office for thirteen days.

Ironically it was the military, which Chavalit had re-habilitated after the 1991-2 debacle, which sapped his power. The military heads succeeded, where Chavalit had patently failed, in persuading a credible technocrat to front the economic team.[42] As Chavalit flip-flopped over support of the constitution, the generals issued a clear approval for the draft. When he proposed a last minute amendment, they forced him to back down to avoid public protest. When he sought assurance of support for his premiership, they withheld. When he proposed a state of emergency to suppress demonstrations, the army chief blocked the move.

The military heads would not risk a repeat of 1991-2. They stayed in the background and repeatedly denied any rumours of a coup. But ministers, lobbyists, and interest groups now called on them every day. The army heads urged Chavalit to accelerate elections under the new constitution. At the inauguration of the reshuffled cabinet, the King delivered the same message. Chavalit undertook to shorten the process from nine months to two or three. Finally the military chiefs also pressed Chavalit to quit.

In late October, Chavalit agreed to step down. His military placemen had turned against him. His coalition partners were lining up to deliver the final blow. Reports had even emerged that the political crisis was making the King sick. The pressure for his resignation had flowed outside the normal boundaries of party political debate. Business and middle-class groups came out in street demonstrations. The quality press argued that no economic recovery was possible without a major change. The cartoons of the tabloid press portrayed Chavalit and his cabinet allies as pirates, jungle animals, dinosaurs, crooks, and clowns.

The Chat Phatthana party tried to maintain the coalition with Chatichai replacing Chavalit as premier. But the cartoons, protests, and press critiques indicated a popular rejection not just of Chavalit but also of the other old-guard politicians. In four parties, younger MPs staged a revolt against their leaders to bring in a new coalition headed by Chuan Leekpai and the Democrat party.

The five months from the baht float to the change of government had been the most heated since the 1991-2 crisis. As the dust settled, it was apparent much had changed. The army had stayed in the background, resisting calls to come forward, and manipulating the political actors from the shadows. The end result was to install the Democrat party, which had a long tradition of opposing military influence. The Democrats had come to power because the urban lobby wanted its economic team (Tarrin and Supachai) to manage the crisis. Many of the old-guard politicians who had dominated the parliamentary scene for the last decade were pushed aside, and others discreetly withdrew.

Chavalit's premiership had turned into a coup by other means, but in an unexpected form. This was a coup *nang talung*, a shadow-puppet coup. The premier had become a shadow projection, jigging to the discordant music of urban protest, manipulated by the generals from the shadows.

Reforming Politics

Thailand's constitution is a battlefield. Since the original charter in 1932, it has been completely revamped eight times. In between there have been numerous amendments, failed amendment attempts, two reversions to the 1932 draft, and many related legal enactments like the political parties laws. Except in the decade when the military totally suppressed parliament, the constitution has been fiddled with constantly.

In 1932, 1946 and 1974, liberals pushed for constitutional reform as a strategy to alter the whole political landscape. Similarly after May 1992, liberal groups pushed for a wholesale overhaul of the charter to usher in the post-military era. The Democrat government passed some amendments but of a limited nature. Reformers protested for more. A famous campaigner staged a hunger strike.

Lawyers, academics, NGOs, and human rights activists argued that although Thailand had some of the forms of a democracy, truly it remained very undemocratic. The state was too strong. Individuals were treated very unequally. Big people could get away with almost anything ("Have we ever seen politicians punished under the current system?"[43]). Little people had little voice, little defence. This was the legacy of a long history of absolute monarchy and military dictatorship. Autocratic habits were built into the mind-sets of the bureaucrats and politicians and into the working systems of major institutions.

The current constitution set out a list of human and civic rights. But then it qualified them as "subject to existing laws". Many of these laws, created under dictatorship, contravened human rights. The reformers wanted a charter which defined human rights and created new judicial institutions to uphold them. Such a charter could act as a base for defending the individual, overhauling outdated institutions, and challenging the power structure.

Against the background of Banharn, the reform movement gathered support and the focus of reform shifted from human rights to the workings of parliament. More people came to feel that Thailand's political development had fallen out of step with its economic success. The provincial bosses used money to buy power and then used power to make money. Little legislation was passed because MPs were not interested. Too little infrastructure was built because the patronage-brokers were squabbling over the spoils. The management of the economy was going to hell because of vested interests.

Ex-premier Anand Panyarachun, who emerged as a leader of this movement, later claimed: "The truth is that the people are sick and tired after 65 years of the current parliamentary system. There is no faith left."[44] The social critic and NGO worker, Dr Prawase Wasi, led a campaign to increase "participation" in the process of reforming the structure of parliament.[45]

The reformers knew that MPs would not amend the charter against their own interests. The reformers demanded drafting by outsiders. The proposal provoked fierce debate which showed that amendment would arouse powerful emotions. Parliament had to compromise. It consented to a drafting process involving an interplay between parliament and outsiders.

The reformers controlled the first stage of the drafting process, begun in early 1997. They put in a charter of rights, three powerful new courts, extensive anti-corruption provisions, and a new blueprint for the parliamentary system. Then they got carried away and threw in a wish-list of other changes. Some clauses tried to dictate the policy of future governments on decentralization, public participation, planning, and environmental management. Others tried to block Thailand's history of coups. The draft was an odd mix of constitutional charter, political manifesto, and historical revisionism.

The document provoked almost everyone influential under the old system. MPs. Police. Military. Judges. Senators. Interior Ministry. Village heads. Many of the objections lodged against the constitution were petty and niggling. But behind them was a broader opposition by the powerful against this spirited challenge.

From the start, the reformers knew they would need public support. They canvassed inputs and opinions through local meetings and opinion surveys. They took the draft on a tour of local reviews. Especially in the provincial towns, meetings were intense and lively. Thousands turned up to listen. Hundreds queued at the microphones to have their say. Participation went far beyond local politicians and activists. Businessmen, professionals, community leaders, and ordinary people took part. The mood was generally supportive. The document might have some quirks and wrinkles. But overall it struck a positive chord among the supporters of this new civic consciousness.

On the other side, the opponents of the draft mobilized through the structures of organized power. Pronouncements by top policemen and military officers. Resolutions passed at meetings of judges and village officials. Statements from the political parties.

The draft was refined and many of the wrinkles removed. But it still promised dramatic changes. It tried to increase the risks and diminish the rewards of treating politics as a business. MPs would have to resign on appointment as ministers. One fifth of MPs would be elected by a form of proportional representation. The senate would change from appointed to elected. Three new courts, an election commission, and a powerful anti-corruption body would check on the abuse of power by politicians and officials. Police, judges, and village heads were relieved of powers which had been too easily abused.

As the drafting process moved towards the final decision, the battle of words became more ideological, more emotional. Anand Panyarachun, who headed the drafting process, claimed the charter would "return power to the people". Banharn complained the drafters had "gone way too far for politicians like me to follow". People around the prime minister sneered at the draft as the work of a gang of French-educated intellectuals who thought they were re-enacting 1789. Conservative opponents claimed the charter gave "too much liberty".[46] It would undermine the monarchy, promote secession, and foment social divisions. The shadowy right-wing group, Apirak Chakri, burned a copy of the draft outside parliament. Snoh Thienthong announced the draft was promoted by communists deploying "the strategy to use towns to surround the jungle".[47]

But popular pressure in support of the draft rose. The press backed it almost unanimously. Many business groups came out in favour. More people had come to understand that the economic crisis had been deepened by bad policy decisions and by corrupt influences. Many invested the draft with the hope for change in the economic trend.

Chavalit had campaigned for election on a platform of political reform. But the draft had run out of his control. He hoped for measures which would strengthen the prime minister by banning no-confidence debates and guaranteeing a four-year term.[48] He was clearly troubled by the draft's attacks on the power of policemen, judges, village officials, and other members of the establishment. He was hostage to the boss politicians who managed his parliamentary majority and who saw the charter as a direct challenge.

But when Chavalit floated the idea of a last-minute amendment, many of the most powerful figures in the land opposed him – the army head, the governor of the central bank, the speakers of the parliament and senate, and the head of the CP conglomerate.[49] On 27 September 1997, the charter draft was approved by parliament with only one MP and sixteen senators voting against. Anand was triumphant: "The quality of politicians will improve. The frauds in elections will decrease and more honest politicians will enter politics. Governments will be more stable."[50]

Wrestling with Democracy

In Southeast Asia in the mid 1990s, democracy was not doing well. Indonesia was a military-backed dictatorship. Cambodia was developing a dictatorial narco-state. Vietnam and Myanmar still had socialist party systems. Malaysia and Singapore favoured one-party regimes. The rhetoric of "Asian values" suggested that democracy was culturally wrong for the region.[51]

Thailand seemed out of step. But with what results? The premiership had become a revolving door. Chatichai. Anand. Suchinda. Chuan. Banharn. Chavalit. An average of eighteen months apiece. Suchinda, Chuan, Banharn, and Chavalit were all hounded out by sharp press campaigns. Political debate at times seemed to be little more than competitive charges of corruption and scandal.

In the early years of the decade, intellectuals were enthusiastic about the development of a "civil society". Five years later, the mood had darkened. Commentators revived the question whether democracy and development were compatible.[52] Chavalit was borne up, at least in part, by forces which sought a return to the certainties of dictatorship.

From 1995 to 1997, urban hopes for change were focused onto the new constitution. But much of its potential lay in the longer term, when legislation and official practice were brought more in line with the principles it laid down. For the short term, the new charter launched torpedoes at some of the worst manipulations of parliament and government, and attempted to tilt the balance of power between the city and provinces.

But was the new charter treating the symptoms rather than the problem?

Thailand's parliamentary democracy is stretched over a sharp divide. Most of the people are in the countryside and most of the wealth in the city. Distributing political power on a headcount basis, even in a very imperfect way, is bound to conflict with the extreme skew of wealth. City and provinces have very different demands from the democratic system.[53]

Chuan and Banharn were both broken over the urban-rural divide. The city-anchored Democrats were brought down over the rural issue of land. Provincial-based Banharn was pilloried for his failure to manage the modern urban economy and to protect it from the depredations of his friends.

Chavalit claimed to bridge the divide. He saw himself as the conciliator between right and left, city and provinces, urban and rural. But in fact his regime was tilted firmly to the right and to the provinces. It was a return to the alliance of generals and godfathers of the 1970s rather than an advance to something new for the millennium. His image of a harmonious orderly society was lifted from the old dictatorial period when order was imposed from above. The image had always been a comforting fiction. It was totally irrelevant to Thailand of the 1990s. It could only be evoked by someone who had spent his career in the regimented society of the military. It exploded when Chavalit himself revived the old anti-Chinese rhetoric.

The spec for a leader of modern, industrializing Thailand is demanding. The leader needs the skills and stature to act as Thailand's representative in the globalizing economy and politics; and also the warmth, accessibility, toughness, and communication skills to appeal to the rural electorate.

Banharn stumbled over the first role. He revelled in chairing a session at the UN, hosting the Asia-Europe summit in Bangkok, and welcoming the English queen. But throughout these appearances, he seemed like a child playing with toys a bit too old for him. Chavalit stumbled over the second role. He claimed the title of "son of the northeast" but failed the first test of speaking the dialect.

The boom and globalization have sharply widened the divisions in Thai society. Thailand needs to develop a political leadership – individual or party – which can span these divisions and which can begin reducing them.

But in many ways, Thai politics advanced a lot between 1992 and 1997. The generals resisted the temptations to intervene. At each election, the leading party won a larger chunk of the seats, and took a more dominant and stabilizing role in the cabinet coalition. The quality of debates improved. Each election brought in more younger MPs with better education (70 percent with a degree in 1995, 73 percent in 1996). Several had been activists in the 1970s. Many others had experienced the political education of those years at a slight remove. The parties were still led by the old guard. But a new generation was rising up to force them aside.

Outside the parliament, the gains were even greater. The press exposed corruption and misgovernment. Many ordinary people had a political education through the series of televised no-confidence debates. The long procedure for amending the constitution mobilized many. The Assembly of the Poor forced a rural agenda into the political arena. The 1997 crisis made many more aware of the close links between politics and the economy.

The convergence of the economic crisis, constitution issue, and Chavalit's decline made the politics of late 1997 especially chaotic. Were these the death throes of a political generation that had failed to keep pace with social change? Like the aftermath of May 1992, the passage of the constitution was another moment of hope.

11 Under the Boom

The boom had a devastating impact on society and environment.

In a decade of boom, the average real income doubled. Many escaped from poverty. But the gap between rich and poor widened very rapidly. In 1981, the top 10 percent of households earned seventeen times as much as the bottom 10 percent. By 1994, the multiple was thirty-seven times.[1]

Over one decade, Thailand became one of the most unequal societies in the developing world.

There were few efforts to limit the impact of growth on the environment. Three decades of boosting agricultural exports stripped away most of the nation's forests. A decade of industrialization brought major problems of pollution.

The government made growth a priority. It shrank from policies about income distribution or environmental protection on grounds that they would slow down growth.

The speed of the economic transformation outpaced non-governmental attempts to cope with the social impact of growth. After a decade of boom, many had come to question the meaning of "development" and to push for change.

Distributing the Gains

Over the decade of the boom, the *average* real per capita income doubled to reach US$2,740 in 1995. In purchasing-power-parity (PPP) terms (which take into account price levels to give more realistic cross-country comparisons), the 1995 figure was US$7,540 – about one-third the level of Japan and two-thirds of Korea.[2]

Most basic social indicators had moved emphatically in the right direction. The infant mortality rate dropped from 22.5 per 1000 in 1971 to 8.3 in 1992. The number of homes with electricity doubled from 43 to 82 percent over the 1980s. The proportion of pre-school children suffering from malnutrition fell from 51 percent in 1982 to 19 percent in 1990. Average life expectancy rose from sixty to sixty-five years over the 1980s.

But in 1994, one-in-ten were still living below the poverty line. And the *distribution* of income had worsened. A lot of people were missing out on the boom.[3]

In the Four Tigers, rapid growth brought better distribution of income. In Singapore and Taiwan, distribution improved throughout the growth phase. In Korea, it zig-zagged – worse for a short time at first but better in the long run.

The Tiger governments used two sorts of policies to improve distribution. First, they prevented rural incomes slipping

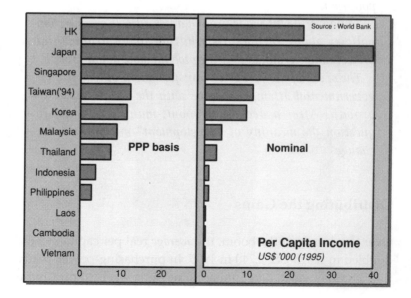

behind the cities by supporting crop prices, spending on rural infrastructure, increasing agricultural productivity, and strengthening the farmers' bargaining power in the market. Second, they evened out urban distribution by investing in education and by increasing welfare and social capital.

In Thailand, the early development efforts paid little attention to distribution. It was assumed the gains of growth would trickle down to the less privileged. In effect the distribution "policy" was the land frontier. Poor peasants could get access to land and hence to income. Largely because of the frontier, and good crop prices, the numbers below the poverty line fell from 57 percent in 1962/3 to 23 percent in 1981.

But the distribution of income grew more skewed. The strategy of agricultural-export-led growth was designed to pull the surplus out of the countryside to build the city. Under this strategy, the income gap between rural and urban grew steadily wider. By 1981, urban per capita income was 2.5 times the rural level.

With the growing income gap went a growing sense of disadvantage, of exploitation. In the 1970s, this resentment fuelled rural support for the communist insurgency and for a spate of protests over crop prices, rents, debt. These protests put the issue of distribution on the policy agenda.

Everyone now took an interest in raising rural incomes. USAID doled out funds for rural infrastructure. Urban politicians promoted schemes to support crop prices. The King and Queen started scores of rural projects. The Bangkok Bank helped design a government scheme to provide rural communities with development funds. The army dabbled in irrigation schemes. The Fourth Plan (1977-81) made poverty alleviation a priority in the interests of "national security". The Fifth Plan included a poverty-eradication scheme which identified the nation's 12,555 poorest villages and provided them with special funds.

But still the economic policy-makers resisted any attempt to change the basic economic strategy. Distribution was not allowed to compromise growth and stability. The anti-poverty projects were just damage control. Some simply did not work. Others had a short-term focus. None were designed to make a serious change in the income gap between village and city.

Once the insurgency had collapsed in the early 1980s, distribution slipped off the agenda again. With the decline in crop prices, the proportion below the official poverty line began to climb again – by one estimate, from 23 percent in 1981 to 30 percent in 1985.[4]

From mid-decade, the urban boom drew all the attention. For many policy-makers, the best way both to grow the economy and to improve distribution was to convert poor, low-productivity peasants into less poor and more productive urban workers. The government closed off the open land frontier. Projects were launched to dispossess farmers who had settled in areas designated as forest reserves. Migration towards the town increased.

After 1986, the numbers below the poverty line began to fall again, down to 10 percent by 1994. But the boom skewed the income distribution further. While many peasants were converted to workers (see chapter 6), over 60 percent of the population was still left behind in the villages. With agriculture stagnant and the city booming, the gap between urban and rural income grew rapidly wider – from around 2.5 times in 1981 to 4 times in 1992.

In the countryside a few families prospered from intensive farming, from trading, from local businesses. But income from agriculture as a whole dropped through the 1980s because of falling crop prices. Rural families struggled to keep up their incomes by earning more off the farm. By 1990, half their income came from outside sources, especially remittance. One in five rural families (almost one in three in the poor northeast) was receiving an average of a thousand baht a month from a son, daughter, or other relative working in the city.[5]

Within the urban economy, too, the income skew increased. At the top end, a few became outrageously rich as businesses boomed and urban land inflated in price. A rather larger handful became very well-off because they had the education and skills which were suddenly in demand. But at the bottom end, the mass of urban-dwellers had little skill or education with which to bargain for a better wage.

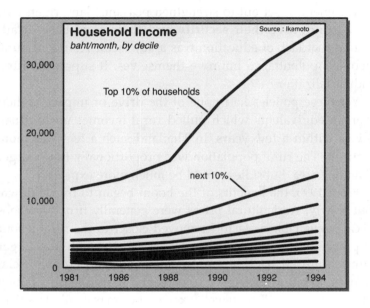

Between 1981 and 1994, the average income of the top 10 percent of the nation's households tripled. By contrast, the incomes of the bottom 10 percent barely changed. The gap between the top and bottom widened from seventeen times to thirty-seven times. *Half of all the income gains of the boom went to just one tenth of the population.*[6]

In the early 1990s, Thailand drifted up the ranking of developing countries with the worst pattern of distribution. By 1994, it had reached the top five, surrounded by Guatemala, Brazil, Honduras, Chile, Colombia, Mexico – countries which had long histories of skewed distribution rooted in slavery, landlordism, and plantation cultures.[7]

The growing gap rekindled rural resentment. The early 1990s saw a growing trend of rural protests (see chapter 8). Once again, protest put distribution back on the agenda.

The post-1992 government returned to policies tried in the 1970s. It paid more attention to supporting rural prices. It increased the flow of development money down to rural local government. It set out to strengthen peasants' land rights as a way to improve their security and their asset base. It admitted that lack of education was a key factor restricting rural people's potential to improve themselves. It supported rural industrialization.

Yet these policies had none of the drive or impact of their Korean equivalents which pulled rural incomes up to urban levels within a few years. In Thailand such a feat was more difficult. The rural population was proportionally much larger than in Korea. Subsidies would be much more expensive.

From 1990, the benefits of the boom began to trickle down. But slowly. Agricultural prices were generally firm. New jobs became available as factories moved closer to the rural labour supply. The growth in urban wages fed through into larger sums remitted back home. In 1992-4, according to official figures, rural incomes grew 10 percent a year. The distribution of income was still massively skewed but marginally less than before.[8]

Yet the economic slowdown from 1996 threatened to halt this trend. The rural poor bear the brunt of urban slowdowns. The postal orders shrink. Laid-off workers come home to share in the family rice bowl. Often that rice bowl has shrunk too.

Poor rural families had become more vulnerable in the boom. Often they had reduced the area cultivated after sons and daughters left for the city. They could not afford the labour-saving machines and expensive input packages promoted by government and agribusiness.[9] They got little benefit from government's price-support schemes which tended to put money in the pockets of merchants rather than farmers. Land titling schemes had become mired in political controversies. The government had made little effort to improve rural productivity as a long-term strategy to overcome the growing income gap.

The boom brought big gains for a small segment of the population. And very meagre gains for the rest.

Environment, Development, People

Over the past generation, Thailand's environment has taken a beating. Forests have been chopped down. The city has become jammed, ugly, polluted. Industrial wastes have poisoned the air, killed off fish in rivers, made some villages scarcely habitable. Some of the country's most beautiful areas have been devastated by tourism.[10]

This has not been the result of simple carelessness. Rather it has been a by-product of the way Thailand has chosen to develop.

Since the 1950s, Thailand's strategy has been to exploit its comparative advantages of abundant land, natural resources, and labour with little thought for long-term sustainable growth. It invited in foreign investment to boost growth. Foreign capital homed in on the resources which could be extracted from Thailand and sold in the markets of the world. Domestic capital took the lead from the foreign investors – linking up with them as joint venture partners or copying what they were doing.

Because the government was committed to economic growth, and because growth was faster when investment was allowed free play, very few restrictions were imposed.

During the phase of agricultural expansion, the government set out a policy to protect the forests. It resolved to keep at least 40 percent of the country under tree cover. It drew maps identifying large areas as "reserved forest". But on the ground it did almost nothing. It stood aside while loggers cut down the trees and peasant settlers swarmed into the "forests" to plant maize and cassava.

In the mid-1980s, agriculture ceased to be important as an engine of growth. Only then did government start trying to reclaim "forests" from the settlers and to protect what remained. By this time, most of the trees had disappeared. Many key watershed areas had been stripped. Two-thirds of cultivated area suffered problems of soil erosion. Erratic river flows increased the incidence of droughts and floods.[11] Logging was formally banned in 1989. Yet over the next six years, another 9 million *rai* of forest disappeared.[12]

Not only trees were vulnerable to agricultural development. Government encouraged farmers to use more chemicals but taught them little about safety. By the 1990s, a Health Department survey found 90 percent of farmers suffering from pesticide poisoning mostly due to cheap and adulterated products.[13]

The pattern was repeated with tourism. Resorts began to develop during the "American era" in the 1960s. When agrarian exports started to flag in the late 1970s, government began to promote tourism. When the second oil crisis wrecked the balance-of-payments, government promoted it harder.

As with the "reserved forests", government pretended to take an interest in protecting the natural and human resources involved in tourism. In fact, it encouraged rapid exploitation. It imposed few planning controls or building restrictions on tourist development. In only twenty years Pattaya was transformed from a set of pretty bays into an environmental disaster. The sea-front was swamped in concrete. The sea filled up with sewage. The ambience was buried under sleaze.

Even when the public complained that tourist businesses were being allowed to develop inside national parks, government usually ignored the protests. The forestry department suggested legalizing such projects because "the resort operators are backed by politicians and influential people. Nobody can evict or punish them."[14]

Again, the human resources suffered as much as the natural ones. While prostitution was technically illegal, government made little attempt to enforce the law because prostitution was a major tourist attraction. The interior minister in the 1960s and the deputy premier in 1980 both publicly championed expansion of the sex industry to promote tourism. For several years government denied the "rumours" of the rising AIDS crisis because they feared it would affect the foreign exchange earnings from tourism.[15] In 1996, the law was modified to penalize patrons of under-age prostitutes more severely. But enforcement was weak. One-in-six women visiting government STD clinics were still aged eighteen or younger.

The pattern of short-term, ruthless development was repeated in the phase of industrialization. Manufacturing firms were attracted to move to Thailand to gain access to good supplies of cheap hard-working labour, and in part also to avoid the environment controls increasing elsewhere. The plunge towards industrialization created new risks for the environment and for the health and safety of those pulled into industrial work.

In 1990, the Thai Development Research Institute (TDRI) reckoned that 55 percent of Thailand's factories produced hazardous wastes and that the volume of these wastes would triple in the next decade. The Ministry of Industry dithered over projects for treatment plants; then decided to privatize; then faced delays when localities protested against siting dumps and treatment plants on their doorstep. A master plan to manage toxic waste was completed only in late 1997.[16]

By this time industry was generating 1.6 million tons of hazardous waste a year. Factories often deposited unmarked containers at municipal dumps. "It was common" said a waste consultant, "to find hazardous waste scattered about even in front of houses or in storage near communities."[17] In the state-owned petroleum corporation, one lone graduate wrestled with the problems of managing the wastes of two large refineries.

In March 1991, there was an explosion at the storage for hazardous materials in the Bangkok port. Twenty-one died. A massive fire destroyed acres of slum dwellings, leaving six thousand homeless. Two thousand residents suffered respiratory and skin diseases for years after.[18]

At an industrial estate in Lamphun, twelve workers died mysteriously. Factory owners and local authorities attributed the deaths to AIDS, even though they had no equipment to establish proof and even though the suddenness of the deaths did not fit the AIDS pattern. Many others believed the more likely agent was hazardous wastes released into the local river. A health worker who championed the case lost her job. An attempt to prosecute the factories failed.[19]

In Lampang, a lignite power plant released so much sulphurous pollution that a shower of rain made thousands in the vicinity fall sick. Even after the plant installed pollution controls, complaints continued. In mid-1996, two-thirds of the children at the local primary school reported sick. Parents suspected the air. The authorities diagnosed a virus. Villagers believed twenty sudden deaths were pollution-related. The authorities cited heart failure.[20]

At the site of the Eastern Seaboard petrochemical complex in Rayong there was a long series of accidents, fires, and leakages resulting in several deaths. In 1997, the air pollution became so bad that forty children at the local school suffered from nausea. A medical team reported that half of the school's pupils and staff had nasal tumors, and most suffered from rashes and dizziness. Investigators found acetic acid fumes resulting from poor waste disposal, toxic residue in the soil, and sulphur dioxide emissions twenty-one times the safety limit.[21]

The water was getting as foul as the air. Surveys in the Gulf of Thailand found high levels of mercury, cyanide, and heavy metals in both water and fish. Unocal admitted releasing ninety kilograms of mercury per year into the sea from its oil-drilling operations. Run-off from waste sites on the Eastern Seaboard was suspected of responsibility for the cyanide.[22]

In the Chaophraya river flowing through Bangkok, domestic and industrial wastes reduced the level of dissolved oxygen close to zero. Residents along the waterways stopped using the water even for washing.[23]

The pollution consequences of headlong development are specially concentrated in the capital. In 1992, the city approved a master development plan. The process of creating the plan had taken thirty years with countless revisions and restarts. The final blueprint was already irrelevant for a city that had multiplied in size and complexity over the past decade.

Transport became the most famous example of the city's dysfunction. On one holiday weekend in 1995, the tailback of vehicles exiting the city stretched 200 kilometres and lasted eighteen hours. The city's most popular radio station features non-stop traffic news and has developed a sideline selling standby in-car urinals. In the late 1980s, government commissioned three above-ground mass-transit systems. Only later did they realize that their routes would have to cross at several points.

The majority of traffic policemen on Bangkok streets suffer from respiratory diseases. Mahidol University reported that the air contained bacteria, fungi, and 3-5 times the acceptable level of dust particles. In some city areas, the lead content in the air has reached dangerous levels. A Health Ministry survey reckoned that all Bangkok street food was contaminated with lead.[24]

"Bangkok is not a place to live," announced the city's governor, "there are fumes, disasters, accidents, uncollected garbage, uncontrolled goods in the supermarket. Big contractors do just whatever they want. Truck drivers drive like hell through the city. This is a jungle, an unorganized place."[25]

The resources most at risk in rapid industrialization are the human ones. At the very bottom of the labour market, illegal immigrants and children work in sweatshops under prison-like conditions. At the next rung up, Thai rural migrants are tipped into the city without the education, experience, or support systems to cope. Even in the relatively organized sectors, labour is poorly defended.

In 1993, the Kader toy factory burned down with the loss of 188 lives. The factory had already suffered a minor fire earlier. Factory inspectors had recommended several changes which had been ignored. Many died simply because the fire doors were deliberately locked to keep them in. Others died because the jerry-built structure began collapsing within fifteen minutes.[26]

The Kader factory had at least been inspected. Many others are not. The labour department lacks both manpower and will. In 1992, safety officers inspected only 4,306 factories, a small fraction of the total number. As many as 2,775 of them were infringing some safety regulation. As few as five were prosecuted. In 1993, 40 percent of the 5,582 inspected factories infringed fire and accident rules, and 20 percent were deemed unsafe on other grounds. The recorded number of industrial accidents had increased by over half in the previous two years.[27] In 1996, the number of industrial workers suffering from environmental illness was estimated as 150,000 or 4 percent of the total. Most problems resulted from exposure to toxic substances. Only a quarter had access to treatment.[28]

This rapid exploitation of human and natural resources has been difficult to resist partly because it is so rapid. Speed is a function of the economy's openness. In any new area of economic opportunity – upland crops, tourism, textile manufacture – the learning process is almost instantaneous. Foreign and domestic investors have access to the world's latest technology. They can import the machines and begin operating immediately in the most efficient manner in the world. The more leisurely process of learning and adjustment in earlier industrializations has disappeared. The society finds it difficult to keep up with the extraordinary pace.

In certain ways the government reacted well to this growing threat. It sponsored research on environmental issues. It encouraged adoption of lead-free petrol through clever pricing. The National Environment Quality Act of 1992 made it easier to prosecute those responsible for damage. The writ of the Science Ministry was extended to include care for the environment. Labour was theoretically protected by a minimum wage law, social security act, and factory inspectorate.

But in practice, enforcement has been poor. In part, this is bureaucratic failure. In part, it results from weakness in legal practice. Attempts to block environmentally damaging projects by bringing cases under the Environment Quality Act regularly failed. The courts ruled that a project could not be proved damaging until it was complete and already causing damage. Judges seemed reluctant to enforce the principle that a polluter should pay for damage caused.[29]

Owning up to AIDS

As elsewhere, AIDS first surfaced in Thailand among gays and drug users in the mid 1980s. At this stage the numbers were small and Thailand had no special significance in the worldwide context of the epidemic.

As elsewhere too, the numbers increased sharply when the virus leapt into the social mainstream. In Thailand, this leap was spectacular, for one key reason: the huge size of the sexual services industry.

Buying women for sex has become part of urban culture. Thai aristocrats used to do it. The single male Chinese migrants did it. Now three-quarters of all urban men have their first sexual experience with a prostitute. Across the whole social spectrum from company executive to taxi driver, men buy girls from cocktail lounges, bars, tea-houses, brothels, and massage parlours as part of everyday socializing. Estimates of the number of women in the sex industry range from 100,000 to two million.[30]

The overlap between the communities of drug users, gays, and sex workers provided AIDS with a bridge into this large sex industry.

For a few years, the authorities tried to deny that anything was happening. Government worried about the impact on tourism which was being promoted hard to earn foreign exchange. In 1989, the prime minister announced AIDS was "no problem" in Thailand.[31]

Both officials and businessmen clung to the fantasy that AIDS was a *farang* disease which somehow spared Asians. One university imposed an AIDS test on its foreign but not its Thai staff. Some massage parlours turned away *farang* at the door.

When the international publicity made the issue unavoidable, authorities still tried to protect the sex tourism industry. First they suggested sex workers found to be HIV-positive should be arrested. Later they insisted sex workers have regular health checks and carry a card. The official stamps presumably would make the client feel his safety was guaranteed.

By the end of the 1980s, the statistics brought this phase of denial to an abrupt end. Some surveys among groups of sex workers found HIV incidence in the range of 40-50 percent. A sample of all males aged 20-22 found 1.7 percent. Between December 1990 and June 1991, the percent of pregnant women infected with AIDS jumped from 0.3 to 0.7.

Mechai Viravaidya, whose birth control campaigns had made *mechai* the Thai translation of condom, predicted that Thailand would have up to 4.3 million HIV-positive by 2001. Thailand had become one of the major centres of the AIDS epidemic.

Government began to campaign against AIDS. It targeted its efforts against gays, drug users, and sex workers. But it kept mass publicity at a minimum level. Tourism still mattered to the economy.

NGOs worked directly with sex workers to popularize condoms. Government traced HIV-positive patients back to brothels and closed them down – encouraging the sex industry to adopt condom use for survival.

In upper urban society, there was a rapid adjustment. Suddenly it was no longer acceptable to entertain clients or colleagues by escorting them to a massage parlour.

But thousands of urban men still bought women on a regular basis. Indeed, rising incomes increased demand. Many men reacted to the growing scare with small and not very sensible changes in habit. Some sought out very young girls in the belief this would improve their odds against infection. Some frequented flashy member clubs, presumably in the belief that the expensive décor guaranteed the girls would be clean. The trade in under-age girls boomed. Member clubs sprung up all over the city.

The epidemic hit hardest at the lower levels of urban society, where the government's discreet publicity and targeted campaigns failed to get through to either sex worker or client. The highest incidence rates were found among hilltribe girls and illegal immigrants drafted into the cheapest level of the sex industry. Infection rates among army recruits ran at around 3 percent. In some northern areas, they peaked at 14 percent.

But the campaigns began to work. Condom usage grew from 10 million to 170 million over a decade. From 1990, the Department of Public Health's annual count of sex workers started to trend gradually downwards for the first time. By 1994, the rates of HIV infection among new births and military recruits peaked and fell back slightly.

Mechai's projection now had to be revised downwards, partly because of these moderate successes, but more because the projection had been based on assumptions disproved by new knowledge of the disease. By 1996, Thailand had an estimated 6-800,000 HIV-positive, 39,161 AIDS cases, and 10,864 deaths. By 2000, the number of HIV-positive cases was expected to reach one million and of AIDS-related deaths, 100,000 a year.[32]

Many feared that the moderate success would lead to complacency. Mechai still predicted a huge social and economic impact: "The tourism industry will collapse and . . . hotels will be changed into hospitals."[33]

But some things never change. In 1997, the minister of interior advised Phuket officials to spruce up the massage parlours and staff them with younger masseuses to boost tourism.[34]

Above and Beyond the Law

To some extent, pollution and environmental destruction are by-products of a crude and primitive phase of industrialization.

In 1992, the Industry Ministry found that two-thirds of all factories in a province adjacent to Bangkok flouted pollution standards. "The air quality", according to a researcher, "is the worst in the Kingdom, and smog levels are often higher than in Los Angeles." The ministry ordered five hundred factories to relocate to new industrial estates. The local chamber of commerce, led by a steel magnate, simply refused to comply.[35]

The province, on the outskirts of Bangkok, was infamous in many ways. Originally a fishing village, it had developed into a smuggling port and sweatshop centre with a lively nightlife of gambling dens and brothels. One family dominated the town's politics, contributing three of the six MPs and acting as a political broker for the surrounding region. The patriarch had been accused of involvement in oil smuggling, refused a US visa on suspicion of drug trading (which he denied), and involved in casino developments on the Burmese border.[36] In the early 1990s, he vied to become the interior minister in charge of the nation's law and order.

He was far from unique. Indeed, he missed the interior post because two very similar figures from other regions also wanted the job.

Entrepreneurs are often tempted to cut corners in the race for profit. The boom years, with new opportunities opening up on all sides, encouraged a ruthless approach to accumulating capital, to getting rich quick by any means.

Some businessmen drifted across the fuzzy line dividing legal and illegal businesses. After the government banned logging in Thailand's forests in 1989, some logging companies continued operating furtively. Others transferred to logging across the borders in Burma, Laos, and Cambodia, often under agreements negotiated by big military figures. Who was to tell which logs had been legally or illegally brought across the borders and which had originated in Thai forests?

The borders housed some other profitable trades. As fighting eased in Cambodia in the early 1990s, miners flocked across to prospect for gems under concessions offered by the Khmer Rouge. The decline of fighting in Cambodia left a stockpile of arms which was in high demand by minority groups fighting the government in Burma. A profitable trade developed in ferrying guns, ammunition, and SAM missiles from the eastern to the western border. Some of the stock was sold into the local market of professional gunmen.

Others dabbled in illegal businesses which expanded with the demand generated by the boom. After government liberalized the oil industry in 1991, smuggling of diesel oil grew rapidly to two billion litres a year, about one-seventh of total demand. Tankers sailed up the gulf and offloaded onto modified fishing boats which delivered the stock to small ports.

Trading in heroin and marijuana had become well established during the Vietnam war. The heroin trade declined as more of the product of the Golden Triangle was exported through China. But amphetamine trading more than compensated. Pills were first manufactured in the central region. Later the supply was taken over by Burmese groups experienced in the heroin trade.

Amphetamines were first popular among truck-drivers incentivized to extend their working hours. But from 1995 usage spread to students seeking a high, slum-dwellers seeking escape, and manual workers seeking a relief from pain. In 1997 police projected a market volume of 200 million pills.

Traffickers dealt not only in drugs but people. Some gangs specialized in exporting Thai women to work illegally in the sex trade in Japan, Taiwan, Malaysia, Singapore, Germany, and the USA. Others brought sex workers and other cheap labour into Thailand from Burma and other neighbouring countries. In the international business of trafficking in people,

Thailand acquired a reputation as a good staging post. Workers were brought out from China to Bangkok for onward shipment. South Asians were infiltrated into Malaysia across the southern border. Gangs used Bangkok as a clearing house for East European and Filipina sex workers.

Other entrepreneurs tapped the super-profits from entertainment businesses which were well-established in society but criminalized by government. Notably, prostitution and gambling. In the boom, the sex trade grew in size and complexity. The public health ministry identified twenty-five different categories of outlet ranging through massage parlours, brothels, restaurants, barber shops, tea-houses, member clubs, karaoke parlours, a-gogo bars, discos, beauty parlours, and escort services, besides a growing part-time involvement of students, factory workers, and salesgirls.

Gambling dens range from large fortified casinos to small "flying" card schools. The underground lottery, in which participants bet on various number combinations of the twice-monthly official lottery draw, has become one of the country's largest businesses with sales networks reaching into every office and village. The new middle class has taken to gambling on international football results aided by satellite television, mobile phones, and electronic bank transfers.

A study reckoned the major illegal businesses generated value-added of 300 to 450 billion baht a year, equivalent to between 8 and 13 percent of the legitimate economy.[37]

Big people invest some of the super-profits of illegal businesses in gaining respectability. One big gambling entrepreneur gave generously to teachers' colleges and was rewarded with an honorary degree presented by the King. Three months later he died when his car was ambushed by assault rifles.[38]

Big people also invest in political protection. Many support politicians and work as vote-banks. Some stand for political office. A northeastern MP was charged in the US for importing tons of marijuana. A general was convicted in Hong Kong for heroin trading. At least three prominent MPs were refused US visas on suspicion of drug trading. In 1996, two political parties exchanged counter-charges on which had more members involved in oil-smuggling.

Big people also invest in gaining immunity from the police. The nature of the police service makes it highly susceptible. For a long time, the government has paid low salaries and tacitly expected the police to augment these in traditional fashion by raising fees for protection offered and services rendered. Over time, these systems of self-remuneration have grown very elaborate. Some policemen collect fees for carrying out their duties and justify these fees on grounds of their low official pay. Some also collect larger fees for *failing* to carry out their duties. They raise unofficial licence fees from all kinds of illegal and semi-legal businesses – ranging from the motorcycle taxi services on every Bangkok soi, to major drug-running operations. Many of these collections are amalgamated and redistributed within the force.[39]

In early 1997, a provincial policeman shot several colleagues and then himself. His family and friends claimed he had lost patience with the corruption: "The police station here functions like a big company. . . . The money comes from raids against *ya baa* (amphetamines) selling rings, gambling dens, and illegal goods smuggling. All in all, several hundred thousand baht a month."[40] Police authorities claimed he was just unstable and refused to investigate the allegations. Ten thousand local people turned out for his funeral.[41]

The organization of these payments can be sophisticated. Truck-drivers regularly pay police to ignore overloading. Collecting these fees is messy – countless roadblocks and other clumsiness. A businessman persuaded the police and trucking industry to regularize the arrangement. He sold window stickers which allowed overloaded trucks to sail through police checkpoints.[42]

Not all policemen are involved in these money flows. But the flows are large and pervasive enough to affect the overall operation of the force. As revealed by a large-scale public poll in 1993, the police are viewed as the most corrupt part of a generally corrupt bureaucracy.[43]

Some police progress from levying protection fees to participating personally in the illegal economy. One officer was sacked for allegedly managing amphetamine factories across the border in Laos. The police chief on the southern border organized special welfare for his men because "I don't want my men earning a living at brothels and gambling dens or from smuggling".[44]

The Saudi jewellery affair cut some narrow windows into the inner working of the police. A Thai migrant worker stole a large quantity of jewellery from the Saudi Arabian palace and shipped it home. When the police arrested the thief, they promptly stole most of the jewels for themselves. Several gangs of policemen then fought to control the loot. As the scandal started to surface, they killed one another to cover their tracks. When the affair was concluded, they competed to put one another in jail.

The softness of law and police tempts big people to believe they can get away with anything. The risks which this creates for little people and for natural resources are huge.

A Just Society?

As society becomes more industrialized, the framework of law and justice becomes more important in regulating the relations among individuals, and between the individual and the state. As Thailand rushes towards industrialization, the legal-judicial framework cannot keep pace. In the absence of law and law-enforcement, might equals right.

In traditional society, there was no concept of individual rights guaranteed by the state, only duties such as the obligation to provide forced labour, to serve in the army, to pay tax. People sought justice by calling on the mercy of the king or begging for the help of an aristocratic patron. The modernizing bureaucrats who overthrew the absolute monarchy in 1932, immediately sat down to write a legal code to replace the feudal structure. The 1932 leader, Pridi Bhanomyong, had studied law in Paris. He used the French code as his model.

From the late 1930s to the 1980s, military governments prevailed. The impetus to modernize the law codes slackened. Pridi's hurried initial effort became less and less relevant to the rapidly changing society. Much of the activity of urban society was not covered by the codes and remained out of reach of judicial arbitration.

Some legal innovations tended to strengthen the power of the state at the expense of the individual and the local community. Earlier law codes, for instance, recognized villagers' customary rights over unoccupied land used in common as community forests and grazing lands. But later laws about forests, highways, mines allowed government departments to lay claim to lands which had no title deed.

The schedule of penalties renders many laws ineffective. In the 1970s, for example, the courts ruled that a Bangkok hotel had infringed building control laws. The maximum penalty it could impose was a fine of 2,000 baht per day. The hotelier happily paid the daily fine and went on running his illegal hotel. When the Phoenix factory polluted forty-two kilometres of the Phong river – killing the fish stocks, poisoning rice fields, and depriving many villages of drinking water – the maximum legal penalty was a 10,000 baht fine or single month in jail.

After the firmer establishment of parliament in the 1980s, the pace of legislation quickened. But it had a long way to catch up, especially given the gathering speed of social and economic change.

Moreover, the impact of legislation depends on how well it is enforced. Thailand's judicial process is not famously efficient.

Like the law codes, the judiciary was modelled on French practice. Although technically separate from the main bureaucracy, it is perceived as part of the same machine and susceptible to the same corruption. Distance, delay, and cost make the courts relatively inaccessible for the ordinary man.

In the early 1990s, the judiciary split into two factions backing rival claimants for the top judicial post. The prime minister (Anand) intervened to settle the dispute. After leaving office he was subject to the harassment of a court action by a member of the losing faction. A famous architect with a gangsterish past was charged with the attempted murder of one of the rivals. The onlooking public could be forgiven for doubting whether such a judiciary would be fair and just.

The administration of criminal justice is especially notorious. Police can detain suspects for long period. They have sole control over investigation, wide powers of search, and a reputation for extracting confessions. Suspects are often forced to re-enact the alleged crime for the benefit of the press, so they appear guilty even before trial. The decision to proceed with a case rests with public prosecutors and the Attorney-General, with no provisions for review and no accountability.[45]

Some cases seemed to be dropped too easily. After the respected administrator Saengchai Sunthornwat was murdered, a powerful figure was arrested but the case was dropped. The public prosecutor said the police had refused to dig up enough evidence. The police said the evidence was sufficient and the prosecutor had given up too easily.[46]

In other cases, convictions seemed driven by mysterious forces. In 1986, four men were convicted of murder on the shaky evidence of one tuk-tuk driver. One of the four died in jail, another became disabled, and a third died from tuberculosis. A decade later, the case was reopened, the four pardoned, and a leading businesswoman convicted.[47]

Because of the deficiencies of law codes and judicial process, much of the day-to-day arbitration of justice falls to the police. To this day, most petty disputes, and many big ones too, are settled by individual police officers. In small matters, the summary justice dispensed by the police can be socially sensitive. Over traffic accidents, minor injuries, and small-scale civil disputes, the officer often penalizes according to the ability to pay. But over larger matters, money and power become the dominating factors.

The judicial system is heavily biased in favour of the rich and powerful. Straightforward corruption – money paid to policemen, prosecutors, judges – plays a large part in this. But there are also forces that run deeper.

The rich and powerful are reluctant to punish one another. This tendency has its roots in the traditional society of lord and slave. Lords protected the social division by protecting one another. The tendency has been modified and sustained through half-a-century of military-bureaucratic domination.

When big people are found doing wrong, they are rarely punished. Elite society may isolate them, push them out of sight, restrain them from doing further wrong. But it usually saves them from public confirmation of guilt, punishment, humiliation. Court proceedings drag on and peter away. Bureaucratic investigations fail for lack of evidence. Accused parties simply disappear. Often this tendency is attributed to Thai tolerance, a Buddhist distaste for retribution. But it also reaffirms the equation: might=right. The powerful can do anything.

The bureaucratic polity codified this tendency. It is especially difficult to bring a case against members of the bureaucracy itself. The procedure is clumsy and the public prosecutor can unilaterally decide that there is no case to answer. Few suits survive this obstacle course and hence very few people even try it. The 1994 constitutional amendments introduced an administrative court to simplify the procedure. But the ambit of the court was defined very narrowly and the amendment never implemented. Usually the worst fate for an errant senior official is to be "removed to an inactive post".

The military has always insisted that soldiers should not be punished by civil process. When a soldier gets caught, the military demands the right to inflict its own rules and punishments. This practice extends right up to wrongs committed by soldiers in their struggles to control the state. Coup-makers have rarely been punished.

The weakness and partiality of law, police, and judiciary are regrettable in themselves. They become more critical as more people are pulled out of village communities and dumped into the city. In the village the community provided some measure of justice and social protection. In the city, people are forced to rely more on the provisions of the state.

This reliance does not make them feel secure. This emerged as a minor theme of the political crisis of May 1992. Young members of the urban underclass were some of the most enthusiastic participants in the demonstrations. They are the most vulnerable to the petty tyrannies and exactions of police and bureaucrat. Truck-drivers and motorcyclists are routinely subjected to minor harassment. During the nights of the demonstrations, gangs of motorcyclists tore round the city smashing up police boxes, traffic lights, and other symbols of police authority.

As a first step of legal reform, human rights groups campaigned to include a better definition of civic rights in the constitution. The constitutional amendment of 1994 made some progress, but not much. The statement of rights was still highly restricted. The constitution also defined civic *duties* which took precedence. It laid down that existing law codes overrode these constitutional rights. And it included a conditional clause which gave the state considerable scope to restrict attempts to exercise these rights.[48]

The project to reform the constitution in 1996-7 concentrated as much on human rights and judicial systems as on the parliamentary framework. The drafters revised and extended the code of human rights; invented three new courts to overcome the difficulty of charging errant politicians and bureaucrats; restricted police powers; and introduced more accountability for judges and prosecutors.

Power to the People

From the 1970s, public concern grew over forest destruction, uncontrolled tourism, pollution, land scandals, corruption, and abuse of power. But until recently movements to impose any social restraint on development ran into fierce resistance. During the long period of military dictatorship, popular movements were readily branded as dangerous, treasonous, communist. Only since the collapse of the Cold War and military dictatorship have organizations begun to grow.

The first NGOs appeared in the 1970s but were crushed after the return of the military in 1976. The movement grew strong only from the early 1980s onwards. The NGOs offered resistance to the mainstream development strategy in four ways.[49]

First, some NGOs attempted to open up alternative development paths. They promoted appropriate technology to replace capital-intensive inputs, mixed farming to replace export-oriented monoculture, community-based organizations to reduce reliance on the market.

Second, some attempted to provide better social and environmental protection. They helped local movements to resist the assaults on the natural environment by businessmen and by government. They created civic groups to give more shape and vision to urban development.

Third, they supplemented the government's skeletal social services. They organized medical services, legal education, schools, and welfare services for the villages and slums.

Fourth, they put pressure on government to change policies – to protect the environment, to control industrial wastes, to allocate forests for community use rather than plantations, to improve labour legislation, to codify civic rights, to liberalize the media.

Much of the force of the NGO movement came from the idealism of the 1973-6 generation. Much of the financing of the movement came from abroad – from international religious and charitable foundations like Redd Barna, the Catholic Council for Development, and the World Wildlife Fund.

This idealism and this funding were the foundations of the movement's success but also the source of its vulnerability. Some military conservatives argued that the NGO movement was run by ex-communists on foreign funds – with implications of outside interference, hidden agendas, and treasonous disloyalty.[50]

In the mid-1990s, the NGO movement went through a crisis. Internally it was racked by an argument over strategy. Should the movement concentrate on local-level work in the villages and slums? Or should it concentrate on trying to change government policies and development strategies? The first (local) route often seemed futile in the face of the powerful forces of industrialization. The second promised to draw the movement back into political confrontation.[51]

At the same time, the movement faced a funding crisis. Some foreign financiers moved away as Thailand moved up the income scale, and countries like Vietnam, Laos, and Cambodia demanded their attention. Many NGOs tried to replace diminishing foreign sources with funds from Thailand's own rising business community. But business donations often came with too many strings attached. Business donors often bridled at the NGOs' wish to restrain the profit principle in pursuit of social benefits.

But the crisis passed. Some international donors stayed on, notably Canada and Denmark. Japanese funding increased. A few Thai companies provided support. More and more money came from government agencies.

The debate over strategy faded. There was plenty of space for different NGOs to play different roles without arguing over which were best. Some organizations became more involved with people's movements in agitations over dams, forests, land, pollution, and waste sites. Others began to work alongside government bodies in health care, slum development, and rural projects. Others became a more established part of policy making. Key figures in the NGO movement played leading roles in the creation of the new draft constitution and of the NESDB's Eighth Plan.

By the late 1990s, Thailand's NGO movement had come of age. It was well-established and no longer under threat. It had a group of wise old leaders who nurtured the movement's vision and served as the movement's voice in the halls of power. It had a network of communication through publications, committed press journalists, and personal contacts. Above all, it had a vision of development done differently which was gradually but relentlessly gaining greater support.

The Eighth Plan

" . . . rapid economic growth has had negative effects on Thai culture, traditional ways of life, family community and social values . . . development based only on economic growth without due consideration of human family, community, social and environmental dimensions cannot be sustained in the long run. If no corrective actions are adopted the people and nature will not be able to coexist harmoniously."[52]

The preamble to the *Eighth National Economic and Social Development Plan (1997-2001)* promised rather more than a standard five-year plan. It claimed to be "a first step towards . . . achieving the long term vision of an ideal Thai society".

The making of the Plan had been unique. The planning board teamed up with an NGO umbrella organization. Together they held nine regional seminars inviting local NGO leaders, development workers, academics, businessmen, community leaders, monks, and bureaucrats. The results were then summarized in a tenth national seminar, compiled by the NGO side into a People's Development Plan, and refined by technocrats into the final version accepted in March 1996. As a planning process, this was a world first.

The planning board inserted a classic macroeconomic plan into the heart of the document. Thailand needed to improve competitiveness and increase savings in order to reduce the current account deficit and sustain annual growth at eight percent.

But this traditional plan was wrapped in a vision of dramatic change, "shifting from growth orientation to people-centred development". The main focus was on development of human resources through education, health care, and social welfare; more equitable sharing through regionalization, participation, and community rights; and rehabilitation of the environment through better management and greater local participation.

The result would be a Thailand which integrated into the globalizing world but remained a society in which "all people learn to live together in an enlightened way, with mutual care for each other, in harmony, peace, justice and freedom; in other words, as Thais."

The authors of the Plan pointed out that the biggest barrier to this vision was the government itself, marked by "very centralized power structure, administrative inefficiency, lax law enforcement, lack of popular participation, unethical and unfair use of administrative power, lack of administrative accountability, and lack of continuity in policy and implementation".[53] Achieving the Plan's targets would need an overhaul of the bureaucracy, and implicitly of politics too, to achieve "good governance".

Within months of the Plan's launch, the eight percent growth target had become a dream. The IMF was in command of the economy. The budgets for the Plan's visionary schemes were being slashed.

The NGOs had stormed the heights of policy planning but found them dwarfed by a much bigger mountain.

Under the Boom

Some did well out of the boom. Some much less so.

Rapid economic growth often leads to greater inequality. But globalization tends to exaggerate the gap. The age of globalization discriminates between those equipped to seize its opportunities and those limited by their education, experience, location, assets.

For society's top ten percent, incomes tripled, amenities increased, horizons expanded to embrace the globe. They became enthusiasts about globalization, development, and all things modern. For those with more ambition than ethics, the careering boom years offered opportunities to get rich very quick, often at the expense of others and of the natural environment.

Further down the social scale, the income gains were modest. At the bottom, they were meagre. Moreover, at these lower levels, the boom often brought greater insecurity. Livelihoods were threatened by land-grabbers, polluting industries, government development projects, damaged ecology. Little people were deprived of the old social safety nets of the village and exposed to a social framework which favoured the wealthy and powerful. Often they stayed afloat by desperate measures. Constantly migrating from job to job. Entering risky occupations. Hocking their daughters. Banding together to defy the rich and powerful.

But by the mid-1990s, there was a strong counter-force, a growing civic and social consciousness expressed mainly through the NGO movement. It pitted localism against globalism, participation against authority, Buddhist moderation against ruthless development. Its networks reached from the village to the councils of power. And it was beginning to make a difference.

12 Boom, Bust and Beyond

Boom

In the mid-1980s, most observers had Thailand marked down as one of the also-rans of Asian development. *Thailand's boom came as a surprise.* No-one in the mid-1980s predicted that Thailand would be the fastest-growing economy in the world over the next decade.

But Thailand did not boom alone. Southeast Asia as a whole was doing well. Indonesia and Malaysia grew almost as fast. A large zone of southern China grew faster. Vietnam changed gear. The Philippines lifted out of a long slump.

Clearly this was not a matter of chance. Economists, business analysts, and sociologists competed to offer explanations.

Some like the World Bank pointed to government policies and the magic of the free market. Unlike in the earlier development strategies of South Asia and Latin America, successful Asian governments had not interfered too much in the working of the economy. They had liberalized markets, invested in infrastructure, removed a few distortions, and let capitalism work.

Others asked *how* governments had been able to achieve such successful policy-making which had eluded other countries. They pointed to a special model of a "developmentalist state", a firm and often dictatorial government prepared to back business to make the economy grow.

Yet others sought a deeper, sociological explanation for the behaviour of Asian businessmen and rulers. They argued that Confucianism played the same role in Asian capitalism that

Protestantism had played in Weber's model of Europe. Both placed a high social value on hard work and business success.

But all these explanations ran up against one basic difficulty: the variety of Asia, the big differences between countries. The World Bank's model fit some countries better than others. Korea might be described as a developmentalist state, but not southern China. It was difficult to claim that a Confucian ethic of capitalism stretched all the way from the South China Sea to the Indian Ocean.

Many Asian countries were doing well *not* because they were all doing the same thing but rather because they were all linked. By simple proximity. By increasing flows of trade, money, ideas, and people. And most of all by the shared influence of Japan.

Since the 1930s, Japanese economists had predicted that Japan's growth would radiate across the region, launching other economies as a flock of "flying geese" behind the Japanese leader. Yet Asia's late-century boom differed from this prediction in two important ways.

First, speed. In the 1980s, barriers to the movement of capital and labour dropped. Markets for technology, skill, and capital funds became more open. The potential – and often the imperative – for firms and money to migrate to new locations increased.

Second, complexity. From the 1980s onwards, Japan was not the only source of the region's dynamism. The Four Tigers had their own momentum. The opening of China created an economic tug very different from that of Japan but in many ways just as powerful.

By the 1990s Asia looked less like a neat echelon of flying geese, and more like a diverse mass migration – the elegant Japanese goose, the lumbering Chinese albatross, the little humming birds of Singapore and Hong Kong, the boisterous ducks of Taiwan and Korea, the fledglings of Thailand, Malaysia, and Indonesia – each flapping in its unique way, but together creating a slipstream that carried them all along.

But Thailand still grew faster than the others, faster than before, faster than the experts predicted.

There were external reasons. Japan had been cultivating its links with Thailand for many years. Foreign investment flowed into Thailand after the mid-1980s realignment of Asian currencies because foreign investors liked Thailand's combination of relative political stability and relatively cheap labour.

But local factors in Thailand multiplied the impact of the foreign investment inflow.

The shift of foreign capital to Thailand was dwarfed by the boom in domestic investment. Local entrepreneurs competed and cooperated with foreign firms for the opportunities in export-oriented industrialization. They seized opportunities in the rising home market. Some leveraged their expertise into other rising markets in China and the Southeast Asian region.

Migrant Chinese communities are scattered across the port cities of the region. In Bangkok, the Chinese have enjoyed some unique advantages. First, they have integrated well into the local society. Thai Buddhism posed no barriers to conversion and inter-marriage. But more important, Thailand has a long tradition as an open trading economy that absorbs immigrants with useful skills. Much of the traditional ruling class has some overseas origins. The rulers welcomed the migrant Chinese because they made the economy grow. They insisted only that the migrants leave their politics behind.

Second, the position of the Bangkok Chinese was not complicated by the strains of colonialism and decolonization. Elsewhere the migrant Chinese were hounded as fellow travellers of colonialism, or persecuted by the ethnic nationalism that followed decolonization. Thailand felt some backwash from these movements in the region, but it was temporary. From the 1940s onwards, the descendants of the Chinese came more and more to dominate the city, its commerce, and eventually its politics and urban culture.

Among all the groups in the Nanyang diaspora, the Bangkok Chinese were uniquely secure.

From the 1940s they prospered on the momentum of a world economy freed from colonialism and pulled along by the prosperity of the USA and Europe. They deployed tactics commonly found amongst Chinese (and other) migrant communities. They saved hard. They cooperated to share risks and opportunities. They suborned the rulers to win access to the best profit opportunities.

Between the 1960s and 1980s, most of the great corporate families went through a transformation. A new generation emerged to take over or share in the management. They had been educated in the USA or Japan. They were more likely to read *Fortune* than *Sin Sian Yit Pao*. They got experience working in joint ventures with the multinational firms arriving to exploit Thailand's protected home market.

When Thailand turned towards export manufacturing and foreign investment, the business community had reached a certain maturity and achieved a critical mass. The leaders of domestic business pushed for the policy change because they sought wider horizons.

By tradition they looked outwards. They had come from overseas. Their success was grounded in trade. They had learnt how to gather in skill, technology, funds from the outside world. They had a track record of working in partnership with the Japanese (and Taiwanese) firms that flooded overseas after the Plaza Accords. They had connections back to the mainland that became more important as a source of dynamism in the 1990s.

This outward orientation was key to the speed at which the Thai economy changed from the early 1980s onwards. In just fifteen years, the economy's main export emphasis moved from crops; to services; to labour-intensive manufactures; to medium-tech manufactures. Local firms rode this roller-coaster by saving and investing more; by securing overseas technology through purchase or partnership; by importing skills; and by supplementing capital from world financial markets.

The businessmen were helped along by government.

In the 1960s and 1970s, Thailand acquired a reputation as a "soft" state with "passive" economic policies marked by highly conservative fiscal and monetary management. When Thailand boomed, some assumed that the government's main contribution was its conservative macro-management. They claimed Thailand's success as a victory for laisser-faire.

Hardly. Thailand acquired a reputation for passive economic management because its policy-makers were doing something different, not because they were doing nothing. In the 1960s and 1970s they concentrated on growing *agricultural* exports. They rigged markets, offered firms incentives, provided cheap credit, subsidized exporting, sponsored technology – all the things that the Tigers were doing to grow industrial exports.

After 1985, they moved quickly to show much the same enthusiasm for promoting *industrial* exports. They managed the baht downwards, revised taxes and tariffs, expanded the financial markets, offered investment incentives, provided some cheap credit, redrew the labour markets, reoriented foreign policy, and reshaped macro-management.

Thailand's technocrats are not much different from those in the Tigers. They see their job as making the economy grow. In the 1960s and 1970s, Thailand's large reserves of land made agricultural-led growth an easier and more promising option than the Tigers' dangerous leap towards industry. Twenty years later, the outlook had changed. The limits of agriculture-led growth were clear. The possibilities of export industrialization had been revealed by the Tigers. Once the technocrats had seen how much the 1984 devaluation boosted industrial exports, they accepted that industry could play the role which agriculture had long played in spearheading Thailand's open economy.

But unlike in the Tiger economies, Thailand's entrepreneurs did not have to be bribed and bullied to embrace export-led industrialization. *Thailand's boom was powered by the animal spirits of private business.* Bangkok's businessmen hooked onto a powerful trend in the international economy. The government supported them where necessary and restricted them hardly at all.

Bust

Thailand's bust in 1997 also came as a surprise.

It was no surprise that the boom came to an end. Only a few were mesmerized into believing that Thailand would escape the business cycle. Many had predicted that Thailand's engine of export growth would falter because of rising wages, increased competition, and the strain on infrastructure and human resources. From 1994 on, export growth had faltered and the current account deficit widened.

The downturn of 1996-7 was not a surprise. But the severity of it was. So was the impact on the region and the world. The growth rate fell lower than in any year since reasonable statistics had been compiled. The collapse of the baht triggered a currency crisis across the region.

The severity of the bust wiped away the memory of the boom. Some outside bankers and analysts claimed the boom had always been an illusion based on easy money. Others exulted that the crash proved the whole "Asian model" of rapid export-led growth was fundamentally flawed. Many in the West had become bored by the enthusiasm for Asian "miracles".

But Asia *had* done spectacularly well. Thailand *had* been through a boom which transformed the economy. The bust was caused by the strains of rapid transformation, magnified by exposure to the erratic behaviour of the over-powerful and under-regulated world of international finance.

From 1986 to 1992, Thailand's boom had been based on growth of export industries promoted by domestic entrepreneurs and direct investments from East Asia. The growth was real. The results were so spectacular that the international merchant banks and portfolio investors wanted a slice of the action. From 1992, Thailand was induced to open up its financial market and welcome foreign inflows. The World Bank, the international finance houses, and the financial press from *Fortune* to *The Economist* touted Thailand and the rest of miraculous Asia as a lucky dip for financial profits.

In the advanced countries, wealthy ageing populations and the privatization of welfare had generated massive pension funds and other savings which sought high returns. But in the early 1990s Japan and Western economies were on the downswing of the business cycle. Returns to investment were low. In Southeast Asia, the cycle was on the upswing. Young and poor populations with new access to technology offered opportunities for high returns to investment. From west and east, money flowed into the region.

Thailand seemed especially attractive. The pegged currency removed any currency risk. Interest rates were high. Everybody was predicting a bright future. Even on the eve of the bust (1997), the IMF praised Thailand's "remarkable economic performance" and "consistent record of sound macroeconomic performance".

Unlike in the 1986-92 phase, only a small part of the inflows came as direct investments in factories and businesses. Most came as portfolio funds, merchant banking loans, and speculative stashes – forms of capital which could move in and out at the speed of an electronic transfer.

Thailand's local financial industry gorged on the inflows. Local firms could not resist the temptation to leverage with loans that seemed so cheap. But the inflows threw the economy off balance. Everyone forgot that Thailand must *grow through trade*, not through money games and concrete fantasies.

Government failed to control the inflows, and failed to direct them towards productive uses. Local entrepreneurs, already under pressure from multinational competitors in export production, were deflected towards service industries, heavy industry projects, and overseas adventures. Too much was borrowed short and lent long. Too much was squandered on condos for housing mosquitos. Some was plunged into over-ambitious and over-protected schemes. Some was simply stolen, as the BBC case revealed. Some was sunk in asset pyramids built by the inflows themselves.

Similar things were happening elsewhere across Asia. International finance wanted a bigger piece of the region's growth. But international finance is out of control. Too many merchant bankers, pension fund managers, and portfolio speculators were drawn by the promise of riches from the Orient. No institutional framework oversees these financial flows and restrains the tendency to fads and panics. Too many believe the illusion that financial markets are rational.

But in the early 1990s, the growth in Thailand and the region was already slowing. The prolonged slump in Japan dulled one of the main drivers of regional growth. The foundation of NAFTA and the strengthening of the EU made world trade more regionalized. Subtle forms of protectionism were spreading. Eventually it was obvious that the returns were less than the dreams. Mosquitos pay no rent.

Thailand triggered the regional collapse because Thailand was the most vulnerable point. Its economic transformation had been especially big and sudden. The inflows from 1993 on were so much larger than anything experienced before. Institutions had found no breathing space to adjust to the extraordinary scale of change. Politicians and technocrats were mesmerized by the bubble, and implicated in the profit-taking. No-one had been through this before and really knew the dangers.

When the bubble imploded, capital fled, liquidity dis-appeared, asset values lurched downwards, and the financial industry caved in. The IMF prescribed the medicine it had developed to cope with crashes caused by profligate government borrowing. It stamped hard on the economic brake. In late 1997, the economy shrank at frightening speed. The baht's value halved. The value of foreign debt rose higher than total GDP. While the benefits of boom were rather unequally distributed, the impact of bust was indiscriminate. From the top conglomerates to the smallest family concern, businesses built up over one, two, three, and four decades faced annihilation.

As capital fled, the same people who had pictured Thailand (and Asia) as the great financial frontier – the World Bank, the international financial analysts, *The Economist* – now blamed the crash on inadequate institutions, corrupt politicians, and imperfect liberalization. All these factors were certainly there. But they had *always been there*. Somehow the bankers and boosters had not noticed them earlier. Their explanation of the bust glossed over the erratic nature of the financial flows themselves.

In retrospect it is easy to see that the financial crisis was avoidable. If Thailand had abandoned the pegged exchange rate at the time of financial liberalization, changes in the baht value would have moderated the inflows. If the central bank had imposed stricter controls on the finance industry, firms would not have become so ridiculously over-exposed. If government had been clever with taxes, money inflows could have been diverted to more productive uses. If the baht had been floated only a few months earlier, it would have avoided the disastrous gambles on the currency market, the generous handouts to doomed finance firms, and the reckless printing of money.

So why did Thailand not avoid the crisis? In the past Thailand had been praised as an example of careful economic management. In 1993, the World Bank singled out Thailand as a model. In 1994, the central bank was ranked third in the region (after Hong Kong and Singapore) for all-round performance. What went wrong?

Partly the macro-managers had tried to have the best of both worlds – the pegged exchange rate which facilitated trade, and the liberalization of finance which stimulated investment. Partly the macro-managers had come to believe the praise accorded them. They refused to heed the advice that this combination would not work.

Partly they seemed dazzled by the glamorous financial world which developed in Bangkok in the early 1990s. The regulators seemed reluctant to impose the constraints which would slow it down.

But partly this reluctance has a murkier side. Powerful people could make easy money because of lax control. The two heads of the economic technocracy, the finance minister and central bank governor, came under intense political pressure. From 1995 onwards, these posts offered only temporary employment. Many good candidates were not keen to apply. Politicians and other powerful people resisted closer supervision of the finance industry, argued against unpegging the currency, and undermined the tradition of fiscal discipline. Up to and beyond the IMF bailout, policies were delayed or distorted at the behest of particular interests.

The bust was not simply the fault of careless lending by international finance. Nor was it simply caused by the pirate instincts of Thai businessmen and politicians. Rather it resulted from the explosive chemistry of mixing the two.

In late 1997, the bust rippled out to the region and the world – prompting even bigger IMF bailouts in Indonesia and Korea, market panics in Philippines and Malaysia, crisis packages in Japan, and nervous tremors in the centres of world finance. This diffusion emphasized that the crisis was both Thai and global. Overcoming the crisis would have to address both sides. Thailand would need to sort out its financial institutions and its politics. But equally the world would have to do something about the erratic money flows or else such crises would recur.

The pattern of boom and bust was not new for Thailand. Over the past three decades, growth has run through three ski-jump cycles, each marked by a steep climb and a plunging descent. The Thai economy was not built to run on a smoother path. The openness to international trends, and the tolerance allowed the animal spirits of private business, give it a swooping trajectory. Over the decades, the swings have become more eccentric.

Along the way, the animal spirits have left their mark in other ways.

Requiem for the Boom

The boom was a triumph for the city and for business.

Urban activities now drive the national economy. The factories clustered in the Bangkok region are the source of GDP growth. The city population is swollen with in-migrants. The confidence of the urban middle class is on display – in domestic and commercial architecture, in youth culture, and most of all on TV. Those who have made money in the city enjoy their new wealth, and enjoy letting others know about it.

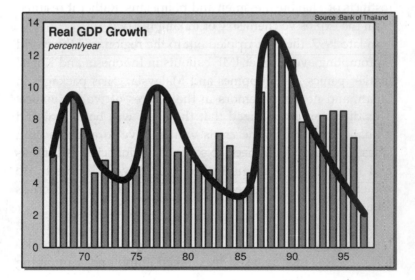

Within the city, business dominates. Businessmen have grown rich and powerful. They have become the heroes of popular culture. The defining fable of the boom is the meteoric rise of Thaksin to the status of billionaire and political leader. The soaps, game-shows, and ads on television revolve around making and displaying wealth. In the early 1990s, students queued up to study finance which seemed the quickest way to make a lot out of nothing. Even illegal businesses seemed legitimate since the practitioners usually escaped punishment and often became famous and powerful.

Politics have been commercialized. Businessmen dominate parliament and cabinet to the exclusion of almost anyone else. Many businessmen treat politics as a business. Elections are major economic events. The parliament is a marketplace for contracts, favours, and deals. Nobody was too surprised when the leader of the "moral force" party presented another politician with a free Daimler as thanks for a business favour. No-confidence debates have become a parade of scandals of escalating value. Economic policy-making is all too obviously distorted by private interests.

In the past, business was balanced against bureaucracy. But this balance has been lost. The culture of the Thai bureaucracy has become outdated and irrelevant to the globalizing world. In the early 1980s, a moderately successful businessmen earned a few times more than a top official. Ten years later, he earned many tens of times more. In the boom, most of the talented and educated young went to business careers rather than government. Many of the experienced old technocrats were head-hunted away by the conglomerates. Gloomy government offices are over-shadowed by the gleaming new towers of commerce. The ethics of public service have been submerged by the belief that getting rich is glorious.

Business unchained has been harsh on Thailand's natural and human resources. Factories have spilled dangerous wastes into rivers, sea, and air. The city has pulled labour out of the villages at invisible but untold cost to structures of family and community. In the city, many have been exposed to new risks. Health and safety at work have become major issues. The escalating pollution weighs heaviest on the poor and unprotected. The spread of AIDS and amphetamines are measures of social risk and dislocation.

The boom has been divisive. It has widened the gap between rich and poor, between city and provinces, between urban and rural. The business lobby has resisted any adjustment in the economic strategy that would compromise the emphasis on growth. Most technocrats have been trained to pursue growth and have difficulty accepting that issues such as distribution, social justice, and environmental protection may be as important.

Neither law nor conscience has been very effective in limiting the social costs of the boom. Business has revelled in the atmosphere of free-for-all. The machinery for social protection has proved very pliable. The legal framework is defective. The judiciary is suspect. The police are unreliable. The authorities have consistently tried to block popular organizations to defend popular rights. Efforts to strengthen the social infrastructure have been brushed aside.

The counterpoint of urban triumph has been rural decline. Within little more than a decade, agriculture has been transformed from the country's main economic engine to a minor part. The land frontier has been closed. The messages radiating out of the city on the TV speak of the city's superiority. The urban economy stakes claims to the land, water, and forests on which the countryside lives. The agrarian economy stagnates through neglect.

Will recovery from the bust just mean a return to the same trajectory, the same risks, the same costs? Or can Thailand move into a pattern of growth which is *sustainable, equitable, and livable*?

Beyond

For a decade, Thailand has been swept along by the momentum of the boom – by the rise in urban wealth, and by the compelling forces of globalization. There has been little chance, little incentive to stop and ponder. Opposing voices have gone unheard.

The bust is an opportunity – to pause for reflection, to question the forces driving the boom, to embark on reforms which during the boom seemed unnecessary, irrelevant, and counter to the interests of people the boom made rich and powerful.

The shift to industrialization is now unstoppable. But there are still choices to be made which will affect the future trajectory of economy, politics, and society. The bust has thrown three of those choices into sharp relief: the balance between inward and outward, globalization and localism; the balance between village and city; and the balance between free enterprise and social constraint.

Outward or inward. At the peak of the boom, globalization was a catch-word, a fad, almost a religion. Globalization offered a chance for a late-comer country like Thailand to catch up fast. It gave entrepreneurs access to the world's money and technology, and consumers an entry into the world's supermarket.

As Thailand slid towards bust, globalization seemed more like a kick in the teeth. Thailand had been tossed around on the wayward currents of international finance, and tipped over the rim of a whirlpool of giddy depth. Globalization now seemed like a dangerous game for a weak late-comer. The salvage gangs were gathering to pick over the wreckage. Thailand had been tempted to open the door only so that the multinational banks and corporations could storm through.

Many foreigners urge that the best solution to the financial crisis is further liberalization. Foreign money flowing in to buy up banks and finance companies will fill the black hole in the finance industry, reverse the capital flight, and bring a fast recovery. Many Thai businessmen and technocrats agree. Globalization is the way of the world. There is no turning back, no sensible alternative. Look at Burma.

But others have doubts. In part they are defending personal interests. In part they argue that local enterprise still needs some protection against outside competition. In part they react with a gut-based nationalism.

In the wider urban society, reaction is more instinctive. The bust has provoked a revival of interest in local culture far stronger than the state-sponsored cultural revivals of recent years. A 24-hour *luk thung* radio station appeared. The Carabao band rewrote and reissued *Made in Thailand*, the anthem which on the eve of the boom had cautioned Thailand about embracing globalization at the expense of local values and traditions. Television drama, the weather vane of urban culture, has dug out nostalgic stories of the pre-globalized past. A series of *luk thung* songs such as "The Floating Baht" have poked fun at the financial crisis and the collapse of globalist dreams. The fact these songs have sold millions of cassettes in the space of a few weeks suggests they tap a very widespread reaction against the enthusiasm for everything modern and global. Maybe, they imply, we just weren't ready.

In the long-run perspective, Thailand looks outward. Seminars in 1997 marked the centennial of King Chula-longkorn's journey to Europe which had marked Siam's entry on the modern world stage. The trauma of the bust is unlikely to deflect Thailand far from the trajectory begun in that period. But there will be some reevaluation of what should be preserved and protected, both in commercial assets and cultural heritage.

City and village. Through the boom, the city stood for everything superior, productive, modern, exciting, desirable. The village seemed backward, dispensable. The bust has forced a reappraisal.

The Floating Baht

The Thai baht is floating, floating here, floating there
Going up and down on the winds of fortune
Will it sail off on the breeze or sink to the bottom of the sea
We have to watch carefully

The baht was floated not long ago, but everything is suddenly
more expensive
Big things or small things, the prices are floating away
Floating up and up. No sign of floating down.

Thai money flows out, but foreign money doesn't flow in. We urban
people like to go abroad, to and fro, spending money for fun.
So what? You have the money.
But it's Thai money. If we spend too much, liquidity disappears.
No money for investment.
How do you know?
Well, its on the news every day and every night.
*I never listen to the news. I watch only big football matches and
Thai boxing. That's more fun!*
You should be more concerned about the fate of your own nation.
*I am! I'm afraid Thai boxers will lose to foreign boxers, that's why
I have to watch. I'm very concerned. How can you say I'm not
concerned.*
You're too playful. Our country has amassed so much external
debt, both long and short term. It's huge.
If it's so huge, only the gods can help. Why should I worry?
Stupid! If you borrow money you have to pay it back.
*Eh? Surely those who did the borrowing have to pay it back. Not
us.*
But you have to help because we are all part of the same family.
Sorry. I don't live around here and I haven't got a family yet.
Don't be stupid!
I'd be stupid if I helped pay the debt...

Ploen Phromdaen, 1997[1]

Urban incomes and employment have shrunk. Estimates of the numbers who will lose their jobs range into millions. In many countries, such a vicious downturn would quickly lead to crime, strikes, political disorder, revolt. If in Thailand this happens only mildly or not at all, there is one reason: the countryside still acts as a shock-absorber, cushioning the bumps and shocks of the urban economy. Many will go back to the village and share in the family rice bowl.

The onset of the bust saw a revival of urban interest in the countryside. Press and TV programmes nervously tracked the stories of village migrants returning home.

The rural shock-absorber still works because the agricultural sector is so large and because the bonds of family and community remain. But the shock-absorber now works less well than in the past. Agriculture has been systematically neglected. The farmers who feed others have remained poor. Most rural families now rely heavily on the income supplement remitted from those sent off to work in the factories, bars, and construction sites of the city. Family and community ties have been weakened by migration. In this bust, the rice bowl will be sorely stretched.

Thai agriculture has huge potential especially in high-value areas which enjoy growing world demand. Thai fragrant rice commands a premium price. There are even better opportunities outside this traditional staple – in organic and chemical free farming, orchards, flora, herbal extracts.

Unlocking this potential demands a new attitude to rural development and a new respect for the farmer. Old-style rural development policy had a strong paternalist streak. In line with the spirit of the Eighth Plan, the new strategy must be to equip the farmer with knowledge, rights, technology, and political power.

In the past, government deliberately denied higher education to the rural population on grounds it was unnecessary if not dangerous. Now government is committed to extending universal education up to twelve years. But it is still reluctant to provide the subsidies which will be necessary to persuade rural families to put their children in school rather than to work. Ironically the state still subsidizes higher education, which mostly benefits the urban wealthy, but not rural secondary education.

Possibly a quarter of all rural families still have problems over land rights. The issue is highly complex. It overlaps with concerns over forest and ecology, and with ambitions for quick wealth. Recent attempts to confront the issue have become political and scandal-ridden. But the problem cannot be ignored. Ironically the collapse of asset values may make it easier to address. Perhaps the new courts and commissions prescribed in the new constitution could be used as a model for creating a land rights commission which would be somewhat insulated from day-to-day political pressures.

Productivity remains very low because investment in agriculture has been so low. Much of the investment has been in large dams geared to paddy farming. Irrigation officials admit they still focus on such projects because that is their expertise. Other investment has been in chemical inputs which are now reckoned to have questionable economic benefits if all the side-effects are computed. Future investment in technology should empower the farmer and respect local knowledge.

Reviving agriculture must also mean breaking down the over-centralization of power. But this will be more difficult than it sounds. The old bureaucracy has resisted decentralization on grounds of security and tradition. Powerful interests are vested in the maintenance of central power. The new constitution (and the Eighth Plan) call for more decentralization of the management of local resources, taxation, administration, education, culture, and environment. But none of these will proceed without popular pressure and political will.

Business and society. Over the boom, business carried all before it. Free enterprise demanded and got a relatively free rein. Business ethics seemed to be legitimated by their own achievement. The bust raises many queries. Free-for-all has meant good-for-some. The benefits have been very badly distributed. Much of what was vaunted as business expertise, especially in the glamorous world of finance, turned out to be little more advanced than hi-lo and pyramid games. The markets have done a bad job of allocating capital for long-t erm growth. Too much was sunk in property, too little in upgrading exports. The business spirit helped to undermine the technocracy and institutionalize money politics.

Business needs some social constraints. The new constitution aims to provide some by defining civic rights, strengthening the judicial system, and challenging those who practice politics as a branch of business. But the passage of the constitution is only a start.

It will need a lot of time and effort to realize the potential of the new charter. The impact of the new courts will depend on the judges chosen, the cases brought, and the judgements delivered. The significance of the statement of rights will depend on the legislation and judicial rulings which are leveraged from it. The many provisions to control corruption and influence will depend on the details of implementation. In all of these areas, there are battles to come.

History also tells that the great reform constitutions of Thailand's past were all rolled back by a conservative reaction. The 1932 charter was never fully implemented before the military took over. The 1946 version was torn up within a year. The 1974 constitution was revoked after the massacre and coup of October 1976.

A similar reaction is predictable this time. Powerful interests from senators to village headmen spoke out against the draft. Parliament's opposition crumbled only because the economic crisis raised the costs and risks of rejection. Even before the parliamentary vote, legislators were plotting how to make amendments as soon as possible. This charter will not survive without strong defence.

Besides, the new constitution is only a step. Much of it is conservative. The social base of the current parliament is very narrow and the new charter will probably broaden it only a little. Parliament will cease to function as a marketplace only when it contains more people who are not there for business.

The hope for a new politics goes along with hope for a new concept of public service.

The bureaucracy was formed in the great reforms a hundred years ago, and remodelled after the Second World War. It served the country well enough. But it has been outpaced by this era of globalization. Good potential recruits and good old hands have been lured away by the salaries and excitement of the private sector. Those that remain behind have become inward-looking. They lack the status, confidence, and credibility to stand up to politicians, businessmen, and influence.

Many problems over the economy, infrastructure, justice, policing, and education stem from the quality of people in government posts. This quality in turn is related to the low pay and declining status of a public-sector career. The Chavalit government passed a resolution on bureaucratic reform and started the formation of a permanent commission to oversee the process. But structure and pay are only part of the problem. How to develop a new breed of public servant for the twenty-first century? How to provide a fast-track route for younger and more capable people to by-pass the old structures of paternalism and patronage?

The model for this new breed lies not in the old bureaucracy with its control mentality and paternalist arrogance, but in the social responsibility and quiet dedication of the welfare and education services run by NGOs.

Two documents composed in the mid-1990s capture this vision. The Eighth Plan highlighted "people-centred de-velopment". The new constitution, its authors claim, was made "by the people and for the people". Both the Plan and the constitution contain emphatic statements of human rights, equality before the law, and the importance of "human dignity".

While one of these documents is a plan and the other a charter, both read much like manifestos. Both resulted from collaboration between reflective members of the old generation of bureaucracy, and activist representatives of the new generation of NGOs and public intellectuals. The two documents seem distilled from the regrets of the former and the hopes of the latter. Both documents are brave attempts to move Thailand rapidly from the past to the future.

In the early 1980s, Thailand had an economy based on rice exports, a political system run by generals, and a reputation for traditional, exotic charm. Over the last decade, the country has been spun through a boom and bust of world-record scale. Industry has overhauled agriculture. The city has replaced the village at the cultural core. Thailand now makes the international headlines as the centre of a crisis of regional and global significance. Like an overnight star, the country seems dazed by the experience, by the extent of change, and by its new international fame. Beyond boom and beyond bust, the challenge is not to get back on the old path of economic growth, but to create the political framework, concept of public service, development strategy, and social values which allow many more people to participate, contribute, and benefit.

ACKNOWLEDGEMENTS

This book is an update of *Thailand's Boom!* published two years ago. We have added two new chapters, on the economic bust (chapter 5) and on politics since 1992 (chapter 10), and redrafted the conclusion. We have also added new material throughout the book to reflect the big changes of the last two-three years. Chapter 3 has been substantially rewritten to extend (but not change) our view of the boom. We have inserted new sections on the Assembly of the Poor, constitutional reform, illegal economy, Eighth Plan, and country music, and have expanded the treatment of NGOs, labour relations, forest politics, pollution, and the debate on Thai identity.

As the book goes to press, the bust is still unfolding. We take the story through to November 1997, the fall of Chavalit, and the closure of fifty-six finance companies.

Thanks to many friends who helped us with information, criticism and encouragement, but especially to Gordon Fairclough, Annette Hamilton, Kevin Hewison, Karel Jansen, Kleo-Thong Hetrakul, Lim Teck Ghee, Paitoon Wiboonchuti-kula, Pichit Patrapimol, Somchai Homla-or, Jim Stent, Sungsidh Piriyarangsam, Ammar Siamwalla, Chatthip Nartsupha, Mingsarn Santikarn, Nualnoi Treerat, Samart Chiasakul, Titima Opasawongkarn, and Michael Vatikiotis. Thanks to Pana Janviroj and *the Nation* for permission to reuse material. Thanks to Add Carabao for allowing us to reproduce the lyrics of *Made in Thailand*, to Phongsit Kamphi for *Home*, and to Ploen Phromdaen for *The Floating Baht*. Very special thanks to Trasvin Jittidejarak.

ABBREVIATIONS

AFTA	ASEAN Free Trade Area
ASEAN	Association of Southeast Asian Nations
BIBF	Bangkok International Banking Facility
BMA	Bangkok Metropolitan Area
BoI	Board of Investment
CNN	Cable News Network
CP	Charoen Pokphand company
EPZ	export processing zone
ESB	Eastern Seaboard Project
GDP	Gross Domestic Product
IC	integrated circuit
IMF	International Monetary Fund
ISEAS	Institute of Southeast Asian Studies
JV	joint venture
LSE	London School of Economics
MBA	Master of Business Administration
MITI	Ministry of Trade and Industry (Japan)
MTV	Music Television
NESDB	National Economic and Social Development Board
NGO	non-governmental organization
NIC	newly industrializing country
PPP	purchasing power parity
SCG	Siam Cement Group
TDRI	Thai Development Research Institute
TPI	Thai Petrochemical Industry
UHF	ultra high frequency
USAF	United States Air Force
USAID	United States Agency for International Development

GLOSSARY

chaebol	Korean business conglomerate
farang	foreigner (westerner)
isan	northeastern region
jao phor	godfather, local political boss
jek	Chinese (pejorative)
jin	Chinese
Khor Jor Kor	acronym of a land resettlement scheme launched by the army in 1991
klong	canal
luk kru'ng	mixed race
luk thung	country music (especially in style of central region)
mor lam	northeastern style of local music
nok rabop	outside the system
peu chivit	for life, describing styles of music and writing
phatthana	development
sae	Chinese clan
sogo shosha	Japanese multinational trading company
SPK 4-01	land document granting conditional occupancy rights
Taejew	(Chaozhou) Chinese dialect from the Swatow (Shantou) region
tambon	sub-district
wat	(Buddhist) temple
ya baa	amphetamine, literally mad drug

READING FURTHER (IN ENGLISH)

For general introductions to modern Thailand, see Charles F. Keyes, *Thailand: Buddhist Kingdom as Modern Nation-State* (Bangkok: Editions Duang Kamol, 1989); John L. S. Girling, *Thailand: Society and Politics* (Ithaca and London: Cornell University Press, 1981); Pasuk Phongpaichit and Chris Baker, *Thailand: Economy and Politics* (Kuala Lumpur: Oxford University Press, 1995); Suchit Bunbongkarn, *State of the Nation: Thailand* (Singapore: ISEAS, 1996).

Four outstanding novels in translation possibly provide an even better introduction: Kampoon Boontawee, *A Child of the Northeast*, trans. Susan Fulop Kepner (Bangkok: Editions Duang Kamol, 1988); Khammaan Khonkhai, *The Teachers of Mad Dog Swamp*, trans. Gehan Wijeyewardene (Bangkok: Silkworm Books, 1992); Khamsing Srinawk, *The Politician and Other Thai Stories* (Kuala Lumpur: Oxford University Press, 1973); Botan, *Letters from Thailand*, trans. Susan Fulop Morell (Bangkok: Editions Duang Kamol, 1977).

The literature on Asian economies, particularly on the Four Tigers, is growing fast. There is a good introduction in Anis Chowdhury and Iyanatul Islam, *The Newly Industrialising Economies of East Asia* (London and New York: Routledge, 1993). On the outflow of Japanese investment, see Pasuk Phongpaichit, *The New Wave of Japanese Investment in ASEAN: Determinants and Prospects* (Singapore: ISEAS, 1990).

On Thailand's pre-modern economic background, the standard work is James C. Ingram, *Economic Change in Thailand, 1850-*

1970 (Kuala Lumpur: Oxford University Press, 1971). See also Sompop Manarungsan, *Economic Development of Thailand, 1850-1950: Response to the Challenge of the World Economy* (Bangkok: Institute of Asian Studies, 1989).

On the role of the Chinese, the classic is William G. Skinner, *Chinese Society in Thailand: An Analytical History* (Ithaca: Cornell University Press, 1957).

On the modern economy, two important new collections are: Peter Warr, ed., *The Thai Economy in Transition* (Cambridge: Cambridge University Press, 1993); and Medhi Krongkaew, ed., *Thailand's Industrialization and Its Consequences* (London: St Martin's, 1995). See also Michael J. G. Parnwell, ed., *Uneven Development in Thailand*, (Aldershot: Avebury, 1996).

Other key works include: Akira Suehiro, *Capital Accumulation in Thailand 1855-1985* (Tokyo: The Centre for East Asian Cultural Studies, 1989); Kevin J. Hewison, *Bankers and Bureaucrats: Capital and the Role of the State in Thailand* (New Haven: Yale University Southeast Asia Studies, 1989); Anek Laothamatas, *Business Associations and the New Political Economy of Thailand: From Bureaucratic Polity to Liberal Corporatism* (Boulder: Westview Press, 1992); Robert J. Muscat, *The Fifth Tiger: A Study of Thai Development Policy* (Helsinki: United Nations University Press, 1994); Karel Jansen, *External Finance in Thailand's Development* (Houndmills: Macmillan, 1997).

Thailand's urban culture is little studied, with the exception of Buddhism on which there is a large literature. See for instance: Peter A. Jackson, *Buddhism, Legitimation, and Conflict: The Political Functions of Urban Thai Buddhism* (Singapore: ISEAS, 1989); and Somboon Suksamran, *Buddhism and Politics in Thailand* (Singapore: ISEAS, 1982). See also William J. Klausner, *Thai Culture in Transition* (Bangkok: The Siam Society, 1997). On music see John Clewley, "The Many Sounds of Siam" in

The Rough Guide to World Music ed. Broughton, Ellingham, Muddyman and Trillo (London: Penguin, 1994).

On the rural transformation, a good place to start is Philip Hirsch, *Political Economy of Environment in Thailand* (Manila and Wollongong: Journal of Contemporary Asia Publishers, 1993). Two recent collections on environmental topics are Hirsch, ed., *Seeing Forests for Trees: Environment and Environmentalism in Thailand* (Chiang Mai: Silkworm Books, 1996), and Jonathan Rigg, ed., *Counting the Costs: Economic Growth and Environmental Change in Thailand* (Singapore: ISEAS, 1995). For the political dimension, see Seri Phongphit, *Back to the Roots. Village and Self-Reliance in a Thai Context* (Bangkok: Rural Development Documentation Centre, 1986). And for the human side, see the two collections of Sanitsuda Ekachai's articles: *Behind the Smile: Voices of Thailand* (Bangkok: The Post Publishing, 1991); and *Seeds of Hope: Local Initiatives in Thailand* (Bangkok: The Post Publishing, 1994).

On modern politics, a good starting point for background is David Morell and Chai-Anan Samudavanija, *Political Conflict in Thailand: Reform, Reaction, Revolution* (Cambridge, Mass.: Oelgeschlager, Gunn & Hain, 1981). On the military see Chai-Anan Samudavanija, Kusuma Snitwongse, and Suchit Bunbongkarn, *From Armed Suppression to Political Offensive* (Bangkok: Institute of Security and International Studies, Chulalongkorn University, 1990). For a useful sketch of the 1980s, see Prudhisan Jumbala, *Nation-building and Democratization in Thailand: A Political History* (Bangkok: Chulalongkorn University Social Research Institute, 1992). See also Pasuk Phongpaichit and Sungsidh Piriyarangsan, *Corruption and Democracy in Thailand* (Bangkok: Chulalongkorn University, Political Economy Centre, 1994; reissued by Silkworm Books, 1996).

NOTES

Chapter 1: A Different Country

1. Over 1985-95, according to the World Bank, real average annual growth of GDP was 8.4 percent. The next-ranked were also in Asia: China (8.3), Korea (7.7), Singapore (6.2). *World Development Report 1997* (Washington: IBRD, 1997), Table 1.

2. *Bangkok Post*, 22 July 1985.

3. The image was first used in the 1930s by Kanamae Akamatsu, and later developed by Saburo Okita and Kojima Kiyochi.

4. World Bank, *The East Asian Miracle* (New York: Oxford University Press, 1993), 142.

Chapter 2: "Pillow and Mat" Capitalism

1. Vichai Suwannaban, *C.P. turakit rai phrom daen* [CP: business without frontiers] (Bangkok: Than Setthakit, 1993); see also Akira Suehiro, *Capital Accumulation in Thailand 1855-1985* (Tokyo: Centre for East Asian Cultural Studies, 1989), 270-1; Kevin J. Hewison, *Bankers and Bureaucrats: Capital and the Role of the State in Thailand* (New Haven: Yale University Southeast Asia Studies, 1989), 143-6.

2. *Bangkok Post*, 24 October 1995.

3. Nidhi Eoseewong (Aeusrivongse), *Watthanatham kradumphi kab wannakam ton rattanakosin* [Bourgeois culture and early Rattanakosin culture] (Bangkok: Thai Khadi Institute, 1982); Sarasin Viraphol, *Tribute and Profit: Sino-Siamese Trade 1651-1853* (Cambridge, Mass.: Harvard University Press, 1977); Jennifer W. Cushman, *Fields from the Sea: Chinese Junk Trade with Siam During the Late Eighteenth and Early Nineteenth Centuries* (Ithaca: Cornell University Press, 1993).

4. Suehiro, *Capital Accumulation*, 42-71; Sompop Manarungsan, *Economic Development of Thailand, 1850-1950: Response to the Challenge of the World Economy* (Bangkok: Institute of Asian Studies, 1989).

5. William G. Skinner, *Chinese Society in Thailand: An Analytical History* (Ithaca: Cornell University Press, 1957).

6. Sir John Bowring, quoted in John L. S. Girling, *Thailand: Society and Politics* (Ithaca: Cornell University Press, 1981), 74.

7. Asvabahu, *Phuak yiew haeng burapha thit lae mu'ang thai jong tuen toet* [The Jews of the Orient and Wake up Thailand] (Bangkok: The Foundation In Memory of King Rama VI, 1985), 83-4. Asvabahu was the King's pen-name.

8. See Nidhi, *Watthanatham kradumphi*; David K. Wyatt, *Studies in Thai History* (Chiang Mai: Silkworm Books, 1994), 98-130.

9. Nakarin Mektrairat, *Kanpatiwat sayam ph. s. 2475* [The 1932 revolution in Siam] (Bangkok: Munnithi khrongkan tamra sangkhomsat lae manutsayasat, 1992), 95; Punee Bualek, "Characteristics of Thai Capitalists between the World Wars" (paper presented at the 5th International Conference on Thai Studies, SOAS, London, 1993).

10. Sungsidh Piriyarangsan, *Thai Bureaucratic Capitalism 1932-1960* (Bangkok: Chulalongkorn University Social Research Institute, 1983); Hewison, *Bankers and Bureaucrats*, 74-6, 81-3.

11. Many of these take-off stories are told in Suehiro, *Capital Accumulation* and Hewison, *Bankers and Bureaucrats*; others in individual biographies such as Somjai Wiriyabanthitkun, *Sahaphat: to laew taek lae taek laew to* [Success story of Sahaphatthanaphibun] (Bangkok: Phujatkan, 1990); Arunee Sopitpongstorn, *Kiarti Srifuengfung: The Boy from Suphanburi* (Bangkok: Sri Yarni Corporation, 1991); Bunchai Jaiyen, *Ruay baep jao sua* [Being rich jao sua style] (Bangkok: Bunchai Press, 1990).

12. Sathian Chantimathorn, *Thanarachan: Chin Sophonpanich* [King of the bank: Chin Sophonpanich] (Bangkok: Matichon, 1988).

13. On the banks, see Sathian, *Thanarachan*; Suehiro, *Capital Accumulation*, 158-78, 242-64; Hewison, *Bankers and Bureaucrats*, 174-5, 200; on the drain of savings to the capital, see Yoko Ueda, *Local Economy and Entrepreneurship in Thailand: A Case Study of Nakhon Ratchasima* (Kyoto: Kyoto University Press, 1995).

14. Sungsidh, *Thai Bureaucratic Capitalism*, 158-63.

15. Suehiro, *Capital Accumulation*, 235.

16. Suehiro, *Capital Accumulation*, 257-9.

17. Hewison, *Bankers and Bureaucrats*, 171.

18. These military-business connections have been described many times. See Sungsidh, *Thai Bureaucratic Capitalism*; Suehiro, *Capital Accumulation*, 130-72; Hewison, *Bankers and Bureaucrats*; David Morell, "The Function of Corruption in Thai Politics" (paper presented at the Meetings of the International Political Science Association, Edinburgh, Scotland, August 1976).

19. On the courtship of the US and the Thai military, see Daniel Fineman, *A Special Relationship: the United States and Military Government in Thailand, 1947-1958* (Honolulu: University of Hawaii Press: 1997).

20. On the Sarit period, see Thak Chaloemtiarana, *Thailand: The Politics of Despotic Paternalism* (Bangkok: Social Science Association of Thailand, 1979); Surachart Bamrungsuk, *United States Foreign Policy and Thai Military Rule, 1947-1977* (Bangkok: Duang Kamol, 1988); Robert J.

Muscat, *Thailand and the United States* (New York: Columbia University Press, 1990).

21. Based on Appendices 2-3 in Suehiro, *Capital Accumulation.*

22. On Japanese attitudes to doing business in Thailand, see Motoko Sakurai, "A Japanese Perspective of Thai Industrialisation" (paper presented at the Conference on the Making of a Fifth Tiger? Thailand's Industrialisation and its Consequences, held at the Australian National University, 7-9 December, 1992).

23. The Hong Kong businessman, Lee Shau Kee, quoted in *Fortune*, 31 October 1994, 52.

Chapter 3: Going Global

1. *Asian Business*, May 1994, 14; *Manager*, February 1994, 24-9; Sorakol Adulyanondha, *Thaksin shinawatra asawin khlu'n luk thi sam* [Thaksin Shinawatra, knight of the third wave] (Bangkok: Matichon, 1993).

2. The Shinawatra family history is told in Prani Sirithorn Na Phatthalung, *Phu bukboek haeng chiangmai* [The pioneers of Chiangmai] (Bangkok: Ruengsin, 1980), 169-223.

3. Olarn Chaiprawat, "Yuk thong khong setthakit thai pi 2529-2533" [The golden age of the Thai economy 1986-1990] in *Kanngoen kanthanakhan lae kandamnoen nayobai setthakit khong prathet* [Finance, banking and economic policies], ed. Nopporn Ruengsakul, Chaiyawat Wibulswadi, and Duangmanee Wongprathip (Bangkok: Chulalongkorn University Press, 1988).

4. Pasuk Phongpaichit, *The New Wave of Japanese Investment in ASEAN: Determinants and Prospects* (Singapore: ISEAS, 1990).

5. "The Thai Economy: First Step in a New Direction" (TDRI Macroeconomic Policy Programme, 26 December 1994).

6. On the industrial boom, see Peter Warr, ed., *The Thai Economy in Transition* (Cambridge: Cambridge University Press, 1993); Medhi Krongkaew, ed., *Thailand's Industrialization and Its Consequences* (London: St Martin's Press, 1995); Paitoon Wiboonchutikula, "Thailand's Industrialization: Past Performance and Future Issues" (Faculty of Economics, Chulalongkorn University, August 1994); Narongchai Akrasanee, David Dapice, and Frank Flatters, *Thailand's Export-led Growth: Retrospect and Prospects* (Bangkok: TDRI, 1993).

7. *Bangkok Post*, 13 July 1995; *The Nation*, 28 January 1995, 10 and 12 March 1977, 26 April 1997, 4 August 1997.

8. *Bangkok Post*, 26 January 1994.

9. *Far Eastern Economic Review*, 12 January 1995; *Asian Business*, June 1995; *The Nation*, 25 October 1995.

10. In chapter 12 of the *General Theory*, Keynes wrote about stock markets: "When the capital development of a country becomes a by-product of the activities of a casino, the job is likely to be ill-done."

11. Paul Handley, "Politics and business, 1987-96" in *Political Change in Thailand: Democracy and Participation*, ed. Kevin Hewison (London and New York: Routledge: 1997), 100.

12. *The Nation*, 25 June 1997.

13. *Business Review*, August 1994, 24-36.

14. *Manager*, February 1994.

15. *The Nation*, 29 April 1996.

16. See for instance, *Bangkok Post*, 24 October 1995.

17. Michael Vatikiotis, "From Chickens to Microchips", *Far Eastern Economic Review*, 23 January 1997.

18. *The Nation*, 29 July 1994.

19. Arunee, *Kiarti*.

20. Both Chai-Anan and Sondhi wrote on the theme in *Phujadkan* in 1993. See Sondhi Limthongkul, *Lokanuwat* [Globalization] (Bangkok: Phujadkan, 1994).

21. Sakurai, "A Japanese Perspective".

22. *Forbes* also published a ranking of the world's richest ethnic Chinese. CP's Dhanin ranked fifth, and in all fourteen Thais made the top fifty. See *Business Review*, October 1995. Thirteen Thai families made the list of dollar billionaires in Geoff Hiscock, *Asia's Wealth Club* (London: Nicholas Brearley, 1997). Of these, four were based in banking, three in telecoms, two in property, and one each in agribusiness, construction, brewing, and petrochemicals. Dhanin ranked twelfth.

Chapter 4: Raising a Tigercub

1. In the huge and ever-expanding literature on the Tigers, Alice H. Amsden, *Asia's Next Giant: South Korea and Late Industrialization* (Oxford: Oxford University Press, 1989) still stands out as the path-breaking interpretation.

2. Thak, *Despotic Paternalism*, 221-34.

3. A reviewer of *Thailand's Boom* in the *Bangkok Post* spent half his review challenging this paragraph. He restated the old argument that Korean economic policy was moulded by the demands of the post-war situation. This has been the conventional view of outside observers. But the newer *Korean* economists concentrate more on the thinking of the key planners. See the analysis by Ha-joon Chang, *The Political Economy of Industrial Policy* (London: St Martin's Press, 1992), ch. 4.

4. Anek Laothamatas, *Business Associations and the New Political Economy of Thailand: From Bureaucratic Polity to Liberal Corporatism*

(Boulder: Westview Press, 1992); Scott R. Christensen, *Capitalism and Democracy in Thailand* (Bangkok: TDRI, 1992).

5. Robert J. Muscat, *The Fifth Tiger: A Study of Thai Development Policy* (New York and Tokyo: M. E. Sharpe and United Nations University Press, 1994), 61-5; Ammar Siamwalla, "Stability, Growth and Distribution in the Thai Economy," in *Finance, Trade and Economic Development in Thailand; Essays in Honour of Khunying Suparb Yossundara*, ed. Puey Ungphakorn et al. (Sompong Press, 1975).

6. Narongchai Akrasanee, "Import Substitution, Export Expansion and Sources of Industrial Growth in Thailand, 1960-1972," in *Essays*, ed. Puey et al.; Narongchai Akrasanee and Juanjai Ajanant, "Manufacturing Industry Protection in Thailand: Issues and Empirical Studies," in *The Political Economy of Manufacturing Protection: Experiences of ASEAN and Australia*, ed. Christopher Findlay and Ross Garnaut (Sydney Boston London: Allen and Unwin, 1975).

7. See for instance the World Bank's critical review of the Thai economy in *Thailand: Managing Public Resources for Structural Adjustment* (Washington D.C: World Bank, 1983).

8. Chaipat Sahasakul et al., *Lessons from the World Bank's Experience of Structural Adjustment Loans (SALs): A Case Study of Thailand* (Bangkok: TDRI, 1992).

9. Anek, *Business Associations*, especially 76-7, 83, 125, 130.

10. Snoh Unakul, *Yutthasat kanpatthana chat adid patjuban anakot* [Strategy for national development: Past, present, future] (Bangkok, 1988), 137.

11. Narongchai and Juanjai, "Manufacturing Industry Protection"; World Bank, *Managing Public Resources*, vol I, 185-6; Muscat, *Fifth Tiger*, 148-9.

12. Paitoon, "Thailand's Industrialization"; Narongchai, Jansen, and Jeerasak, *International Capital Flows*.

13. This is clear from the insider account in Pisit Leeahtham, *From Crisis to Double Digit Growth* (Bangkok: Dokkya, 1991).

14. Ammar, "Stability".

15. Figures from the World Bank, *World Development Report, 1993*, Table 1.

16. TDRI, "The Thai Economy".

17. Ammar, "Stability", 30.

18. Karel Jansen, *Finance, Growth and Stability: Financing Economic Development in Thailand, 1960-1986* (Aldershot: Avebury, 1990).

19. Pranee Tinakorn, "Industrialisation and Welfare: How Poverty and Income Distribution Are Affected," in *Thailand's Industrialization*, ed. Medhi; Suganya Hutaserani and Somchai Jitsuchon, "Thailand's Income Distribution and Poverty Profile and their Current Situations" (paper presented at the Year-End Conference on Income Distribution and Long-Term Development, TDRI, Bangkok, 1988).

20. Pisit, *From Crisis*.

21. Mingsarn Santikarn and Adis Israngkura, "Industrial Policies of Thailand," in *Economic Development Policy in Thailand, A Historical Review*, ed. Warin Wonghanchao and Yukio Ikemoto (Tokyo: Institute of Developing Economies, 1988); Suehiro, *Capital Accumulation*, 193-8.

22. Christensen, *Capitalism and Democracy*.

23. Mingsarn and Adis, "Industrial Policies".

24. For the automobile case, see Richard F. Doner, "Politics and the Growth of Local Capital in Southeast Asia: Auto Industries in the Philippines and Thailand," in *Southeast Asian Capitalists*, ed. Ruth McVey (Ithaca: Cornell, 1992); on sugar, see Ansil Ramsay, "The Political Economy of Sugar in Thailand", *Pacific Affairs* 60, no. 2 (Summer 1987); for several other examples, see Hewison, *Bankers and Bureaucrats*.

25. Anek, *Business Associations*, 76-83, 125.

26. Rathakorn Asadorntheerayuth, *Boonchu Rojanastien* (in Thai) (Bangkok: Dokbia, 1993).

27. *Transport & Communications*, August 1991, 79. Thanks to Sakkarin Niyomsilpa.

28. The ESB history is summed up in Somchai Ratanakomut, Samart Chiasakul, and Shigeru Itoga, *Manufacturing Industry in Thailand: A Sectoral Analysis* (Tokyo: Institute of Developing Economies, 1995).

29. *Bangkok Post*, 8 May 1995.

Chapter 5: Bubbling Over

1. *The Nation*, 13 June 1996.

2. Arporn Chewakrengkrai, quoted in *Asiaweek*, 4 October 1996. On the general problem, see Narongchai, Dapice, and Flatters, *Thailand's Export-Led Growth*, 31-5.

3. Government barred the BIBF banks from raising capital in the Thai market, so inevitably they concentrated on one-way lending (out-in) which unbalanced the financial market.

4. *Bangkok Post*, 24 December 1994.

5. "The Way Out of the Economic Crisis", paper by Phatra Research Institute, 30 September 1997, 5.

6. Somchai Krusuansombat (Zoom) in *Thai Rath*.

7. *The Nation*, 10, 13 and 17 March 1997.

8. *The Nation*, 1 March 1997.

9. "The Way Out", 11-12.

10. *The Nation*, 20 May 1997.

11. Especially Suchart Tancharoen, Chucheep Harnsawasdi, Newin Chidchob, Chattawat Muttamara, and Pairoj Piempongsant.

12. On the role of Vijit in the affair see *The Nation*, 20 February 1997, and Cholada Ingsrisawang in *Bangkok Post*, 26 February 1997.

13. *The Nation*, 23 May 1996, 2, 4, 13 July 1996, 20, 26 February 1997; *Bangkok Post*, 13 May 1996, 26 February 1997

14. *Asia Times*, 5 November 1996.

15. *Bangkok Post*, 26 March 1997; *Far Eastern Economic Review*, 10 April 1997.

16. *Bangkok Post*, 6 January 1997, 20, 21, 24 February 1997; *The Nation*, 23 November 1996.

17. When Vijit Supinit was assigned by the central bank as a director of Siam City Bank, he acquired several thousand shares in a subsidiary finance company at par value. He later chaired the meeting of the Securities Exchange Commission which approved the subsidiary's listing on the stock market. *The Nation*, 27 June 1996; *Bangkok Post Mid-Year Economic Review 1996*, 35.

18. Chalongphob Sussangkarn, quoted in *Far Eastern Economic Review*, 15 August 1996.

19. On the Ekamol firing controversy see the lead story in *The Nation*, 10 January 1996.

20. *The Nation*, 10 August 1996.

21. *The Nation*, 18 June 1996.

22. Phisit Pakkasem in *The Nation*, 31 August 1996.

23. *Far Eastern Economic Review*, 15 October 1996.

24. *Bangkok Post*, 19 June 1997.

25. *Bangkok Post*, 23 December 1996; *The Nation*, 23 December 1996.

26. *The Nation*, 21 December 1996.

27. Economists who publicly backed devaluation included Pisit Lee-ahtam, Narongchai Akrasenee, Virabhongse Ramangkura, and Ammar Siamwalla.

28. Quite how much was not clear. See Ivory Tower in *The Nation*, 8 September 1997.

29. "The Way Out", 11-12.

30. After writing this, we discovered Peter Warr and Bhanupong Nidhiprabha had used a similar metaphor about Thai technocrats, but with rather different meaning; see their *Thailand's Macroeconomic Miracle* (Washington and Kuala Lumpur: World Bank and Oxford University Press, 1996), 228.

Chapter 6: Manpower and Womanpower

1. All the figures on labour come from the *Labour Force Surveys* by the National Statistical Office. A useful review of recent changes is Chalongphob Sussangkarn, "Labour Markets," in *Thai Economy*, ed. Warr.

2. There are lots of little studies of this migration, but no single overview. See for instance T. D. Fuller et al., *Migration and Development in Modern Thailand* (Bangkok: The Social Science Association of Thailand, 1983); S. Goldstein, *Migration and Urban Growth in Thailand* (Bangkok: Institute of Population Studies, Chulalongkorn University, 1974).

3. Chalongphob, "Labour Markets", 359.

4. S. D. Bamber, K. J. Hewison, and J. Underwood, "A History of Sexually Transmitted Diseases in Thailand: Policy and Politics", *Genitourinary Medicine*, 159 (1993); Wathinee Boonchalaksi and Philip Guest, *Prostitution in Thailand* (Nakhon Pathom: Mahidol University, Institute for Population and Social Research, 1994). Many agree on a figure of around 200,000 female sex workers.

5. Daniel Ray Lewis, "Impact of Development on the Thai Rural Population" (Southeast Asia Studies Program, Ohio University, 1995).

6. Calculated from the wage data in the *Labour Force Surveys*.

7. Said at the conference on Women and the Management of Natural Resources, organized by the Committee for Crafts and Women's Development in the Northeast, held at Surin on 1-3 October 1995.

8. Quoted in Chatthip Nartsupha and Phonphilai Lertwichai, *Watthanatham muban thai* [Thai village culture] (Bangkok: Sangsan, 1994), 76.

9. Apichat Chamratrithirong, *National Migration Survey* (Bangkok: Mahidol University, 1994).

10. Real wages calculated from data in Niphon Poapongsakorn and Surachai Khitatrakun, "Kan sang dachani kajang mattrathan khong prathet thai" [Creating a standardized wage index for Thailand], TDRI working paper, August 1996.

11. The history of Thai labour is covered by Kanchada Poonpanich, "The Making of Third World Workers: A Cultural Analysis of the Labour Movement in Thailand, 1920s-1950s" (Ph.D. thesis, Bielefeld University, 1989); Sungsidh Piriyarangsan, "The Foundation of a Workers Strategic Group: An Analysis of the Labour Movement in Thailand (1956-1976)" (Ph.D. thesis, Bielefeld University, 1989).

12. This period is described in Sungsidh, "Foundation"; David Morell and Chai-Anan Samudavanija, *Political Conflict in Thailand: Reform, Reaction, Revolution* (Cambridge, Mass.: Oelgeschlager, Gunn & Hain, 1981); Vichote Vanno, "The Role of Trade Unions in the Political Development in Thailand: 1958-1986" (Ph.D. thesis, City University of New York, 1991).

13. Sungsidh, "Foundation", 197, 206, 212-23; Kittipak Thavisri, "Trends Toward Corporatist Labour Controls in Thailand and Malaysia" (Ph.D. thesis, Northern Illinois University, 1991), 241-2; Vichote, "Role of Trade Unions", 190-1, 218-23.

14. Sungsidh Piriyarangsan and Kanchada Poonpanich, "Labour Institutions in an Export-Oriented Country: A Case Study of Thailand," in *Workers, Institutions, and Economic Growth in Asia*, ed. Gerry Rodgers (Geneva: ILO, International Institute for Labour Studies, 1994), 232-4; Sungsidh Piriyarangsan and Kitti Limsakul, *Khajang khan tam* [Minimum wages] (Bangkok: Faculty of Economics, Chulalongkorn University, 1994); Pasuk Phongpaichit, "Nu, Nit, Noi and Thailand's Informal Sector in Rapid Growth," in *Human Resources Development*

Strategy in Thailand: Past, Present, and Future, ed. Chira Hongladarom and Shigeru Itoga (Tokyo: Institute of Developing Economies, 1991).

15. Sungsidh and Kanchada, "Labour Institutions", 238.

16. See Kritaya Archawanitkul, Wanna Jarusomboon, Anchalee Warangrat, "Khwam sapson lae khwam sapson ruang khon khamchat nai prathet thai" [The complexity and confusion over the numbers of transnational workers in Thailand], and other papers presented at the Seminar on Policy Options for the Importation of Foreign Labour into Thailand: A Study of Interest Parties, Legal Issues and the State Management System, organized by Institute of Population and Social Research, Mahidol University, Bangkok, 27-29 May 1997.

17. Banthit Thamatrirat, "Chiwit khabuankan sahaphap raengngan thai phaitai rabob ro so cho" [The Thai labour movement under the National Peace Keeping Council] in *Chomna raengngan thai* [The face of Thai labour] (Bangkok: Arom Phongphangan Foundation, 1991).

18. *Bangkok Post*, 7 May 1997.

19. Sungsidh Piriyarangsan, "Borisat thai suzuki motor: ton tun khong kan khad rabop raeng ngan samphan thi prongdong" [Thai Suzuki Motors: the cost of not having a peaceful labour relations system], presented at the Political Economy Forum, Chulalongkorn University, 30 August 1996.

20. "Has the Sanyo Torching Case Really Destroyed the Investment Atmosphere?", seminar organized by the Political Economy Centre, Chulalongkorn University, reported in *The Nation*, 18 January 1997.

21. Chira and Itoga, *Human Resource Development Strategy*.

22. Phitsanes Jessadachatr et al., "Education Management: Public and Private Sector Roles in the Provision of Education," in *The 1991 Year-End Conference: Educational Options for the Future of Thailand* (Bangkok: TDRI, 1991).

23. Thanks to Mark Turner for these figures.

24. *Bangkok Post*, 30 March 1997.

25. Information from the Ministry of Labour.

26. H. Warrington Smyth, *Five Years in Siam* (London: 1898, reprinted by White Lotus, Bangkok, 1994), 281.

27. Suteera Thomson and Maytinee Bhongsvej, *Profile of Women in Thailand* (Bangkok: Gender and Development Research Institute, 1995).

28. *The Nation*, 11 and 13 October 1995. Oranuj was transferred to the Prime Minister's Office and elevated to the top C-11 grade.

Chapter 7: City Thais

1. See for instance National Identity Office, *Thailand in the 1980s* (Bangkok: Muang Boran, 1984); Craig J. Reynolds, ed., *National Identity and its Defenders, Thailand, 1939-1989* (Melbourne: Monash University, 1991), 16-17.

2. *The Nation Weekend,* 11 April 1997.

3. On the urban transformation of Buddhism see Peter A. Jackson, *Buddhadasa – A Buddhist Thinker for the Modern World* (Bangkok: Siam Society, 1988) and *Buddhism, Legitimation, and Conflict: The Political Functions of Urban Thai Buddhism* (Singapore: ISEAS, 1989); Somboon Suksamran, *Buddhism and Politics in Thailand* (Singapore: ISEAS, 1982); Suwanna Satha-Anand, "Religious Movements in Contemporary Thailand: Buddhist Struggles for Modern Relevance", *Asian Survey,* 30, nos. 1-3 (April 1990); J. L. Taylor, "New Buddhist Movements in Thailand: An 'Individualist Revolution', Reform, and Political Dissonance", *Journal of Southeast Asian Studies,* XXI, no. 1 (March 1990), and *Forest Monks and the Nation-State: An Anthropological and Historical Study in Northeastern Thailand* (Singapore: ISEAS, 1993). See also Gordon Fairclough in *Far Eastern Economic Review,* 4 May 1995.

4. Jackson, *Buddhadasa.*

5. Suwanna, "Religious Movements", 400-2; Jackson, *Buddhism, Legitimation and Conflict,* 199-217; Taylor, "New Buddhist Movements", 140-3.

6. Taylor, *Forest Monks;* Kamala Tiyavanich, *Forest Recollections: Wandering Monks in Twentieth-century Thailand* (Chiang Mai: Silkworm Books, 1997).

7. *The Nation,* 21 September 1995.

8. Quoted by Sanitsuda Ekachai in *Bangkok Post,* 9 January 1995. The phrase "goddess of trade" came from Nidhi Eoseewong (Aeusrivongse).

9. *The Nation,* 16 October 1993.

10. Suwanna, "Religious Movements", 395, 402; Taylor, "New Buddhist Movements", 141.

11. Skinner, *Chinese Society.*

12. See especially Fred W. Riggs, *Thailand: The Modernisation of a Bureaucratic Polity* (Honolulu: East-West Center Press, 1966). Riggs used the term "pariah entrepreneur".

13. *M.R. Kukrit Pramoj: His Wit and Wisdom. Writings, Speeches and Interviews,* comp. Vilas Manivat, ed. Steve Van Beek (Bangkok: Duang Kamol, 1983).

14. Botan, *Letters from Thailand,* trans. Susan Fulop Morell (Bangkok: Duang Kamol, 1977).

15. See Kasian Tejapira, *Lae lortlai mangkorn* [Through the dragon's pattern] (Bangkok: Khopfai, 1994). Chai-Anan publicly rediscovered his Chinese origins in his *Phujadkan* column.

16. Kasian Tejapira, "In Thailand, being ethnic Chinese is chic" in *The Nation,* 7 February 1997.

17. Craig J. Reynolds, "Tycoons and Warlords: Modern Thai Social Formations and Chinese Historical Romance," in *Sojourners and Settlers: Southeast Asia and the Chinese,* ed. Anthony Reid (London: Allen and Unwin, 1996).

18. Thanks to Wannee Ruttanaphon of Lintas Thailand for information on dates and audience data for these series.

19. National Identity Office, *Thailand in the 1980s*, 91.

20. Among his many works see Sulak Sivaraksa, *Siam in Crisis* (Bangkok: Komol Keemthong Foundation, 1980).

21. See especially Nidhi, *Watthanatham kradumphi*; Charnvit Kasetsiri, *The Rise of Ayudhya* (Kuala Lumpur: Oxford University Press, 1976); Srisakara Vallibhotama reported in *The Nation*, 4 November 1995.

22. Nidhi Eoseewong (Aeusrivongse), *Kanmu'ang thai samai phrajao krung thonburi* [Thai politics in the reign of King Taksin], (Bangkok: Phikanet Printing Centre, 1993 reprint of 1985 original), 16.

23. Sujit Wongthes, *Jek bon lao* [Chinese mixed with Lao], *Sinlapa Wattanatham*, special issue, 1987.

24. Kasian Tejapira, "The Postmodernization of Thainess", *Proceedings of the 6th International Conference on Thai Studies, Theme II, Cultural Crisis and the Thai Capitalist Transformation*, Chiang Mai, 14-17 October 1966, 394.

Chapter 8: The Abandoned Village

1. Editorial of the *Bangkok Times* quoted in Benjamin A. Batson, *The End of the Absolute Monarchy in Siam* (Singapore: Oxford University Press, 1984), 245.

2. On Thailand's rural history see David Feeny, *The Political Economy of Productivity: Thai Agricultural Development, 1880-1975* (Vancouver: University of British Columbia Press, 1982); David Bruce Johnston, "Rural Society and the Rice Economy in Thailand, 1860-1930" (Ph.D. thesis, Yale University, 1975); Anan Ganjanaphan, "The Partial Commercialization of Rice Production in Northern Thailand (1900-1981)" (Ph.D. thesis, Cornell University, 1984); Chirmsak Pinthong, ed., *Wiwatthanakan khong kanbukboek tidin thamkin nai khet pa* [Study of land occupancy in forest areas] (Bangkok: Rural Development Institute, 1991); Hans Uhlig, ed., *Spontaneous and Planned Settlement in Southeast Asia* (Hamburg, Institute of Asian Affairs, 1984); Witayakorn Chiengkul, *The Effects of Capitalist Penetration on the Transformation of the Agrarian Structure in the Central Region of Thailand (1960-1980)* (Bangkok: Chulalongkorn University Social Research Institute, 1983); Philip Hirsch, *Development Dilemmas in Rural Thailand* (Singapore: Oxford University Press, 1990).

3. Oey A. Meesook, *Income, Consumption, and Poverty in Thailand, 1962/63 to 1975/76* (Washington, D.C.: World Bank, 1979).

4. A CPT pamphlet quoted by Pravit Rojanaphruk in *Bangkok Post*, 19 August 1994.

5. Saiyud Kerdphol, *The Struggle for Thailand: Counter Insurgency 1965-1985* (Bangkok: S. Research Center, 1986); Ruth T. McVey, "Change

and Consciousness in a Southern Countryside," in *Strategies and Structures in Thai Society*, ed. H. Brummelhuis and J. H. Kemp (Amsterdam: University of Amsterdam, 1984); Gawin Chutima, *The Rise and Fall of the Communist Party of Thailand (1973-1987)* (Canterbury: University of Kent, 1990).

6. Morell & Chai-Anan, *Political Conflict*, 152-4, 217-25; Kanoksak Kaewthep, *Bot wikhro sahaphan chaona chao rai haeng prathet thai* [Analysis of the Peasants' Federation of Thailand] (Bangkok: Chulalongkorn University Social Research Institute, 1986); Andrew Turton, Jonathan Fast, and Malcolm Caldwell, eds., *Thailand: Roots of Conflict* (Nottingham: Spokesman, 1978).

7. Morell and Chai-Anan, *Political Conflict*, 225-9.

8. Chai-Anan Samudavanija, Kusuma Snitwongse, and Suchit Bunbongkarn, *From Armed Suppression to Political Offensive* (Bangkok: Institute of Security and International Studies, Chulalongkorn University, 1990), 67-87; Saiyud, *Struggle*, 183-4; Gawin, *Rise and Fall*.

9. Pinkaew Leungaramsri and Noel Rajesh, *The Future of People and Forests in Thailand after the Logging Ban* (Bangkok: Project for Ecological Recovery, 1992).

10. Ammar Siamwalla has calculated that between 1989 and 1995, numbers working in agriculture in the age range 15-24 dropped 55 percent, and in the age-range 25-34 by 15 percent. *The Nation*, 17 October 1997.

11. On these protests, see for instance *Thai Development*, the regular newsletter from the Thai Development Support Committee.

12. Philip Hirsch, *Political Economy of Environment in Thailand* (Manila and Wollongong: Journal of Contemporary Asia Publishers, 1993).

13. Karuna Buakumsri in *Bangkok Post*, 1 October 1995; Walakkamon Eamwiwatkit in *The Nation*, 19 October 1995; Malee Traisawasdichai in *The Nation*, 18 October 1995; Noel Rajesh, "Local participation and the Kaeng Sua Ten dam controversy", *Watershed*, vol. 2 no. 3, March-June 1997; *Kan seuksa pon kratop dan niveswitaya krongkan kaeng sua ten* [Ecological impact assessment of Kaeng Sua Ten dam project], prepared by the Faculty of Science, Chulalongkorn University, May 1997.

14. The story of forest depletion is told in Hirsch, *Political Economy*; Pinkaew and Rajesh, *Future*; Chirmsak, *Wiwatthanakan*; Pramool Pejsawang, *Pamai kab tidin tamkin: khotetjing panha lae khosanoenae* [Forest vs. land for cultivation: Facts, problems, and recommendations] (Bangkok: Social Science Association of Thailand, 1991).

15. Suthawan Sathirathai, "The Adoption of Conservation Practices by Hill Farmers, with Particular Reference to Property Rights: A Case Study in Northern Thailand" (Ph.D. thesis, University of Cambridge, 1992), 56-7; MIDAS Agronomics Company Limited, *Conservation Forest Area Protection, Management, and Development Project, Pre-investment Study, Final Report, Vol. 2, Main Report* (Bangkok: 1993) 10-11.

16. Santita Ganjanapan, "Indigenous and Scientific Concepts of Forest and Land Classification in Northern Thailand" in *Seeing Forests for Trees: Environment and Environmentalism in Thailand,* ed. Philip Hirsch (Chiang Mai: Silkworm Books, 1996), 263. See also the articles by Rapin, Pratuang and Anan in the same volume.

17. Pratuang Narintarangkul Na Ayuthaya, "Community Forestry and Watershed Networks in Northern Thailand" in *Seeing Forests for Trees,* ed. Hirsch.

18. A village headman speaking at the Chulalongkorn University Political Economy Centre's seminar on "Environment and Eucalyptus", April 1995.

19. Apichai Puntasen, Somboon Siriprachai, and Chaiyuth Punyasavatsut, *Wikhro nayobai eucalyptus jak ngae mum phon prayote thang setthakit lae kanmu'ang* [The political economy of eucalyptus: A case of business cooperation by the Thai government and its bureaucracy] (Bangkok: Social Science Association of Thailand, 1991); Pinkaew and Rajesh, *Future,* 72-3; Hirsch, *Political Economy,* 19.

20. Local Development Institute, "Khrong kan jat thi thamkin hai kap ratsadorn phu yak rai nai phuen thi pa sa-nguan suemsom (Khor Jor Kor)" [Fact sheets about Khor Jor Kor] (Bangkok, 1992); Chai-Anan Samudavanija and Kusuma Snitwongse, *Sing waedlom kap khwam mankhong: khwam mankhong khong rat kap khwam mai mankhong khong ratsadon* [Environment and security: Security for the state, insecurity for the people] (Bangkok: Institute of Security and International Studies, Chulalongkorn University, 1992), 61-9.

21. Chai-Anan and Kusuma, *Sing waedlom;* Hirsch, *Political Economy,* 21-23; Pinkaew and Rajesh, *Future,* 184-8; Suthawan, "Adoption of Conservation Practices", 59.

22. *Bangkok Post,* 29 January 1995.

23. Wanida Tantiwithiyapitak in *Bangkok Post,* 4 May 1997.

24. *The Nation,* 23 April 1997.

25. Suchira Playulpitak of the Dhammanaat Foundation.

26. Prayang Dok-lamyai of the Northern Farmers Network in *The Nation,* 26 April 1997.

27. Bamrung Kayotha in *The Nation,* 13 March 1997.

28. Chatthip Nartsupha, "The 'Community Culture' School of Thought," in *Thai Constructions of Knowledge,* ed. Manas Chitkasem and Andrew Turton (London: School of Oriental and African Studies, 1991); see also Seri Phongphit, *Back to the Roots. Village and Self-Reliance in a Thai Context* (Bangkok: Rural Development Documentation Centre, 1986); Bunthian Thongprasan, *Naewkit watthanatham chumchon nai ngan phatthana* [The community culture strategy in development work], comp. Kanjana Kaewthep (Bangkok: Catholic Council of Thailand for Development, 1988).

29. Chatthip and Phonphilai, *Watthanatham mu ban thai.*

30. Chalongphob Sussangkarn, *Towards Balanced Development: Sectoral, Spatial, and Other Dimensions* (TDRI Year-End Conference, 1992).

31. Snoh Thientong, Chavalit's Interior Minister, dubbed them "seasonal migratory birds".

Chapter 9: Opening Up Politics

1. Riggs, *Thailand* started it off in 1966.

2. The development of the modern bureaucracy is covered in Tej Bunnag, *The Provincial Administration of Siam, 1892-1915* (Kuala Lumpur: Oxford University Press, 1977); Riggs, *Thailand*; Chai-Anan Samudavanija, *The Co-Evolution of State Power and Political Power* (Bangkok: Chulalongkorn University, Research Division, 1992); Likhit Dhiravegin, *The Bureaucratic Elite of Thailand* (Bangkok: Thai Khadi Research Institute, 1992).

3. Surachart, *United States Foreign Policy*; Frank C. Darling, *Thailand and the United States* (Washington, D.C.: Public Affairs Press, 1965); Daniel Fineman, *A Special Relationship*.

4. Scot Barmé, *Luang Wichit Wathakan and the Creation of a Thai Identity* (Singapore: ISEAS, 1993); Chalermkiet Phiu-Nual, *Prachathippatai bab thai: Khwamkhit thang kanmu'ang khong thahan thai 2519-2529* [Thai style democracy: The political thought of the Thai military 1976-1986] (Bangkok: Thai Khadi Institute, Thammasat University, 1990); Thak, *Thailand*, 295-6.

5. Thak, *Thailand*, 335-8; Surachart, *United States Foreign Policy*, 171.

6. Ubonrat Siriyuvasak, "Radio Broadcasting in Thailand: The Structure and Dynamics of Political Ownership and Economic Control", *Media Asia*, 19, no. 2 (1992).

7. Anthony Diller, "What Makes Central Thai a National Language", in *National Identity* ed. Reynolds.

8. Thongchai Winichakul, *Siam Mapped: A History of the Geo-body of a Nation* (Honolulu: University of Hawaii Press, 1994).

9. The current version of textbooks is reviewed in Niels Mulder, *Thai Images: The Culture of the Public World* (Chiang Mai: Silkworm, 1997).

10. Charles F. Keyes, *Isan: Regionalism in Northeastern Thailand* (Ithaca: Cornell University Southeast Asia Program, 1967); Surin Pitsuwan, "Elites, Conflicts, and Violence: Conditions in the Southern Border Provinces", *Asian Review*, 1 (1987).

11. Barmé, *Luang Wichit*.

12. Phraya Anuman Rajadhon, *Essays on Thai Folklore* (Bangkok: Thai Inter-Religious Commission for Development and Sathirakoses Nagapradipa Foundation, 3rd ed., 1988).

13. Morell and Chai-Anan, *Political Conflict*, ch. 5.

14. Noranit Setthabut, *Phak prachathipat* [The Democrat Party] (Bangkok: Thammasat University Press, 1987).

15. This period is well covered in Morell and Chai-Anan, *Political Conflict*.

16. Puey Ungphakorn, "Violence and the Military Coup in Thailand", *Bulletin of Concerned Asian Scholars*, 9, no. 5 (1977); Benedict R. O'G. Anderson, "Withdrawal Symptoms: Social and Cultural Aspects of the October 6 Coup", *Bulletin of Concerned Asian Scholars*, 9, no. 5 (1977); Surachart, *United States Foreign Policy*; Morell and Chai-Anan, *Political Conflict*, chs. 9-10.

17. Chai-Anan, Kusuma, and Suchit, *From Armed Suppression*; Katherine R. Bowie, *Rituals of National Loyalty: An Anthropology of the State and the Village Scout Movement in Thailand* (New York: Columbia University Press, 1997).

18. Likhit Dhiravegin, *Demi Democracy: The Evolution of the Thai Political System* (Singapore: Times Academic Press, 1992); Prudhisan Jumbala, *Nation-building and Democratization in Thailand: A Political History* (Bangkok: Chulalongkorn University Social Research Institute, 1992); Christensen, *Capitalism and Democracy*.

19. There is a good case study of this period in Ueda, *Local Economy*.

20. James Ockey, "Business Leaders, Gangsters and the Middle Class" (Ph.D. thesis, Cornell University, 1992), ch. 6.

21. Sombat Chantornvong (1993), "Local Godfathers in Thai Politics: A Preliminary Observation" (paper presented at the 5th International Conference on Thai Studies, SOAS, London, 1992); Pasuk Phongpaichit and Sungsidh Piriyarangsan, eds., *Rat thun jaophor thongthin kap sangkhom thai* [State, capital, local godfathers, and Thai society] (Bangkok: Political Economy Centre, Chulalongkorn University, 1992); Pasuk Phongpaichit, Sungsidh Piriyarangsan, and Nualnoi Treerat, *Guns, Girls, Gambling, Ganja: Thailand's Illegal Economy and Public Policy* (Chiang Mai: Silkworm, forthcoming).

22. Ockey, "Business Leaders", ch. 4.

23. *The Nation*, 7 April 1991; *Naew Na*, 27 April 1990; *Matichon Sutsapda*, 10 June 1990; Somrudee Nicrowattanayingyong, "Development Politics and Paradox: A Study of Khon Kaen, a Regional City in Northeast Thailand" (Ph.D. thesis, Syracuse University, 1991).

24. Viengrat Natipho, "Thurakit nakleng + nakleng thurakit = nak thurakit ku'ng nakleng" [Semi-businessmen, semi-gangster] *Jotmai Khao Sangkhomsat*, August-October 1989.

25. See the description of Sia Leng's networks of friends in *Siam Rath*, 22 April 1990, 16 May 1990; *Matichon Sutsapda*, 10 June 1990; *Naew Na*, 27 April 1990; *Banmuang*, 17 April 1990.

26. Viengrat, "Thurakit nakleng"; Ockey, "Business Leaders", ch. 5.

27. The best description is in Ockey, "Business Leaders", ch. 5.

28. Ueda, *Local Economy*, 12-5.

29. Pasuk Phongpaichit, "Technocrats, Businessmen and Generals: Democracy and Economic Policy-making in Thailand," in *The Dynamics of Economic Policy Reform in Southeast Asia and the Southwest Pacific* ed. A

MacIntyre and K. Jayasuriya (Kuala Lumpur: Oxford University Press, 1992).

30. Pasuk Phongpaichit and Sungsidh Piriyarangsan, *Corruption and Democracy in Thailand* (Bangkok: Political Economy Centre, Chulalongkorn University, 1994; reissued by Silkworm Books, 1996). The gift cheque story is told in David Murray, *Angels and Devils* (Bangkok: White Orchid, 1996), 59-68.

31. Cynthia Owens, "Thai Military's Financial Power Remains", *Asian Wall Street Journal*, 16 June 1992.

32. *Matichon Sutsapda*, 4 March 1984, 12 October 1986.

33. *The Nation*, 7 April 1991; *Matichon*, 7 January 1992; Viengrat, "Thurakit nakleng".

34. *Matichon Sutsapda*, 4 March 1984, 12 October 1986.

35. Benedict R. O'G. Anderson, "Murder and Progress in Modern Siam", *New Left Review*, 181 (1990): 47-8.

36. *Thai Rath*, 23 and 24 March 1993.

37. *Thai Rath*, 7 October 1995; *Bangkok Post*, 6 October 1995; *The Nation*, 15 October 1995.

38. *Matichon Sutsapda*, 25 May 1986; Viengrat, "Thurakit nakleng"; Sombat Chantornvong, "Botbat khong jaophor thongthin nai setthakit lae kanmuang thai: kho sangket buangton" [Role of jao phor in Thai economy and politics: Observations], in *Rat thun jaophor thongthin*, ed. Pasuk and Sungsidh.

39. Gawin, *Rise and Fall*; Morell and Chai-Anan, *Political Conflict*, 292-4.

40. Gawin, *Rise and Fall*; Pornpirom Iamtham, "The Student-Led Democratic Movement after the 14 October 1973 Incident and its Relations with the Communist Party of Thailand", *Asian Review*, 1 (1987).

41. On Chamlong see Duncan McCargo, "The Three Paths of Major-General Chamlong Srimuang", *South East Asia Research*, 1, no. 1 (1993); and "Towards Chamlong Srimuang's Political Philosophy", *Asian Review*, 7 (1993).

42. Surin Maisrikrod, *Thailand's Two General Elections in 1992: Democracy Sustained* (Singapore: ISEAS, 1992); Murray, *Angels and Devils*.

43. *A Memoir of His Majesty King Bhumibol Adulyadej of Thailand* (Bangkok: The Office of His Majesty's Principal Private Secretary, 1987), 52.

44. Thak, *Thailand*, 309-31.

45. On 15 March 1969, quoted in Morell and Chai-Anan, *Political Conflict*, 69.

46. *Far Eastern Economic Review*, 26 October 1995, 25.

47. *A Memoir*, 7.

48. In an interview with the BBC in 1981.

49. The phrase was used by Chai-Anan Samudavanija.

50. Closed door discussion in the Economics Faculty, Chulalongkorn University on 5 June 1992. The speaker is a leader of the finance industry.

Chapter 10: Wrestling with Democracy

1. One prominent political financier described elections as "auctions", and explained that politicians were bound to recover the investment: "How else do they expect to survive if they don't set out to recoup their losses?". Sia Leng in *Bangkok Post*, 27 October 1996. On elections, see W. Callahan and D. McCargo, "Vote-buying in Thailand's Northeast: the July 1995 General Election", *Asian Survey* 36(2).

2. *The Nation*, 30 September 1996.

3. Urban attitudes are summarized and exemplified in Suchit Bunbongkarn, *State of the Nation: Thailand* (Singapore: ISEAS, 1996).

4. On the rise of Chamlong, see Duncan McCargo, "The Three Paths of Major-General Chamlong Srimuang," *South East Asia Research*, 1(1).

5. "For example, for the July 2 election last year [1995] I dumped a nine-digit sum of my own money. I won't say exactly how much because the issue is related to electoral laws." Vatana Asavaheme in *The Nation*, 17 October 1996.

6. *The Nation*, 5 November 1996. The official spending limit was one million baht per candidate.

7. "If the candidates are elected, the canvassers receive gifts such as pick-up trucks as a bonus." An anonymous canvasser in *The Nation*, 16 November 1996.

8. *The Nation*, 21 May 1994.

9. Amnuay Virawan founded the Nam Thai party. Thaksin Shinawatra joined Palang Dharma and was made leader.

10. Ockey, "Business Leaders", ch. 6.

11. *Far Eastern Economic Review*, 26 October 1996.

12. *The Nation*, 25 July 1995. Newin was the ultimate gravel-pit politician. His family home was built in the middle of their gravel pit. (Thanks to Gordon Fairclough for this information).

13. *Bangkok Post*, 11 February 1996, 8 September 1996.

14. *The Nation*, 19 January 1996.

15. Duncan McCargo, "The international media and the domestic political coverage of the Thai press", in *Proceedings of the 6th International Conference on Thai Studies, Theme I, Globalization: Impact on and Coping Strategies in Thai Society*, Chiang Mai, 14-17 October 1996.

16. *The Nation*, 18 January 1997; *Thai Rath*, 18 January 1997.

17. On many of these issues, see the reporting of the no-confidence debate on 8-11 May 1996.

18. *The Nation*, 19 May 1996.

19. See a short-list of recent projects in Suphanburi in *The Nation*, 16 May 1996.

20. Newin's speech was published in *The Nation*, 25 May 1996.

21. Even at their last, outgoing meeting, Banharn's Cabinet approved 60 construction projects worth 35 billion baht. See *Bangkok Post*, 26 September 1996.

22. *The Nation*, 14 February, 1996.

23. Assistant Profesor Sukhum Chaloeysub in *Bangkok Post*, 10 March 1996.

24. Over a year later, an ex-MP was sentenced to death for the murder. Saengchai had stated his intention to revoke several concessions to run radio stations, including one controlled by the ex-MP. *The Nation*, 26 September 1997.

25. Chai-Anan Samudavanija, *The Thai Young Turks* (Singapore: ISEAS, 1982), ch. 1.

26. See the lead story in *Bangkok Post*, 5 February 1996.

27. *Thai Rath* on 11 May 1996 ran the banner headline: "Disgrace". *The Nation* (12 May 1996) quoted a Chumphon resident: "I prefer to let the military rule rather than a thief."

28. Television and press coverage on 7-8 May 1996. The nationality issue was a sting; the Democrats had been fed wrong information.

29. *The Nation*, 18 October 1996.

30. *The Nation*, 30 September 1996; *Thai Rath*, 30 September 1996.

31. *The Nation*, 10 September 1997.

32. Chavalit originally stood from the Bangkok suburb of Nonthaburi. In 1995, he shifted base to Nakhon Phanom, his birthplace. Within one year he got funding for a teachers' college, a technical college, an occupational college, two university campuses, an upgrade of the airport, widening of the main street, and several major roads. His local party boasted that the total government funding amounted to 4.6 billion baht. "People in the province really admire him," said the mayor. See *The Nation*, 4 November 1996. After the election, PollWatch estimated that "a certain party" spent 50 million baht on vote buying in the province. *The Nation*, 18 November 1996.

33. Chavalit described himself as "70 percent soldier, 30 percent politician". Thanks to Michael Vatikiotis for this quote.

34. *Bangkok Post*, 17 and 18 March 1997; *Matichon*, 17 March 1997.

35. *Bangkok Post*, 2 April 1997; *Thai Rath*, 2 April 1997.

36. *The Nation*, 29 March 1997.

37. *Bangkok Post*, 14 January 1997.

38 *Bangkok Post*, 14 September 1997.

39. "There is no law left in the country. No one has reasons any more. Do we really want to see the country in chaos?. . . The economy is falling apart and it's all because of the word 'freedom'. The media also wants freedom. But can they control themselves?" Snoh Thienthong reported in *Bangkok Post*, 14 September 1997.

40. *The Nation*, 18 September 1997.

41. *The Nation*, 24 October 1997.

42. Virabhongse Ramangkura, who had been an adviser to Prem in the mid-1980s, and served briefly as Finance Minister under Chatichai. The military pressure is described by Suvit Suvit-Swasdi in *Bangkok Post*, 24 August 1997. Virabhongse later said: "I'm a non-partisan minister forced by the Royal Thai armed forces to work with the World Bank and the IMF for the country." *The Nation*, 24 October 1997.

43. Bovornsak Uvanno in *The Nation*, 5 June 1997.

44. *The Nation*, 13 July 1997.

45. Banharn's government bowed to pressure to alter the old constitution to allow re-drafting by a non-parliamentary body. The 100-member (one resigned) Constitution Drafting Assembly was partly elected, but by an indirect system which allowed parliament to vote on the final choice. The draft could not be amended by parliament and, if voted down, would go to referendum.

46. *The Nation*, 25 August 1997.

47. *Bangkok Post*, 24 August 1997.

48. *Bangkok Post*, 20 January 1997.

49. All the press on 5 September 1997.

50. *Bangkok Post*, 28 September 1997.

51. Michael R. J. Vatikiotis, *Political Change in Southeast Asia: Trimming the Banyan Tree* (London and New York: Routledge, 1996).

52. Anek Laothamatas ed., *Democratization in Southeast and East Asia* (Sinagpore: ISEAS, 1997).

53. On the urban-rural theme in Thai politics, see Anek Laothamatas, *Song nakhara prachathippatai* [Two cities of democracy] (Bangkok: Matichon, 1995).

Chapter 11: Under the Boom

1. Yukio Ikemoto, "Income Distribution and Malnutrition in Thailand", *Chulalongkorn Journal of Economics*, 5, no. 2 (1993). In Ikemoto's revised figures (personal communication, August 1997) the multiple was thirty-nine times in 1992 easing to thirty-seven times in 1994.

2. Figures (except Taiwan) from the World Bank, *World Development Report 1997* (Washington: IBRD, 1997).

3. Suganya and Somchai, "Thailand's Income Distribution"; Pra-nee "Industrialisation and Welfare"; Lewis, "Impact of Development".

4. Suganya and Somchai, "Thailand's Income Distribution".

5. Lewis, "Impact of Development".

6. Ikemoto, "Income Distribution".

7. TDRI, "Thai Economy".

8. Nanak Kakwani and Medhi Krongkaew, "Big Reduction in Poverty", *Bangkok Post Economic Review Year-end 1996*. Nanak and Medhi suggested that the poverty line should be raised, which would still leave 14.3 percent or 8.4 million below in 1994.

9. Guy Trébuil, "Farmer Differentiation in Southern and Central Thai Agrarian Systems: Who Benefits from Agricultural Growth?" in *Uneven Development in Thailand*, ed. Michael J. G. Parnwell (Aldershot: Avebury, 1996).

10. Hirsch, *Political Economy*; Hirsch ed., *Seeing Forests for Trees*; Jonathan Rigg, ed., *Counting the Costs: Economic Growth and Environmental Change in Thailand* (Singapore: ISEAS, 1995).

11. Guy Trébuil in *Counting the Costs*, ed. Rigg, 76-7.

12. Supara Janchitfah reporting a Project for Ecological Recovery study in *Bangkok Post*, 25 May 1997.

13. *Bangkok Post*, 28 February 1996.

14. Sathit Sawintara, director-general of the forestry department, recommending illegal resorts be given 30-year leases. Environmentalists called the idea "a bonus for rapists who are still at large". *The Nation*, 23 October 1997.

15. Bamber, Hewison, and Underwood, "A History of Sexually Transmitted Diseases".

16. Timothy Forsyth "Industrial Pollution and Government Policy in Thailand: Rhetoric versus Reality" in *Seeing Forests for Trees*, ed. Hirsch; Phanu Kritiporn, Theodore Panayotou, and Krerkpong Charnprateep, "The Greening of Thai Industry: Producing More and Polluting Less" (paper presented at TDRI Year-End Conference, December 1990); *Bangkok Post*, 1 January 1995. For an example of dumping in Bang Pu, see *The Nation*, 18 July 1996.

17. *Bangkok Post*, 14 September 1997.

18. These and other incidents are summarised in *Bangkok Post*, 1 January 1995.

19. Forsyth, "Industrial Pollution", 195-6.

20. *Bangkok Post*, 2 October 1996, 30 June 1997.

21. *The Nation*, 5, 8, 15, and 24 July 1997; *Bangkok Post*, 30 June, 6, 18, and 24 July 1997.

22. James Fahn in *The Nation*, 12 January 1996, 9 and 28 October 1996.

23. Churai Tapvong, "Environmental Economics and Management: Water Pollution Control in Thailand" in *Counting the Costs*, ed. Rigg.

24. *Phujadkan raisapda*, 19-25 June 1995; *The Nation*, 11 May 1995, 27 July 1995; *Bangkok Post*, 7 January 1996.

25. Bhichit Rattakul reported in *The Nation*, 25 May 1997.

26. Voravidh Charoenlert, "Industrialisation and Fragmentation of Labour Movement" (paper presented at Political Economy Centre, Chulalongkorn University, Bangkok, 1993).

27. These data are from the official *Yearbook of Labour Statistics*.

28. Oraphan Methadilokkul reported in *Bangkok Post*, 8 February 1996.

29. "Public has no chance in fighting govt projects" in *Bangkok Post*, 4 August 1997. James Fahn in *The Nation*, 17 August 1997.

30. Wathinee Boonchalaksi and Philip Guest, *Prostitution in Thailand* (Nakhon Pathom: Mahidol University, 1994). Many researchers agree on a figure around 200,000.

31. Bamber, Hewison, and Underwood, "A History of Sexually Transmitted Diseases".

32. Bhassorn Limanonda, "Understanding Sexual Subcultures for AIDS Prevention: A Case Study of Rural Communities in Sanpatong District, Chiang Mai", in *Proceedings of the 6th International Conference on Thai Studies, Theme III, Family, Community, and Sexual Sub-cultures in the AIDS Era*, Chiang Mai, 14-17 October 1996.

33. Mechai's comments were widely reported in the press in the lead-up to the international AIDS conference in Chiang Mai in September 1995. See also Gordon Fairclough in *Far Eastern Economic Review*, 21 September 1995.

34. *Bangkok Post*, 17 August 1997. The minister was Snoh Thienthong.

35. Charles Greenberg, "The Varied Responses to an Environmental Crisis in the Extended Bangkok Metropolitan Region" in *Seeing Forest for Trees*, ed. Hirsch, 173.

36. *The Nation*, 27 September 1994, 16 and 17 July 1995.

37. Pasuk Phongpaichit, Sungsidh Piriyarangsan, and Nualnoi Treerat, *Guns, Girls, Gambling, Ganja: Thailand's Illegal Economy and Public Policy* (Chiang Mai: Silkworm, forthcoming).

38. Pasuk, Sungsidh, and Nualnoi, *Guns, Girls*, ch. 2.

39. Pasuk and Sungsidh, *Corruption*, ch. 4; *Bangkok Post*, 14 December 1997, perspective section.

40. *Bangkok Post*, 6 July 1997.

41. *The Nation*, 18 June 1997.

42. The system was exposed by an ITV documentary.

43. Pasuk and Sungsidh, *Corruption*, chs. 4-5.

44. Police-colonel Sompol Ratthakarn in *Bangkok Post*, 28 July 1997.

45. William J. Klausner, "Law and Society," in *Thai Culture in Transition* (Bangkok: The Siam Society, 1997), .

46. Suvit Suvit-Sawasdi in *Bangkok Post*, 8 September 1996. The son-in-law of the original suspect was eventually convicted.

47. The case concerned the murder of a young girl, Sherry Ann Duncan, who had been lover of the businesswoman's husband.

48. "A person cannot use the right and freedom according to the constitution to harm the nation, religion, monarchy and constitution." *The Civil and Commercial Code*, comp. and trans. Kamol Sandhikshetrin (Bangkok: fifth edition, 1993).

49. On the NGOs, see Surichai Wun'Gaeo, "Non-Governmental Development Movement in Thailand," in *Transnationalisation, the State and the People: The Case of Thailand* (United Nations University, 1985); Ernst W. Gohlert, *Power and Culture: The Struggle against Poverty in*

Thailand (Bangkok: White Lotus, 1991); *Thai NGOs: The Continuing Struggle for Democracy* (Bangkok: Thai NGO Support Project, 1995).

50. See for instance Pulsak Wanphong, ex-dean of law at Ramkhamhaeng University and a lecturer at the military academy in *Phujadkan raisupda*, 13-19 September 1993.

51. See for instance the debates reported by Sanitsuda Ekachai in *Bangkok Post*, 11 July 1994; and the debate in the journal *Thai Development*, especially No. 27-28 (1995) "After three decades of development: It's time to rethink", and No. 29 (1995) "NGOs in the year 2000".

52. Government of Thailand, *The Eighth National Economic and Social Development Plan (1997-2001)* (Bangkok: NESDB, n.d.), ii-iv.

53. *Eighth Plan*, 121.

Chapter 12: Boom, Bust and Beyond

1. This is a short extract from a much longer song. The dialogue portion is between a sophisticated "urban" voice and a couple of "local" voices. Ploen Phromdaen is a highly accomplished lyricist, and this translation does little justice to his puns, rhymes, and word-plays.

INDEX

Beijing, 212-3
Black Friday, 41
Board of Investment (BoI), 36,
     60, 64, 66, 68, 70, 82, 83
Bodi Chunnananda, 119
Boonchu Rojanastien, 84, 223,
     227
Boonrawd brewery, 53, 56
Botan, 174
Buddhadasa Bhikkhu, 166-7
Buddhism, 151, 166-72, 234
budget, 73, 76, 78-80, 119, 260-1
Budget Bureau, 22, 60, 65
bureaucracy, 6, 146, 173-4, 217-
     20, 228-9, 267, 303, 321-2, 329
Buriram, 206, 259, 260
Burma, 16-17, 29, 30, 32, 49, 51,
     140, 221, 226, 297, 298, 324;
     see also: Myanmar
business community; and
     economic policy, 74, 76-7,
     81-7, 90-3; and government,
     6, 56, 67, 70-2; and politics,
     15-17, 21-2, 222-31, 241-2,
     265, 269, 320-2; and society,
     327-30
BZW, 102

California Ville, 160
Cambodia, 29, 33, 51-2, 140, 259,
     277, 297, 306
Canada, 108, 109, 306
Canton, 54
Carabao, 154-6, 158, 182, 184,
     261, 324
Caravan, 182
cassava, 63
Catholic Council for
     Development, 306
Cayman Islands, 106-7
cement industry, 64
Central Department Stores, 18,
     45, 161
Centrepoint, 160
Chachoengsao, 136
chaebol, 81

Chai-Anan Samudavanija, 55,
     236, 262
Chaiyapruek, 160
Chamlong Srimuang, 236-8, 248
Chantima Sudasunthorn, 156
Chaophraya river, 62-3, 196, 291
Charnvit Kasetsiri, 179
Charoen Pattanadamrongjit (Sia
     Leng), 226
Charoen Pokphand (CP) group,
     10-11, 24, 45, 49-50, 53, 57,
     86, 125, 277
Chat Phatthana party, 239, 247,
     257-8, 272
Chat Thai party, 109, 223, 225,
     227-8, 239, 247, 257-8, 266
Chatichai Choonhavan, 50, 177,
     227-30, 237, 239, 277;
     government (1988-91), 50-1,
     70, 228-31, 258, 260
Chatri Sophonpanich, 121
Chavalit Yongchaiyudh, 170,
     247, 262-4, 276-80, 354;
     government (1996-7), 119,
     206-7, 264-73, 329
chemical industries, 36, 44
Chevron, 89
Chiang Mai, 30, 136, 201, 208
Chiaravanont family, see
     Charoen Pokphand, Dhanin
     Chiaravanont
Chin Sophonpanich, 19-21
China, 30, 94, 130, 140, 147, 223,
     297, 310; economy, 5, 96;
     investment in, 11, 51, 53
Chinese (in Thailand), 10-22,
     24-7, 150-2, 162, 164, 172-6,
     179-80, 271, 293, 312-14;
     migration, 13-15
Chirathiwat family (Central), 18,
     24; see also: Central
     Department store
Chonburi, 7, 9, 226, 231-3
Chrysler, 37, 45
Chuan Leekpai, 211, 216, 223,
     224, 252, 257, 259, 263, 272,

277-8; government (1992-5), 51, 117, 248, 252-7, 265
Chulalongkorn University, 121, 145, 198, 218
Chulalongkorn, King, 170-1, 324
Cold War, 7, 219, 222-3, 245, 271, 305
colonial era, 12-13
comedy, 180-1, 183-4
Commerce Ministry, 70, 152
Communications Ministry, 86
communism, 60, 136, 137, 190-1, 224, 271, 306
Communist Party of Thailand (CPT), 153
community culture movement, 209-11
Community Forestry Bill, 208
computers, see electrical and electronic
conglomerates, 24-6, 32, 82
constitution, 6, 253, 270-1, 273-80, 303-5, 328-330
consumerism, 9
Cornell, 61
corruption, 229, 256-7, 259-60, 262-3, 266, 268
Crown Property Bureau, 43, 48
currency (baht), 68-71, 97-8; depreciation, 5, 124; policy, 66-7, 72, 116

Daewoo, 37
dams, 194-8, 207
debt, overseas, 75-6, 79, 122-3
decentralization, 254, 265
Democrat party, 103, 223, 225, 239, 247, 248-9, 262, 272-3; see also: Chuan Leekpai
Department of Export Promotion, 70
devaluation, see currency
Development Board, see National Economic and Social Development Board

Dhammagai movement, 168, 172
Dhanin Chiaravanont, 53, 340; see also: Charoen Pokphand
disk drives, 35
Dongyai forest, 202
Dow, 89
drug trade, 226, 255, 267-8, 294, 297-9, 322
Dusit Thani hotel group, 51

Eastern Europe, 147, 298
Eastern Seaboard, 8-9, 87-9, 141, 231, 290-1
Economist, The, 5, 100, 316, 318
education, 128, 133, 145-7, 149, 151-2, 221, 285
Eighth Plan, 207, 307-8, 327, 329-30
elections, 245-52, 279, 353; in 1992, 239; in 1995, 257-8; in 1996, 263-4, 267-8
electrical and electronics industries, 33-6, 64, 95
electricity generation, 44, 89, 196, 290
Elephant Building, 160
environment, 6-7, 193-203, 281, 287-93, 296-7, 305-8
Esso, 89
eucalyptus, 201-2, 207, 212
Europe, 5; business in Thailand, 12-13, 82; union (EU), 5, 317
export of capital, 50-3
export oriented strategy, 67-72
exports, 4, 5, 31-8, 95-8

Fashion Island, 161
Federation of Small-scale Farmers, 204, 208
finance companies, 40, 46-7, 68, 85, 99-105, 112-13, 124-5, 130, 143
Finance One, 103-4, 121, 122
finance, international, 41-2, 98-9, 102-3, 105

King of Thailand, 6, 12, 14, 238, 240-2, 259, 272, 283, 298
Korat, 136, 228
Korea, 1, 17, 59-61, 65, 67, 76, 81, 84, 124, 211, 282, 286, 311, 319
Krirk-kiat Jalichandra, 106-10
Kuan Yin cult, 170
Kukrit Pramoj, 223-4

labour, 127-52, 292; Acts, 137; in-migration, 140; internal migration, 128, 130-6, 180-1, 192, 213-14; overseas migration, 129-30; politics, 4, 136-44; white collar, 144-7
Laddawan, 160
Laem Chabang, 8
Lampang, 194, 290
Lamphun, 201, 290
Lamsam family, 20, 24
Lamtakong reservoir, 204-5
land, 23, 60, 63, 75, 93, 127, 132, 188-94, 201-4, 206-8, 213-14, 255-7
Land & House company, 46, 112, 172
Lao people, 179, 220
Laos, 29, 51-2, 140, 234, 297, 306
Latin America, 53, 64, 117, 130, 310
law, 7, 273-4, 300-2
Le Chateau, 160
leather goods industry, 33
Leeson, Nick, 98, 105
liquor industry, 18, 24
Loei, 194
logging, 51, 288, 297
London, 53
Long Ju Kiang, 231-2
Lord lai mangkorn, 162, 174-5
LSE, 61
Luang Phor Koon, 168, 172
luk kruûng (mixed race), 156, 158
luk thung, see *phleng luk thung*
Luna Lanai, 160

macro policy, 72-81, 115-21, 317-20
Mae Moh, 194
Mahidol University, 145, 291
Mai Charoenpura, 157-8
Makro, 11
Malacca, 12
Malaysia, 1, 2, 11, 12, 16-17, 34, 49, 51, 56, 76, 111, 221, 277, 298, 310, 319
Manager group, 48, 51-2, 125, 236
manufacturing, 17-18, 23; exports, 4, 31-8, 57, 66, 67, 70, 79
Mass Communications Organization of Thailand (MCOT), 261-2
May 1992 crisis, 238-9, 304
Mazda, 37
Mechai Viravaidya, 294-5
media industry, 47-9, 249-50, 253-4
Merrill Lynch, 100
Mexico crisis, 105, 117, 124
Micropolis, 35
middle class, 149, 233-8, 266, 320
Middle East, 75, 95, 129, 144, 147
migration, see Chinese or labour
military, Thai, 2, 304; and forests, 198, 202-3; and politics, 21-2, 137-8, 216-7, 218-20, 224-5, 228-31, 237-8, 242-3, 254-5, 264, 2
Minebea, 35
Ministry of Finance, 60, 64, 66, 68, 71, 87-261
Ministry of Industry, 84, 289
Ministry of Interior, 219
Mitrapharp highway, 203-5
Mitsubishi, 34, 38, 89
moh lam, 181-4
Mong Dtang Mum, 261
Mongkut dok som, 164, 175
Monsit Khamsoi, 183
Montri Pongpanich, 227, 259